INSTRUCTOR'S RESOURCE GUIDE FOR

Intermediate Algebra

FIFTH EDITION

INSTRUCTOR'S RESOURCE GUIDE FOR

Intermediate Algebra

FIFTH EDITION

Mervin L. Keedy
Purdue University

Marvin L. Bittinger
*Indiana University-
Purdue University at Indianapolis*

ADDISON-WESLEY PUBLISHING COMPANY
Reading, Massachusetts • Menlo Park, California • Don Mills, Ontario
Wokingham, England • Amsterdam • Sydney • Singapore • Tokyo
Madrid • Bogotá • Santiago • San Juan

ISBN 0-201-15380-7
CDEFGHIJ-BK-943210

TABLE OF CONTENTS

I ALTERNATE TESTS, FORMS A, B, C, D, E, AND F 1

There are six <u>NEW</u> alternate test forms for each chapter and the final examination. They are not repeats of the Fourth Edition. If a pre-test for the book is desired, instructors may use form A, B, or C of the final examination for this purpose.

The questions on Forms A, B, and C of the final examinations are grouped by chapters. On Forms D, E, and F the questions are organized by type. For example, all the problem solving is together.

The last question of each chapter test and the last two questions of each final examination are extension questions which are meant to be more challenging. They are like the more challenging questions in the last part of each exercise set. Four skill maintenance questions precede the extension question on each test for Chapters 2-10. They cover skills taught in earlier chapters. Both the extension and the skill maintenance questions have been placed at the end to make it easy to omit them if the instructor wishes to do so.

Chapter 1 1

Chapter 2 13

Chapter 3 25

Chapter 4 37

Chapter 5 49

Chapter 6 61

Chapter 7 73

Chapter 8 85

Chapter 9 97

Chapter 10 109

Final Examination 121

II ANSWER KEYS FOR ALTERNATE TESTS, FORMS A, B, C, D, E, AND F 157

III CUMULATIVE TESTS, FORMS A AND B 199

To stress the importance of skill maintenance, two forms of a cumulative test are provided for use with each of the Chapters 2-9. They can also be used for midterm exams and review for the final examination. The last two questions on each test are extension questions.

Chapters 1-2 199

Chapters 1-3 203

Chapters 1-4 207

Chapters 1-5 211

Chapters 1-6 215

Chapters 1-7 219

Chapters 1-8 223

Chapters 1-9 227

IV   ANSWER KEYS FOR CUMULATIVE TESTS, FORMS A AND B 231

 V   EXTRA PRACTICE SHEETS 241

These sheets provide extra drill on the hardest topics in the text. The instructor can use them for lecture examples or additional homework assignments. Students will find them to be excellent review for tests. They provide an excellent source of practice and reteaching for students who have done poorly on a test and who are going to retest.

Section(s)

  1.3   Addition and Subtraction of Real Numbers 241

  2.3   Solving Problems Using Linear Equations 243

2.5-2.7   Graphing Linear Equations 245

  3.2   Solving Systems of Linear Equations 249

  3.3   Solving Problems Using Systems of Linear Equations 251

  4.2   Solving Inequalities with Both Principles 253

  4.5   Solving Equations and Inequalities with
           Absolute Value 255

5.5,5.6
5.8,5.9   Factoring Polynomials 257

  6.3   Addition and Subtraction of Fractional Expressions 259

6.4,6.5   Solving Fractional Equations Including Problem
           Solving 261

  6.8   Simplifying Complex Fractional Expressions 263

  6.9   Division of Polynomials 265

7.3,7.4   Multiplying, Dividing, and Simplifying Radical
           Expressions 267

  7.9   Solving Radical Equations 269

  8.2   Solving Quadratic Equations Using the Quadratic
           Formula 271

8.1,8.3   Solving Problems Using Quadratic Equations 273

  8.6   Solving Equations Reducible to Quadratic 275

8.8,8.9   Graphing Quadratic Functions 277

9.4,9.5   Solving Systems of Equations When One or Both
           Equations are Second-degree 281

 10.5   Solving Exponential and Logarithmic Equations 283

 VI   ANSWER KEYS FOR EXTRA PRACTICE SHEETS 285

VII   ANSWERS FOR THE EVEN EXERCISES OF THE EXERCISE SETS IN THE TEXT 299

These answers can be copied and given to students if the instructor wants them to have all the answers to the exercises in the exercise sets in the text. The odd answers are in the text.

VIII   COMPUTER PROGRAMS   337

These programs are in BASIC computer language. They are meant to
give the student an idea of the power and utility of the computer,
but are not intended to provide a full course in programming. Not
all BASIC languages are the same. The student should try the program on his computer. If it does not run, the user's manual might
be consulted. Some of these programs will run on an APPLE. All of
these programs will run on an IBM-PC, IBM-XT, and IBM-AT.

The authors wish to thank Randy Becker for his creative leadership
in the preparation of these programs.

IX   INDEX FOR VIDEO CASSETTE REVIEWS   349

Videotaped lectures by Professor John Jobe of Oklahoma State
University are designed to supplement lectures or for use in
individualized instruction. The lectures are keyed to specific
objectives in Basic Mathematics, Introductory Algebra, and
Intermediate Algebra, Fifth Editions. Counter readings were provided
by Sandra Judith Costello, Adjunct Professor of Mathematics, Somerset
County College, Somerville, New Jersey. For further information
concerning these tapes contact your local Addison-Wesley sales
representative.

X   TRANSPARENCY MASTERS AND TEST-MAKING AIDS   363

Transparencies of large rectangular coordinate grids and number
lines make graphing easier for the instructor and more easily
understood by the student during the lectures. The small grids and
number lines are useful when writing additional tests.

Special thanks are extended to Patsy Hammond for her excellent typing.
Her skill and efficiency made the authors' work much easier.

Name _____

Class _____ Score _____ Grade _____

1. Evaluate $\dfrac{a + b}{3}$ for a = 14 and b = 4.

ANSWERS

Find decimal notation.

2. $-\dfrac{9}{5}$ 3. 49.2%

Find fractional notation.

4. 0.56   5. 4.7%

Find percent notation.

6. $\dfrac{11}{5}$ 7. 0.226

8. Simplify: $|-34|$

Compute.

9. 8 + (-6)   10. -6.6 + (-1.5)

11. $\dfrac{3}{4} - \dfrac{5}{6}$ 12. -4 - 7

13. -2(8)   14. (-2.1)(-5.6)

15. $\dfrac{10}{9} \div -\dfrac{2}{3}$ 16. $\dfrac{-12}{4}$

1. _____

2. _____

3. _____

4. _____

5. _____

6. _____

7. _____

8. _____

9. _____

10. _____

11. _____

12. _____

13. _____

14. _____

15. _____

16. _____

Name _____

ANSWERS	
17._____	17. Insert > or < to make a true sentence: -3 ___ 2
18._____	Multiply.
	18. 3(2a + b)
	19. 2rs(3t - 1)
19._____	Factor.
	20. 4x - 8y + 12z
	21. abc + abd
20._____	
21._____	22. Collect like terms: 9a - 7b - 6a + 5b
22._____	23. Find an equivalent expression: -(-8a - 6b + 3c)
23._____	
24._____	Simplify.
	24. 6a - [9 - 5(a + 3)]
	25. 3(2x - 1) - 2(x + 1)
25._____	
26._____	26. 4 · 3 - 5²
	27. $\left(\dfrac{3x^{-2}y^5}{2x^3}\right)^3$
27._____	Multiply or divide and simplify.
28._____	28. $(3x^2y^{-4})(-5x^{-3}y^9)$
	29. $\dfrac{8a^3b^{-4}}{-18a^{-5}b}$
29._____	
30._____	30. Simplify: $2(4^2 \cdot 4^{-2} - 4^{-2} \cdot 4^0)$

Name _____

Class _____ Score _____ Grade _____

1. Translate to an algebraic expression:

    3 more than y

2. Insert > or < to make a true sentence:

    -5   -9

Compute.

3. $\frac{9}{10} + \left(-\frac{1}{5}\right)$ 4.   -12 + 8

5.   -5 - 4   6.   -12.4 - (-4.9)

7. $-\frac{2}{3}\left(-\frac{9}{8}\right)$ 8.   -6(5)(3)

9.   -42 ÷ 6   10.   -12.1 ÷ 1.1

Find fractional notation.

11.   180%   12.   0.323

Find decimal notation.

13. $\frac{4}{9}$ 14.   14.3%

Find percent notation.

15.   0.014   16. $\frac{7}{20}$

ANSWERS

1._____

2._____

3._____

4._____

5._____

6._____

7._____

8._____

9._____

10._____

11._____

12._____

13._____

14._____

15._____

16._____

Name _____

ANSWERS	

17. Find $-a$ when a is $\frac{3}{4}$. (In other words, find the additive inverse.)

17. _____

18. Simplify: $\left| -\frac{8}{7} \right|$

18. _____

19. Collect like terms: $3a + 2b + a - 7b$

19. _____

Multiply.

20. _____

20. $-6(x - 5y)$

21. $2ab(c + d)$

21. _____

Factor.

22. _____

22. $18m - 9n - 6p$

23. $xy + 2x - xz$

23. _____

Simplify.

24. _____

24. $-2(5x + 3) + 3(2x - 3)$

25. $5a - [1 - 3(a + 6)]$

25. _____

26. $3^4 - 11 + 5 \cdot 4$

27. $(-4x^3y^{-1}b^{-5})^{-2}$

26. _____

Multiply or divide and simplify.

27. _____

28. $(-5x^6y^{-7})(4x^{-3}y^{-2})$

29. $\dfrac{42a^{-5}b^2}{-12a^3b}$

28. _____

29. _____

30. Evaluate when $x = -1$ and $y = 2$:

$(x + y)(x - y)(x^{x-y} - y^{y-x})$

30. _____

Name _____

Class _____ *Score* _____ *Grade* _____

Find percent notation.

1. 0.298   2. $\frac{6}{5}$

ANSWERS

1._____

Find decimal notation.

3. $\frac{5}{16}$ 4. 3.67%

2._____

3._____

Find fractional notation.

5. 51.7%   6. 1.19

4._____

5._____

7. Evaluate $\frac{2x}{y}$ for x = 6 and y = 4.

6._____

7._____

8. Insert > or < to make a true sentence:
          -4.5   -5.4

8._____

9._____

Compute.

9. -8.7 + 5.9   10. -6 + (-6)

10._____

11. 2 - 8   12. $-\frac{5}{9} - \frac{5}{12}$

11._____

12._____

13. (-3.4)(4.3)   14. -9(-6)

13._____

14._____

15. $\frac{-72}{-8}$ 16. $-\frac{2}{3} \div \frac{4}{9}$

15._____

16._____

Name _____

ANSWERS

17. _____

18. _____

19. _____

20. _____

21. _____

22. _____

23. _____

24. _____

25. _____

26. _____

27. _____

28. _____

29. _____

30. _____

17. Simplify: $|0|$

18. Find $-a$ when a is $-\frac{18}{7}$. (In other words, find the additive inverse.)

Multiply.

19. $4(3x - y)$

20. $mn(2s + 3)$

21. Collect like terms: $2m + 3n - 5m + n$

Factor.

22. $15a + 5b - 20c$

23. $4\pi r - 2\pi$

24. Find an equivalent expression: $-(6m - 5n - 2p)$

Simplify.

25. $3^2 - 2^4 + 5 \cdot 4$

26. $\left(\frac{2x^{-1}y^3}{5x^2y}\right)^2$

27. $9a - [7 - 2(3a + 4)]$

Multiply or divide and simplify.

28. $(-2x^{-3}y^{-5})(4x^2y^{-1})$

29. $\frac{-15a^5b^{-3}}{20a^7b^{-2}}$

Δ ——————————————————————

30. Suppose $x = 3^a$ and $y = 3^{3a-4}$. Find $x^{-2}y$.

Name _____

Class _____ *Score* _____ *Grade* _____

1. Insert > or < to make a true sentence:

        $0 \quad -7$

ANSWERS

2. Evaluate $\dfrac{a - b}{5}$ for $a = 16$ and $b = 6$.

1._____

2._____

3._____

Find percent notation.

3. $\dfrac{3}{40}$ 4. 5

4._____

5._____

Find decimal notation.

5. 5.4%   6. $-\dfrac{3}{2}$

6._____

7._____

Find fractional notation.

7. 0.47   8. 62.3%

8._____

9._____

Compute.

9. $-\dfrac{1}{3} + \dfrac{1}{2}$ 10. $3 + (-6)$

10._____

11._____

11. $-19 - (-12)$ 12. $-8.6 - 2.3$

12._____

13._____

13. $4(-7)$ 14. $-\dfrac{3}{4}\left(\dfrac{5}{6}\right)$

14._____

15._____

15. $\dfrac{7}{8} \div -\dfrac{3}{4}$ 16. $\dfrac{-60}{-15}$

16._____

Name _____

ANSWERS

17. Simplify: $|5|$

17._____

18. Find an equivalent expression: $-(-5m - 3n + 6p)$

18._____

19. Collect like terms: $4x + 2y - 3x + y$

19._____

Multiply.

20._____

20. $-2(4x - 3y)$ 21. $4ab(c - 2d)$

21._____

Factor.

22._____

22. $16a + 8b - 4c$ 23. $np + p$

23._____

Simplify.

24. $2a - [3 - 2(2a + 3)]$ 25. $2(x - 1) - 3(x + 2)$

24._____

25._____

26. $2^3 - 4^2 + 3 \cdot 2$ 27. $(-3x^{-2}yz^3)^{-2}$

26._____

Multiply or divide and simplify.

28. $(4x^5y^{-4})(-3xy^2)$ 29. $\dfrac{-18a^6b^{-3}}{10a^{-4}b^2}$

27._____

28._____

Δ————————————————————

29._____

30. Simplify: $\left[\dfrac{(-3x^3y^2)(-4xy)}{(3x^3y^{-2})(-4x^4)}\right]^{-3}$

30._____

CHAPTER 2

Name _____

Class _____ *Score* _____ *Grade* _____

Graph.

ANSWERS

1. $y = -2x + 3$

2. $y = 3x$

1.___See graph.___

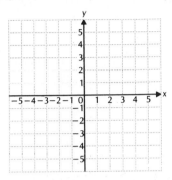

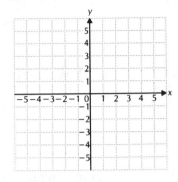

2.___See graph.___

3.___See graph.___

3. $y = 3$

4. $2y - 3x = 6$

4.___See graph.___

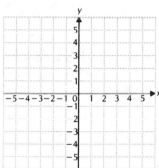

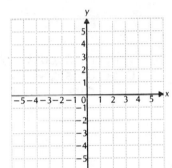

5._____

5. Find the slope and y-intercept: $y = 4x + 2$

6. Find the slope, if it exists, of the line containing the points (3,9) and (3,1).

6._____

7. Find an equation of the line with slope -4 and containing the point (-8,-10).

7._____

8. Find an equation of the line containing the points (3,6) and (-2,1).

8._____

9. Find an equation of the line containing the point (-3,4) and parallel to the line $2x - y = 5$.

9._____

10. Solve for a: $T = a + abc$

10._____

Name _____

ANSWERS	

Solve.

11. $9 - 7x = -5$ 12. $(5x - 3)(x + 6) = 0$

11. _____

13. $4(x - 2) = 5 - (x + 6)$

12. _____

Solve.

13. _____

14. Six plus seven times a number is nine times the number. What is the number?

14. _____

15. The total cost for tuition plus room and board at City U is $4870. Tuition costs $540 more than room and board. What is the tuition fee?

15. _____

[✓]————————————————————————————

16. Subtract: $\dfrac{5}{6} - \dfrac{4}{9}$ 17. Factor: $6y - 9$

16. _____

Divide.

17. _____

18. $-6.3 \div 2.1$ 19. $\dfrac{24ab^{-3}c^5}{-6a^2b^{-4}c^3}$

18. _____

Δ————————————————————————————

20. Three numbers are such that the second is five less than four times the first, and the third is three more than two-fifths the second. The sum of the three numbers is 65. Find the largest number.

19. _____

20. _____

Name _____

Class _____ Score _____ Grade _____

ANSWERS

1. Solve using the substitution method:

$$2x - 3y = 9$$
$$y = -4x + 11$$

1._____

2. Solve using the addition method:

$$2x + 3y = -13$$
$$3x - 4y = 6$$

2._____

3. Solve graphically:

$$3x + y = 3$$
$$2x + y = 1$$

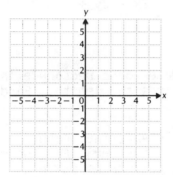

3.____See graph.____

Evaluate.

4. $\begin{vmatrix} -3 & 5 \\ 4 & -2 \end{vmatrix}$

5. $\begin{vmatrix} 0 & 1 & -3 \\ 2 & 4 & -1 \\ 0 & -2 & 1 \end{vmatrix}$

4._____

5._____

6. Solve using Cramer's rule. Show your work.

$$5x + y = 7$$
$$3x - 2y = -1$$

6._____

7. Solve: $2x + y - 3z = 8$

$$4x - y + 2z = -12$$
$$-3x + 2y - z = 13$$

7._____

8. Find a) the profit and b) the break-even point:

$$C = 450x + 105,000$$
$$R = 800x$$

8.a)_____

b)_____

27

Name _____

ANSWERS	
9._____	**9.** Determine whether the system is dependent or independent:
	$$2x - 5y = 3$$
	$$-6x + 15y = -9$$
10._____	**10.** Determine whether the system is consistent or inconsistent:
	$$x + 2y - z = 5$$
	$$2x - y - z = 1$$
11._____	$$2x + 2y + z = 9$$

Solve.

11. The perimeter of a rectangle is 50 cm. The width is two-thirds the length. Find the dimensions.

12._____

12. In triangle ABC, the measure of angle B is 5° more than four times angle A. The measure of angle C is twice the measure of angle A. Find the angle measures.

13._____

[✓]──────────────────────────────

13. Simplify: $4[3(x - 1) - 5] - [5(x + 2) - 8]$

14._____

14. Solve: $5x + 3 = -7$

15. Solve for a: $b = \frac{2}{5}a + 3$

15._____

16. Money is borrowed at 12% simple interest. After one year $2800 pays off the loan. How much was originally borrowed?

Δ──────────────────────────────

16._____

17. Two solutions of the equation $y = mx + b$ are (1,-2) and (2,1). Find m and b.

17._____

Name _____

Class _____ *Score* _____ *Grade* _____

1. Solve using the addition method:

$$2x - 3y = 5$$
$$5x + 4y = 1$$

2. Solve using the substitution method:

$$y = 3x + 2$$
$$x + 2y = 11$$

3. Solve graphically:

$$x - y = 2$$
$$2x - y = 5$$

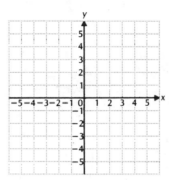

Solve.

4.
$$3x + 2y - 3z = -8$$
$$x - y + z = 0$$
$$2x - 3y + 4z = 4$$

5. The difference of two numbers is 41. Twice the larger plus three times the smaller is 2. Find the numbers.

6. For a theater production, the costs of tickets for students, adults, and children were $2.50, $4.00, and $1.00, respectively. The total number of children's and adult tickets sold was 10 more than twice the number of student tickets sold. The number of children's tickets sold was 20 more than half the number of student tickets. The total receipts from ticket sales were $520. How many of each type of ticket was sold?

Evaluate.

7. $\begin{vmatrix} 2 & -4 \\ 3 & -5 \end{vmatrix}$

8. $\begin{vmatrix} 3 & -1 & 1 \\ 1 & 2 & 0 \\ -2 & 4 & 1 \end{vmatrix}$

ANSWERS

1._____

2._____

3.___See graph.___

4._____

5._____

6._____

7._____

8._____

Name _____

ANSWERS	
9._____	9. Solve using Cramer's rule. Show your work.$$3x - y = 7$$$$2x + 3y = 1$$
10._____	10. Determine whether the system is consistent or inconsistent:$$x + y - z = 5$$$$x - y - z = 3$$$$2x - 2z = 7$$
11._____	11. Determine whether the system is dependent or independent:$$x + 2y = -3$$$$-2x - 4y = 6$$
12.a)_____	
b)_____	12. Find a) the profit and b) the break-even point:$$C = 27x + 30,000$$$$R = 52x$$
13._____	[✓]──────────────────13. Simplify: $5(x + 3) - 2(x + 4)$
14._____	14. Solve: $3 - 4x = 15$15. Solve for m: $p = \frac{1}{2}n(m - r)$
15._____	16. The sum of two consecutive odd integers is 304. Find the integers.
16._____	Δ────────────────────17. A beaker contains 15 mL of alcohol and water. This mixture is 40% alcohol. How much of this mixture should be poured out and replaced with pure alcohol so that the beaker will contain a solution that is 60% alcohol?
17._____	

Name _____

Class _____ *Score* _____ *Grade* _____

	ANSWERS

1. Solve graphically:

$$2x + 3y = 6$$
$$x + 2y = 4$$

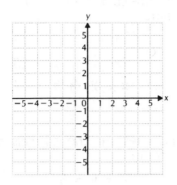

1. ___See graph.___

2. Solve using the substitution method:

$$y = 3x + 5$$
$$2x - 3y = 6$$

2. _____

3. Solve using the addition method:

$$2x + 5y = -3$$
$$3x - 2y = 5$$

3. _____

4. Solve: $x + 6y + 3z = 4$

$$3x - 2y + z = 0$$
$$2x + y + 2z = 3$$

4. _____

Evaluate.

5. $\begin{vmatrix} 3 & -1 \\ 4 & 6 \end{vmatrix}$ 6. $\begin{vmatrix} 2 & -2 & 3 \\ 0 & -1 & 1 \\ 1 & 4 & 1 \end{vmatrix}$

5. _____

6. _____

7. Solve using Cramer's rule. Show your work.

$$2x - 3y + z = 0$$
$$-x + 4y + 3z = -14$$
$$3x - y - z = 10$$

7. _____

8. Find a) the profit and b) the break-even point:

$$C = 100x + 200,000$$
$$R = 150x$$

8.a) _____

   b) _____

Name _____

ANSWERS

9._____

9. Determine whether the system is dependent or independent:

$$x + y + z = 13$$
$$2x + y - z = 15$$
$$x - 2y + z = -2$$

10._____

10. Determine whether the system is consistent or inconsistent:

$$x + y = 5$$
$$2x - 2y = -10$$

11._____

Solve.

11. A collection of dimes and quarters is worth $32.50. There are 205 coins in all. How many of each kind of coin are there?

12._____

12. The sum of three numbers is 209. The second is 12 less than twice the first. The third is 18 more than 4 times the first. Find the numbers.

13._____

[✓]──────────────────────────────

13. Simplify: $3a - [4 - 2(5a + 1)]$

14._____

14. Solve: $5x + 7 = 2x - 2$

15._____

15. Solve for R: $T = 4Q - 7R$

16. A store drops the price of a lamp 30% to a sale price of $59.50. What was the former price?

16._____

Δ──────────────────────────────

17. Find a three-digit number such that the sum of all three digits is 13, the unit's digit is one more than twice the hundred's digit and the ten's digit is three times the unit's digit.

17._____

Name _____

Test Form E   Class _____ Score _____ Grade _____

ANSWERS

1. Solve using the substitution method:
$$3x + 2y = 2$$
$$x = y + 9$$

1._____

2. Solve using the addition method:
$$3x + 5y = 1$$
$$4x + 3y = -6$$

2._____

3. Solve graphically:
$$2x - 3y = -5$$
$$x + y = 5$$

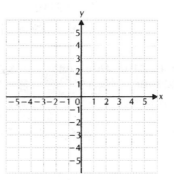

3.___See graph.____

4. Solve: $3x + 5y - 2z = 7$
$$2x + y - 3z = -5$$
$$4x - 2y + z = 3$$

4._____

Evaluate.

5. $\begin{vmatrix} -3 & 1 \\ 2 & 5 \end{vmatrix}$

6. $\begin{vmatrix} 4 & -1 & 2 \\ 1 & -2 & 0 \\ -1 & 3 & 1 \end{vmatrix}$

5._____

7. Solve using Cramer's rule. Show your work.
$$x + y + z = 4$$
$$x - 2y - z = 3$$
$$3x - y - 4z = 2$$

6._____

Solve.

8. Toni is 4 years older than her brother David. Eight years from now David will be five-sixths as old as Toni. How old are they now?

7._____

8._____

Name _____

ANSWERS

9. _____

10. _____

11. _____

12.a) _____

   b) _____

13. _____

14. _____

15. _____

16. _____

17. _____

9. One year an investment of $100,000 was made by an investment club. The investment was split into three parts and lasted one year. The first part of the investment earned 8% interest, the second 9%, and the third 10%. Total interest from the investments was $9150. The interest from the third investment was twice the interest from the first. Find the amount of each part of the investment.

10. Determine whether the system is consistent or inconsistent:

$$3x + 6y = -9$$
$$x + 2y = 3$$

11. Determine whether the system is dependent or independent:

$$x + y - 2z = 3$$
$$x - y + z = 1$$
$$2x - z = 4$$

12. Find a) the profit and b) the break-even point:

$$C = 27x + 46,000$$
$$R = 50x$$

[✓]────────────────────────────

13. Simplify: $3(a - 2) - 4(a - 3)$

14. Solve: $\frac{3}{4}x - \frac{5}{6} = \frac{2}{3}$

15. Solve for b^2: $A = b^2c$

16. Six plus five times a number is eight times the number. What is the number?

Δ────────────────────────────

17. The numerator of a fraction is 7 more than the denominator. The sum of the numerator and denominator is 2 less than three times the denominator. What is the reciprocal of the fraction?

Name _____

Class _____ *Score* _____ *Grade* _____

Evaluate.

ANSWERS

1. $\begin{vmatrix} -2 & 1 \\ -3 & 2 \end{vmatrix}$

2. $\begin{vmatrix} 1 & -3 & 2 \\ -1 & 1 & 3 \\ 4 & 0 & -2 \end{vmatrix}$

1._____

3. Solve using Cramer's rule. Show your work.

$$3x - y + 2z = -1$$
$$x + y - 3z = 6$$
$$2x + 2y + z = 5$$

2._____

4. Find a) the profit and b) the break-even point:

$$C = 24x + 16,000$$
$$R = 32x$$

3._____

5. Solve graphically:

$$x + y = -3$$
$$3x - 2y = 1$$

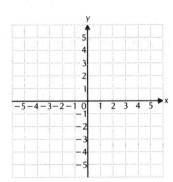

4.a)_____

b)_____

5.___See graph.___

6. Solve using the substitution method:

$$x = 2y - 3$$
$$3x - 4y = -1$$

6._____

7. Solve using the addition method:

$$3x + 2y = 3$$
$$4x + 3y = 3$$

7._____

Solve.

8. Two investments are made totaling $7500. For a certain year the investments yielded $690 in simple interest. Part of the $7500 is invested at 8% and part at 10%. Find the amount invested at each rate.

8._____

Name _____

ANSWERS

9. _____

10. _____

11. _____

12. _____

13. _____

14. _____

15. _____

16. _____

17. _____

9. Max has a total of 242 on three tests. The sum of the scores on the second and third tests exceeds his first score by 68. His second score exceeds his third by 5. Find the three scores.

10. Solve: $2x + 4y + 3z = 0$
$$-5x - y + z = -1$$
$$x + 3y - 2z = -9$$

11. Determine whether the system is dependent or independent:
$$x + y = 3$$
$$2x - 2y = 6$$

12. Determine whether the system is consistent or inconsistent:
$$2x + 3y = 4$$
$$x + 2y + z = 1$$
$$x + y - z = 3$$

[✓]────────────────────────────────

13. Simplify: $4(y - 1) - 2(y + 5)$

14. Solve: $2x - 1 = 7$

15. Solve for P: $R = 3P - Q$

16. The sum of two consecutive even integers is 206. Find the integers.

Δ────────────────────────────────

17. Solve: $\begin{vmatrix} 2 & 0 & -1 \\ 1 & x & 3 \\ -2 & 1 & 2 \end{vmatrix} = 10$

Name _____

Test Form A

Class _____ *Score* _____ *Grade* _____

Solve.

1. $x - 5 > 12$

2. $-3y \leqslant 18$

3. $4x - 3 < x + 6$

4. $-4 < 3y + 2 \leqslant 5$

5. $5x - 3 < -2$ or $5x - 3 > 2$

6. $|2y - 3| = 7$

7. $|4a + 1| \geqslant 5$

8. Find the intersection: $\{-5,0,5,10\} \cap \{0,10,20\}$

9. Find the union: $\{1,2,3,4\} \cup \{2,4,6,8\}$

Graph on a number line.

10. $-3 < 2x - 1 < 1$

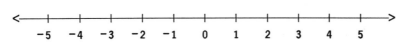

11. $x \leqslant -2$ or $x > 3$

ANSWERS

1._____

2._____

3._____

4._____

5._____

6._____

7._____

8._____

9._____

10._____See graph._____

11._____See graph._____

Name _____

ANSWERS	

Determine whether true or false.

12. $11 \; \epsilon \; \{1,3,5,7,9\}$ 13. $\{1,2\} \subset \{-2,-1,0,1,2\}$

12. _____

Graph on a plane.

14. $x + 3y \leqslant 3$ 15. $-1 \leqslant x < 2$

13. _____

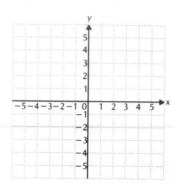   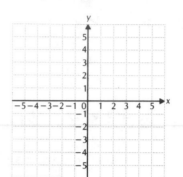

14. See graph.

15. See graph.

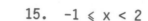

16. Graph: $5x - 2y = 10$

16. See graph.

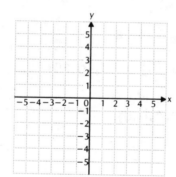

17. _____

Solve.

17. $(x - 3)(2x + 1) = 0$ 18. $x + y = 4$
                                    $x + 2y = 2$

18. _____

19. A collection of dimes and nickels is worth $7.50. There are 15 more dimes than nickels. How many of each type of coin are there?

19. _____

Δ_____

20. Solve: $|3x - 4| = x + 1$

20. _____

Name _____

Class _____ Score _____ Grade _____

1. Find the union: {-7,-3,-1,0} ∪ {-3,3,9}

2. Find the intersection: {1,5,6,9} ∩ {0,1,2,4,5,6,8,9}

Determine whether true or false.

3. Ø ⊂ {1}   4. 3 ε The set of whole numbers

Graph on a number line.

5. $|2x + 5| > 1$

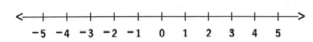

6. $-3 \leqslant x \leqslant 2$

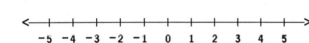

Graph on a plane.

7. $-1 \leqslant y < 1$ 8. $x - y > 4$

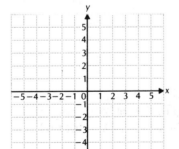   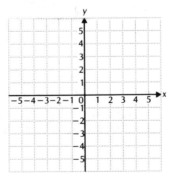

Solve.

9. $y + 3 < 7$ 10. $4y \geqslant 24$

ANSWERS

1._____

2._____

3._____

4._____

5.___See graph.___

6.___See graph.___

7.___See graph.___

8.___See graph.___

9._____

10._____

Name _____

ANSWERS

Solve.

11._____

11. $5x - 7 > 3x + 1$

12. $-5 \leqslant 3 - 4y < -1$

12._____

13. $|2a - 1| < 7$

14. $|2x + 1| = 2$

13._____

15. $3y + 2 < -1$ or $3y + 2 > 1$

14._____

[✓]————————————————————————

16. $2(x - 1) = 3(x - 2)$

17. $2x - 3y = 7$
     $3x + 4y = 2$

15._____

18. Graph: $4x - 3y = 12$

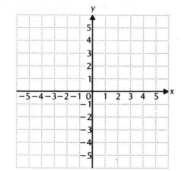

16._____

17._____

19. One solution is 80% alcohol and a second is 65% alcohol. How much of each should be mixed together to make 1000 L of a solution that is 74% alcohol?

18.___See graph.___

19._____

Δ————————————————————————————

20. Solve: $3a - 7 < a + 3 < 2a + 5$

20._____

Name _____

Class _____ Score _____ Grade _____

Graph on a number line.

1. $-2 \leqslant x \leqslant 3$

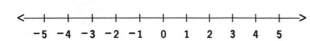

2. $|2x - 1| > 3$

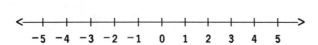

3. Find the intersection: $\{2,3,4\} \cap \emptyset$

4. Find the union: $\{1,4\} \cup \{-2,-1\}$

Solve.

5. $4x + 2 > x + 1$ 6. $-5y < 15$

7. $-4 < 1 - y < 2$ 8. $x - 4 \geqslant 10$

9. $|3y - 5| < 8$ 10. $|5x + 2| = 7$

11. $2a + 3 \leqslant -5$ or $2a + 3 \geqslant 5$

ANSWERS

1. __See graph.__

2. __See graph.__

3. _____

4. _____

5. _____

6. _____

7. _____

8. _____

9. _____

10. _____

11. _____

Name _____

ANSWERS	Graph on a plane.

12. ___See graph.___

12. $2x - y \geqslant 4$

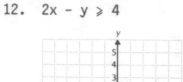

13. $-2 < x \leqslant 1$

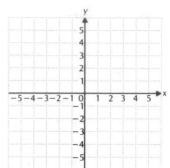

13. ___See graph.___

14. _____

Determine whether true or false.

14. $1 \; \varepsilon \; \{-9,-6,-2,0,1,5\}$

15. $\{x \mid x < 1\} \subset \{x \mid x \leqslant 2\}$

15. _____

[✓]

16. Graph: $3x + 2y = 6$

16. ___See graph.___

17. _____

Solve.

17. $(4x - 1)(x + 5) = 0$

18. $x - 3y = 9$
$3x - 2y = 13$

18. _____

19. _____

19. The difference of two numbers is 18. The larger is one more than twice the smaller. Find the numbers.

Δ

20. Solve: $|2x + 3| \geqslant -1$

20. _____

Name _____

Class _____ Score _____ Grade _____

Solve.

1. $-8x \geqslant 48$

2. $5x + 2 \leqslant 2x + 8$

3. $y + 7 < -2$

4. $-6 \leqslant 2y - 4 < 8$

5. $|4y + 3| = 7$

6. $|2a + 4| > 10$

7. $3a - 4 \leqslant -4$ or $3a - 4 \geqslant 4$

Graph on a number line.

8. $x < -2$ or $x \geqslant 0$

9. $2x - 3 \leqslant 5$

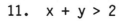

Graph on a plane.

10. $y \leqslant 1$

11. $x + y > 2$

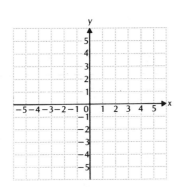
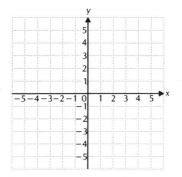

ANSWERS

1._____

2._____

3._____

4._____

5._____

6._____

7._____

8.___See graph.

9.___See graph.

10.___See graph.

11.___See graph.

Name _____

ANSWERS

Determine whether true or false.

12. _____

12. $\{x | x > -2\} \subset \{x > -1\}$

13. $2 \in \{-5,-2,0,2,4,7\}$

14. Find the union: $\{1,5,10,12\} \cup \emptyset$

13. _____

15. Find the intersection: $\{1,2,3\} \cap \{1,2,3\}$

[✓]

Solve.

14. _____

16. $5(x + 3) = 2(x - 3)$ 17. $2x + 3y = 7$
                                        $3x + 2y = 3$

15. _____

18. Graph: $x - 4y = 4$

16. _____

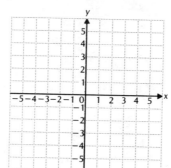

17. _____

19. The perimeter of a rectangle is 134 m. The width is 11 m less than the length. Find the dimensions.

18. _See graph._

Δ——————————————————————————————

19. _____

20. Solve: $|x - 2| \leqslant |x + 1|$

20. _____

Name _____

Class _____ Score _____ Grade _____

Determine whether true or false.

ANSWERS

1. 18 ε The set of even integers

1._____

2. {2,3} ⊂ {0,2,4}

3. Find the intersection: {-4,-3,1,4,9} ∩ {-3,-2,2,4,5}

2._____

4. Find the union: {-1,1} ∪ {0}

Graph on a number line.

5. |x + 3| < 2

3._____

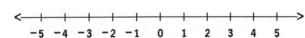

4._____

6. -4 ≤ x < 2

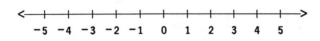

5.____See graph.____

Graph on a plane.

6.____See graph.____

7. x > 2   8. 3x + y ≤ 3

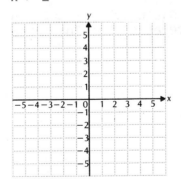   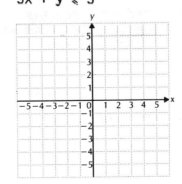

7.____See graph.____

8.____See graph.____

Solve.

9. 7x < 21   10. 2x - 1 ≤ 5x + 8

9._____

10._____

Name _____

ANSWERS

Solve.

11. _____

11. y − 4 ⩾ −5

12. −1 < 3x + 2 ⩽ 4

13. |2y − 7| = 9

14. |3a + 5| > 1

12. _____

15. 4a + 5 < −3 or 4a + 5 > 3

[✓]──────────────────────────────────

16. Graph: x − y = 4

13. _____

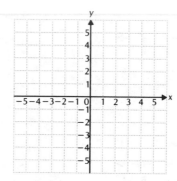

14. _____

15. _____

Solve.

17. (x − 7)(2x + 5) = 0

18. 5x + 2y = 7
     2x + 3y = −6

16. See graph.

19. Fred is three times as old as his daughter Sue. In twelve years Fred will be twice as old as Sue. Find their ages now.

17. _____

Δ──────────────────────────────────

20. Graph on a plane: y ⩾ |x| − 1

18. _____

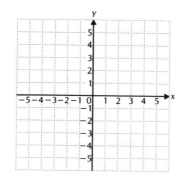

19. _____

20. See graph.

Name _____

Class _____ Score _____ Grade _____

Solve.

1. $z + 3 < -7$

2. $7x + 2 \leqslant 5x + 4$

3. $-3 < 4x - 7 < 5$

4. $-6x \geqslant -42$

5. $5y + 4 < -9$ or $5y + 4 > 9$

6. $|3a + 4| = 7$

7. $|2y - 3| > 5$

Graph on a number line.

8. $x < -2$ or $x \geqslant 1$

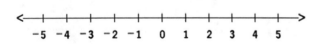

9. $|2x + 5| < 3$

10. Find the intersection: $\{-3,4,9\} \cap \{-4,3,5\}$

11. Find the union: $\{1,2,3\} \cup \{1,3,5\}$

ANSWERS
1._____
2._____
3._____
4._____
5._____
6._____
7._____
8.__See graph.__
9.__See graph.__
10._____
11._____

Name _____

ANSWERS	Determine whether true or false.

12. _____

12. $25 \in \{5,10,15,20\}$

13. $\{x \mid x < 3\} \cup \{x \mid x < 5\}$

Graph on a plane.

13. _____

14. $x - 2y \geqslant 2$

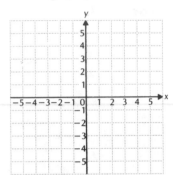

15. $y < 3$

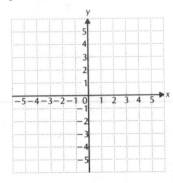

14. _____See graph._____

15. _____See graph._____

[✓]────────────────────────────

16. Graph: $x + 3y = 3$

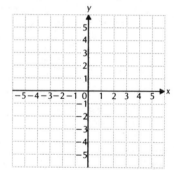

16. _____See graph._____

17. _____

Solve.

17. $3(2x - 1) = 10 - (x + 5)$ **18.** $2x + 3y = -3$
$5x + 4y = 3$

18. _____

19. For a certain year, $1040 interest is received from two investments. A certain amount is invested at 8% and $4000 more than that is invested at 9%. Find the amount invested at each rate.

19. _____

Δ────────────────────────────

20. Determine whether this statement is true or false. If false, give a counterexample.

For any real numbers a, b, c, and d, if
$a < b$ and $c < d$, then $ac < bd$.

20. _____

Name _____

Class _____ *Score* _____ *Grade* _____

Multiply.

1. $(3ab + c)(3ab - c)$ 2. $(4x - 3y)(x + 2y)$

3. $(2x - 1)(5x^2 - 2x + 1)$

Factor.

4. $6m^2 + 11m + 4$ 5. $4y^2 - 9$

6. $3y^3 - 3$ 7. $12x^2 + 16x$

8. $49a^2 + 56a + 16$

9. Factor by completing the square. Show your work.
    $$x^2 - 30x + 200$$

10. Arrange the polynomial $5a^3b - 2ab^4 - a^5b^2 + 3a^2b^3$ in descending powers of b.

11. Collect like terms: $3x + 2 - 9x^3 - 3 + 2x - 5x^3$

12. Subtract: $(5xy - 3x^2y + 2x^2y^2) - (4x^2y + 2x^2y^2 - 7xy)$

Solve.

13. $x^2 + 12x = -32$

14. The perimeter of a square is half its area. Find the length of a side.

ANSWERS

1._____

2._____

3._____

4._____

5._____

6._____

7._____

8._____

9._____

10._____

11._____

12._____

13._____

14._____

Name _____

ANSWERS

15._____

16.a)_____

b)_____

c)_____

d)_____

e)_____

17.___See graph.___

18._____

19._____

20._____

21._____

22._____

15. Given the function h described by $h(y) = 4y^2 - y - 5$, find $h(-2)$.

16. Given the functions $f(x) = x + 2$ and $g(x) = x^2 - 1$ find a) $(f + g)(x)$ b) $(f - g)(x)$ c) $(fg)(x)$ d) $(f/g)(x)$ e) $(ff)(x)$

17. Graph: $f(x) = x^2 + 2$

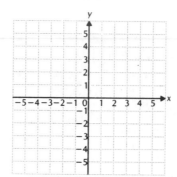

[✓]———————————————————————————

Solve.

18. $5y - 4 < y + 4$ 19. $|2x + 3| \geqslant 5$

20. $x + 2y + z = 3$
    $2x + 5y - 2z = 1$
    $x - y - z = 4$

21. A student has a total score of 264 on three tests. The sum of the scores on the second and third tests exceeds the first score by 80. The second score is 3 less than the first. Find the three scores.

Δ———————————————————————————

22. Solve: The sum of two numbers is 24, and the sum of their squares is 306. Find the numbers.

Name _____

Class _____ Score _____ Grade _____

1. Evaluate the polynomial $3x^5y^2 - 4xy + 5x^3y^3$ for
   $x = -1$ and $y = 2$.

ANSWERS

2. Add: $(4xy^2 - 2xy + 3x^2y) + (3xy - 5x^2y + 3xy^2)$

1._____

2._____

3. Subtract: $(2a^2 - 5ab + 3b^2) - (-2ab + a^2 - 3b^2)$

3._____

Multiply.

4. $(2x + y)^2$ 5. $(5y^3z^4)(-4y^2z^6)$

4._____

6. $(4x - 5)(3x + 5)$

5._____

6._____

Factor.

7. $3x^2 - 10x - 8$ 8. $9m^2 - 48m + 64$

7._____

9. $y^4 - 16$ 10. $2x^3 + 250$

8._____

11. $2x^3 + 4x^2 - 3x - 6$

9._____

12. Complete the square: $x^2 - \frac{2}{3}x$

10._____

11._____

Solve.

13. $4 = a(3a + 1)$

12._____

14. The base of a triangle is 3 cm less than the height.
    The area is 27 cm². Find the height and base.

13._____

14._____

Name _____

ANSWERS	
15.	See graph.

15. Graph: $f(x) = |x| - 1$

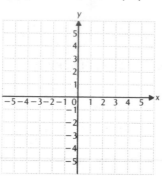

16.a)_____

b)_____

16. Given the functions $f(x) = x^2 + 3$ and $g(x) = x - 4$, find a) $(f + g)(x)$ b) $(f - g)(x)$ c) $(fg)(x)$ d) $(f/g)(x)$ e) $(gg)(x)$

c)_____

d)_____

17. Given the function f described by $f(x) = x^3 - 1$, find $f(-3)$.

e)_____

[✓]————————————————

17._____

Solve.

18. $|2x - 3| = 5$ 19. $y - 7 \geqslant 4y + 2$

18._____

20. $x + y + z = 3$

     $2x - 2y + z = -5$

     $3x + 2y + 2z = 4$

19._____

21. The sum of three numbers is 113. The second is two more than twice the first. The third is six more than four times the first. Find the numbers.

20._____

Δ————————————————

21._____

22. Factor: $x^2 + 2xy + y^2 - a^2 + 4ab - 4b^2$

22._____

CHAPTER 5

Name _____

Test Form E

Class _____ Score _____ Grade _____

1. Add: $(13x^2y - 4xy^2 + 3xy) + (4xy^2 - 7x^2y - 2xy)$

2. Subtract: $(5m^3 - 3m^2 + 6m + 3) - (6m - 9 - m^2 + 4m^3)$

3. Arrange the polynomial $4xy^5 - 3x^6y^2 + x^2y^3 - 2y$ in descending powers of x.

ANSWERS

Multiply.

4. $(x^2 - 1)(x^2 - 2x + 1)$ 5. $(2y + 5z)(4y - z)$

6. $(a + 3b)(a - 3b)$

Factor.

7. $4x^2 + 4x - 3$ 8. $50m^2 + 40m + 8$

9. $4y^6 + 4y^3$ 10. $a^2 + 6a + 8$

11. $x^2 - 6x + 9 - 49y^2$

12. Factor by completing the square. Show your work.
$$x^2 - 4x - 221$$

Solve.

13. $6m + 8 = 9m^2$

14. The square of a number is 35 more than twice the number. Find the number.

1._____

2._____

3._____

4._____

5._____

6._____

7._____

8._____

9._____

10._____

11._____

12._____

13._____

14._____

Name _____

Test Form E

ANSWERS	

15.a)_____

15. Given the functions $f(x) = x - 2$ and $g(x) = x^2 + 4$, find a) $(f + g)(x)$ b) $(f - g)(x)$ c) $(fg)(x)$ d) $(f/g)(x)$ e) $(ff)(x)$

b)_____

16. Given the function P described by $P(x) = 2x^2 - 3x + 1$, find $P(-1)$.

c)_____

17. Graph: $f(x) = x - 3$

d)_____

e)_____

16._____

17.___See graph.___

[✓]————————————————————————

Solve.

18. $2y + 1 \geqslant 3y - 4$ 19. $|3x - 4| < 5$

18._____

20. $2x + 2y - z = 3$
     $x + 3y + z = -1$
    $3x + 4y - 2z = 7$

19._____

21. Pam picked apples on three days. She picked a total of 64 bushels. On Monday she picked 7 bushels less than on Tuesday. On Wednesday she picked 12 bushels more than on Monday. How many bushels did she pick each day?

20._____

Δ————————————————————————

21._____

22. Factor: $x^{9a} - y^{6b}$

22._____

Name _____

1. Find the LCM: $4x - 4$, $x^2 - 2x + 1$

ANSWERS

1._____

Perform the indicated operation and simplify.

2. $(4y^5 + 3y^4 - 8y^3 + 3) \div (y^2 + 1)$ 3. $\dfrac{y + 6}{2y + 8} \cdot \dfrac{3y + 12}{y^2 - 36}$

2._____

3._____

4. $\dfrac{x^3 + 8}{x^2 + 3x - 40} \div \dfrac{x^2 + 5x + 6}{x^2 - 2x - 15}$ 5. $\dfrac{2}{x^2 - 16} - \dfrac{1}{x - 4}$

4._____

6. $\dfrac{2}{3x + 6} + \dfrac{x}{x^2 - 4}$ 7. $\dfrac{y}{y + 1} + \dfrac{2}{y - 1} - \dfrac{y + 1}{y^2 - 1}$

5._____

8. Divide. Use synthetic division. Show your work.
$(y^2 - 8y + 16) \div (y + 4)$

6._____

7._____

Solve.

9. $\dfrac{5}{y^2 - 25} = \dfrac{4}{y + 5} - \dfrac{1}{y - 5}$ 10. $\dfrac{x}{4x - 16} = \dfrac{1}{x - 4}$

8._____

11. Simplify: $\dfrac{4 - \dfrac{4}{y}}{4 + \dfrac{4}{y}}$

9._____

10._____

12. Solve for p: $\dfrac{mn - p}{np} = R$

11._____

12._____

Name _____

ANSWERS

13. _____

14. _____

15. _____

16. _____

17. _____

18. _____

19. _____

20.   See graph.

21. _____

13. Find an equation of variation where y varies inversely as x and y = 0.2 when x = 0.8.

Solve.

14. The number of plastic cups produced by a machine varies directly as the amount of time the machine is operating. The machine produces 14,000 cups in 7 hours. How many cups can be produced in 30 hours?

15. The speed of train A is 15 mph faster than the speed of train B. Train A travels 315 miles in the same time it takes train B to travel 270 miles. Find the speed of each train.

16. Mark can paint a room in 6 hours. Working together, Mark and Marie can paint the room in 2 hours. How long would it take Marie to paint the room by herself?

[✓]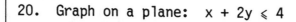

Factor.

17. $3x^2 + 12x + 9$ 18. $27b^3 - 1$

19. Solve: $x^2 = 6x$

20. Graph on a plane: $x + 2y \leqslant 4$

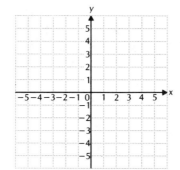

△ _____

21. Find the reciprocal and simplify:

$$\frac{x + 1}{\frac{1}{x} + 1}$$

Name _____

Class _____ *Score* _____ *Grade* _____

	ANSWERS
1. Find the LCM: $3x^3$, $2x^2 + 4x$	
	1._____
Perform the indicated operation and simplify.	
2. $\dfrac{4}{y^2 + 10y + 25} - \dfrac{3}{y^2 - 25}$ 3. $\dfrac{a}{a + b} + \dfrac{2ab}{a^2 - b^2}$	2._____
	3._____
4. $\dfrac{y}{y^2 - 36} + \dfrac{1}{y^2 + 7y + 6} - \dfrac{y}{y^2 - 5y - 6}$	
	4._____
5. $\dfrac{5y^2 - 5}{3y + 9} \cdot \dfrac{y^2 - 9}{15y + 15}$ 6. $\dfrac{x^2 - 36}{x^3 - 8} \div \dfrac{x^2 - 4x - 12}{x^2 - 4}$	
	5._____
7. $(y^2 - 10y + 20) \div (y + 2)$	
	6._____
8. Simplify: $\dfrac{\dfrac{y^2 + 8y + 7}{y^2 + 2y + 1}}{\dfrac{y^2 - 49}{y^2 + 11y + 10}}$	7._____
9. Solve for a: $\dfrac{a + b}{ab} = F$	8._____
	9._____
Solve.	
10. $\dfrac{x}{7} + \dfrac{x}{8} = 1$ 11. $\dfrac{4}{5a + 8} = \dfrac{a}{a + 3}$	
	10._____
12. Divide. Use synthetic division. Show your work. $(4x^4 - 6x^2 - 5x + 4) \div (x - 2)$	11._____
	12._____

Name _____

ANSWERS	
13._____	
14._____	
15._____	
16._____	
17.__See graph.__	
18._____	
19._____	
20._____	
21._____	

13. Find an equation of variation where y varies directly as x and y = 24 when x = 8.

Solve.

14. A study showed that school attendance varied inversely as the outside temperature. When the temperature was 70° F, 92% of the students attended class. What percentage of students attended class when the temperature was 80° F?

15. A boat can travel at a speed of 12 km/h in still water. The boat travels 50 km downstream in a river in the same time it takes to travel 10 km upstream. What is the speed of the river current?

16. Bob can unload a truckload of melons in 5 hours. Working together, it takes Bob and Jack 2 hours to do the same job. How long would it take Jack to unload the truck by himself?

[✓]──────────────────────────

17. Graph on a plane: $x + y \geqslant 3$

Factor.

18. $a^3 + 125$ 19. $6x^2 + 11x - 10$

20. Solve: $x^2 + 6x + 5 = 0$

Δ──────────────────────────

21. Simplify: $\dfrac{y^2 - z^2}{z^2 - z + y^2 + y - 2yz}$

Name _____

Class _____ *Score* _____ *Grade* _____

	ANSWERS

1. Find the LCM: $4y + 24$, $y^2 + 12y + 36$

1. _____

Perform the indicated operation and simplify.

2. $\dfrac{2y + 4}{7y^2 - 28} \cdot \dfrac{7y - 14}{16}$ 3. $(y^2 - 8y + 21) \div (y - 4)$

2. _____

4. $\dfrac{2x^2 - 98}{x^2 + 15x + 50} \div \dfrac{x^2 + 2x - 35}{x^2 - 25}$ 5. $\dfrac{a + b}{a - b} + \dfrac{a - b}{a + b}$

3. _____

6. $\dfrac{2}{y^3 - 64} - \dfrac{2}{y^2 + 4y + 16}$

4. _____

5. _____

7. $\dfrac{5}{y^2 - 25} - \dfrac{1}{y^2 + 6y + 5} + \dfrac{3}{y^2 - 4y - 5}$

6. _____

8. Divide. Use synthetic division. Show your work.

$(3y^3 - 2y + 5) \div (y + 3)$

7. _____

9. Simplify: $\dfrac{a + \dfrac{1}{b}}{b + \dfrac{1}{a}}$

8. _____

9. _____

Solve.

10. $\dfrac{2}{y + 4} - \dfrac{2}{y^2 - 16} = \dfrac{4}{y - 4}$ 11. $\dfrac{x}{3x - 27} = \dfrac{3}{x - 9}$

10. _____

12. Solve for a: $B = \dfrac{P}{a(c - d)}$

11. _____

12. _____

ANSWERS	
13._____	13. Find an equation of variation where y varies directly as x and y = 0.25 when x = 16.

Solve.

14. The amount of tread left on a tire varies inversely as the number of miles the tire has traveled. A tire that has traveled 30,000 mi has $\frac{1}{8}$ in. of tread left. How much tread will be left on a tire that has traveled 24,000 mi?

14._____

15. Two pipes are being used to drain a tank. One of them can drain the tank alone in 3 hours. The other can drain the tank alone in 6 hours. How long will it take them together to drain the tank?

15._____

16. The speed of a stream is 3 mph. A boat travels 49 mi downstream in the same time it takes to travel 35 mi upstream. Find the speed of the boat in still water.

16._____

[✓]————————————————————————————

Factor.

17. $8y^3 - 64$ 18. $4x^2 - 12xy + 9y^2$

17._____

19. Solve: $3x^2 - 4x = 0$

20. Graph on a plane: $y < 1$

18._____

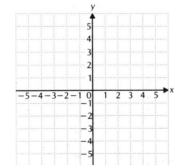

19._____

20. __See graph.__

Δ————————————————————————————

21. Simplify: $1 + \dfrac{1}{x + \dfrac{1}{x + 1}}$

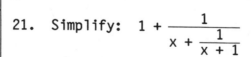

21._____

Name _____

Class _____ **Score** _____ **Grade** _____

1. Find the LCM: $x^3 - 2x^2$, $2x^2 - 6x + 4$

ANSWERS

1. _____

Perform the indicated operation and simplify.

2. $\dfrac{5}{y^2 + 8y + 16} - \dfrac{4}{y^2 + 9y + 20}$ 3. $\dfrac{a - 1}{1 - a} + \dfrac{3a + 3}{a^2 - 1}$

2. _____

4. $\dfrac{2}{y + 8} + \dfrac{24}{y^2 - 64} - \dfrac{3}{2y - 16}$

3. _____

5. $\dfrac{y^2 - 8y - 33}{y^2 - 6y + 8} \div \dfrac{y^2 + y - 6}{y^2 - 15y + 44}$

4. _____

6. $(3y^4 + 1) \div (y^2 + 2y + 1)$

5. _____

7. $\dfrac{y^2 + 6y + 9}{3y^2 - 27} \cdot \dfrac{2y - 6}{y^2 + 4y + 3}$

6. _____

8. Simplify: $\dfrac{\dfrac{2y^2 + 8y + 8}{y^2 + y - 2}}{\dfrac{y^2 + 6y + 8}{y^2 - 9y + 8}}$

7. _____

9. Divide. Use synthetic division. Show your work.

$(y^2 - 6y + 30) \div (y + 2)$

8. _____

9. _____

Solve.

10. $\dfrac{x}{11} + \dfrac{x}{6} = 2$ 11. $\dfrac{3}{y + 7} - \dfrac{6}{y^2 + 10y + 21} = \dfrac{4}{y + 3}$

10. _____

12. Solve for b: $M = \dfrac{ab + c}{ab}$

11. _____

12. _____

Name _____

ANSWERS	
13._____	**13.** Find an equation of variation where y varies inversely as x and y = 5 when x = 3.
	Solve.
14._____	**14.** The amount of concrete necessary to construct a patio varies directly as the area of the patio. It takes 4.5 yd³ of concrete to construct a 200 ft² patio. How many cubic yards of concrete will be needed to construct at 250 ft² patio?
15._____	**15.** Airplane A travels 50 km/h faster than airplane B. Airplane A travels 875 km in the same time it takes airplane B to travel 700 km. Find the speed of each airplane.
16._____	**16.** One typist can type a report in 4 hours. Another typist can type the same report in 3 hours. How long would it take them to type the report working together?
	[✓]————————————————————
17. See graph.	**17.** Graph on a plane: $3x - 4y < 12$ 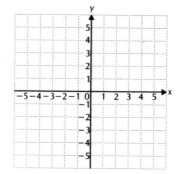
18._____	
19._____	Factor.
	18. $4x^2 - 4x - 48$ **19.** $y^3 - 8$
	20. Solve: $2x^2 = x + 6$
20._____	Δ————————————————————
	21. Find the reciprocal and simplify: $$\frac{1 - \dfrac{1}{x^2}}{x - 1}$$
21._____	

Name _____

Class _____ Score _____ Grade _____

ANSWERS

1. Simplify: $(-2x^{-5}y^3)(5x^3y^{-6})$

1._____

Simplify. Assume that letters can represent ANY real number.

2. $\sqrt{64x^2}$ 3. $\sqrt[3]{-27}$ 4. $\sqrt[6]{y^6}$

2._____

In the remaining questions, assume that ALL expressions under radical signs represent positive numbers.

5. Divide and write scientific notation for the answer:

$$\frac{4.5 \times 10^6}{9.0 \times 10^{11}}$$

3._____

4._____

6. Use a calculator or Table 1. Approximate to three decimal places.

$$\sqrt{148}$$

5._____

6._____

7. Simplify: $\sqrt{72} + 4\sqrt{98} - 3\sqrt{50}$

7._____

Multiply and simplify.

8. $\sqrt{128x^3} \ \sqrt{2y^4}$ 9. $(2 + 3\sqrt{3})(2 - 3\sqrt{3})$

8._____

10. Divide. Then simplify by taking roots if possible.

$$\frac{\sqrt{48x^2y^5}}{\sqrt{6xy^2}}$$

9._____

11. Rationalize the denominator: $\dfrac{\sqrt{2} + \sqrt{a}}{\sqrt{3} + \sqrt{a}}$

10._____

11._____

12. Rewrite with fractional exponents: $\left(\sqrt[3]{2x^2y}\right)^5$

12._____

Name _____

ANSWERS

13. _____

14. _____

15. _____

16. _____

17. _____

18. _____

19. _____

20. _____

21. _____

22. _____

23. _____

24. _____

25. _____

13. Use fractional exponents to write a single radical expression:

$$\sqrt[3]{x}\ \sqrt[4]{x}$$

14. Solve: $\sqrt{x + 7} = 4 - \sqrt{x - 1}$

In Questions 15 and 16, give an exact answer and an approximation to three decimal places.

15. In a right triangle with a = 5 and b = 3, find the length of side c.

16. How long is a guy wire reaching from the top of a 10 ft pole to a point on the ground 7 ft from the pole?

17. Express in terms of i and simplify: $\sqrt{-12}$

18. Add: $(5 + 7i) + (3 - 4i)$

19. Multiply: $(3 - i)(4 + 5i)$

20. Divide: $\dfrac{4 + 3i}{1 - 2i}$

[✓]————————————————————

21. Multiply: $\dfrac{x^2 - 1}{2x - 6} \cdot \dfrac{x^2 - 6x + 9}{x^2 - 4x + 3}$

22. Solve: $\dfrac{2}{x - 2} = \dfrac{3x}{2x + 4}$

23. Complete the square: $x^2 - 3x$

24. Find two consecutive even integers whose product is 168.

Δ————————————————————

25. Multiply and simplify.

$$(\sqrt{7} + \sqrt{3} - \sqrt{10})(\sqrt{7} + \sqrt{3} + \sqrt{10})$$

Name _____

Class _____ Score _____ Grade _____

Simplify. Assume that letters can represent ANY real number.

	ANSWERS

1. $\sqrt{x^2 - 8x + 16}$ 2. $\sqrt[8]{(-3)^8}$ 3. $\sqrt[3]{-\dfrac{1}{8}}$

1._____

2._____

In the remaining questions assume that ALL expressions under radical signs represent positive numbers.

4. Use a calculator or Table 1 to approximate to three decimal places:
$$\sqrt{135}$$

3._____

Simplify.

4._____

5. $\dfrac{3^{-2}a^3b^{-5}}{2^{-3}a^{-3}b}$ 6. $2\sqrt{12} + 3\sqrt{75} - \sqrt{300}$

5._____

7. Multiply and write scientific notation for the answer:
$$(3.1 \times 10^8)(3.5 \times 10^{-2})$$

6._____

Multiply and simplify.

7._____

8. $(3\sqrt{5} + 1)(2\sqrt{5} - 3)$ 9. $\sqrt{3a^2b^5}\ \sqrt{6ab^3}$

8._____

10. Divide. Then simplify by taking roots if possible.
$$\dfrac{\sqrt{125a^5b^2}}{\sqrt{5ab}}$$

9._____

11. Rewrite without fractional exponents: $(4x)^{2/3}$

10._____

12. Use fractional exponents to write a single radical expression:
$$\sqrt[4]{3x}\ \sqrt[6]{x - 2}$$

11._____

13. Rationalize the denominator: $\dfrac{2 + \sqrt{3}}{3 - \sqrt{2}}$

12._____

13._____

Name _____

14. _____

14. Solve: $\sqrt{x + 7} = \sqrt{x + 12} - 1$

15. Subtract: $(-2 + 9i) - (3 + 4i)$

15. _____

16. Divide: $\dfrac{3 + 6i}{2 + 3i}$

16. _____

17. Multiply: $(6 - 7i)(2 + 2i)$

18. Determine whether $-1 - 2i$ is a solution of $x^2 + 2x + 5 = 0$.

17. _____

In Questions 19 and 20, give an exact answer and an approximation to three decimal places.

19. In a right triangle with $a = 4$ and $c = 9$, find the length of side b.

18. _____

20. The diagonal of a square has length 5 m. Find the length of a side of the square.

19. _____

[✓]────────────────────────────────

20. _____

21. Divide and simplify: $\dfrac{2y - 8}{y^2 - 1} \div \dfrac{y^2 - 5y + 4}{3y + 3}$

22. Factor by completing the square. Show your work.
$$x^2 + 6x - 91$$

21. _____

23. Solve: $\dfrac{4}{x - 8} = \dfrac{x}{2x - 16}$

22. _____

24. The length of a rectangle is 5 cm more than the width. The area is 84 cm². Find the width and length.

23. _____

Δ────────────────────────────────

24. _____

25. Simplify: $\dfrac{9\sqrt{36ab}}{6\sqrt{a^{-3}b^{-5}}} \dfrac{\sqrt{x^3y^2}}{\sqrt{81x^2y^{-3}}}$

25. _____

Name _____

Class _____ Score _____ Grade _____

1. Divide and write scientific notation for the answer:

$$\frac{1.1 \times 10^{18}}{4.4 \times 10^{7}}$$

Simplify. Assume that letters can represent ANY real number.

2. $\sqrt[3]{-64}$ 　　　　　3. $\sqrt{100a^2}$ 　　　　　4. $\sqrt[7]{x^7}$

In the remaining questions assume that ALL expressions under radical signs represent positive numbers.

Multiply and simplify.

5. $\sqrt[4]{mn^2} \; \sqrt[4]{m^3n^3}$ 　　　　　6. $(3 - \sqrt{5})^2$

7. Divide. Then simplify by taking roots if possible.

$$\frac{\sqrt{21a^9}}{\sqrt{7a^3}}$$

Simplify.

8. $(4x^{-5}y^7)(-3x^4y^{-2})$ 　　　9. $5\sqrt{8} - \sqrt{200} + 3\sqrt{50}$

10. Rationalize the denominator: $\dfrac{\sqrt{2} + \sqrt{3}}{\sqrt{6} + \sqrt{5}}$

Solve.

11. $4 = \sqrt{5 + 3x}$ 　　　　　12. $\sqrt{5x} - 3 = \sqrt{x - 1}$

13. Rewrite with fractional exponents: $(\sqrt[3]{2a^2b})^7$

ANSWERS
1._____
2._____
3._____
4._____
5._____
6._____
7._____
8._____
9._____
10._____
11._____
12._____
13._____

Name _____

ANSWERS
14. _____
15. _____
16. _____
17. _____
18. _____
19. _____
20. _____
21. _____
22. _____
23. _____
24. _____
25. _____

14. Use fractional exponents to write a single radical expression:

$$\sqrt[6]{a} \ \sqrt[8]{a-3}$$

In Questions 15 and 16, give an exact answer and an approximation to three decimal places.

15. In a right triangle with $b = 4$ and $c = 10$, find the length of side a.

16. Find the length of a diagonal of a square with sides of length 4 cm.

17. Add: $(4 + 3i) + (2 - 6i)$

18. Multiply: $(-2 + 5i)(3 + 7i)$

19. Divide: $\dfrac{9 - i}{3i}$

20. Express in terms of i and simplify: $-\sqrt{-27}$

[✓]————————————————————————

21. Factor: $y^2 - 12y + 36 - 16z^2$

22. Multiply and simplify: $\dfrac{x^2 - 4x}{x^2 + 3x - 4} \cdot \dfrac{x^2 + 8x + 16}{x^2 - 16}$

23. Solve: $\dfrac{4}{y^2 - 1} - \dfrac{1}{y + 1} = \dfrac{2}{y - 1}$

24. Find three consecutive integers such that the product of the first and third integers is 11 less than the product of the second and third integers.

Δ————————————————————————

25. Divide: $\dfrac{3\sqrt{5} + 2\sqrt{3}\,i}{3\sqrt{5} - 2\sqrt{3}\,i}$

Name _____

　　　　　　　Class _____ Score _____ Grade _____

	ANSWERS

Simplify. Assume that letters can represent ANY real number.

1. $\sqrt{x^2 - 2x + 1}$　　　　2. $\sqrt[3]{-1}$　　　　3. $\sqrt[8]{y^8}$

1. _____

In the remaining questions, assume that ALL expressions under radical signs represent positive numbers.

2. _____

4. Use a calculator or Table 1 to approximate to three decimal places:
$$\sqrt{104}$$

3. _____

5. Multiply and write scientific notation for the answer:
$$(3.0 \times 10^{-12})(3.5 \times 10^6)$$

4. _____

Multiply and simplify.

5. _____

6. $\sqrt{27x}\ \sqrt{3x^2}$　　　　　7. $(3 + 4\sqrt{2})(1 - 2\sqrt{2})$

6. _____

Simplify.

7. _____

8. $\dfrac{3^{-1}x^{-7}y^4}{2^{-2}x^3y^{-1}}$　　　　9. $3\sqrt{24} - 2\sqrt{150} + 5\sqrt{54}$

8. _____

10. Divide. Then simplify by taking roots if possible.
$$\frac{\sqrt{42x^5}}{\sqrt{6x^2}}$$

9. _____

11. Rationalize the denominator: $\dfrac{4 + \sqrt{a}}{3 + \sqrt{a}}$

10. _____

12. Rewrite without fractional exponents: $(4ab^3)^{\frac{1}{5}}$

11. _____

13. Use fractional exponents to write a single radical expression:
$$\sqrt{y}\ \sqrt[5]{y + 1}$$

12. _____

13. _____

Name _____

ANSWERS

14._____

15._____

16._____

17._____

18._____

19._____

20._____

21._____

22._____

23._____

24._____

25._____

14. Solve: $\sqrt{3x + 4} - \sqrt{3x - 3} = 1$

15. Express in terms of i and simplify: $-\sqrt{-25}$

16. Add: $(7 - 5i)(2 + 3i)$

17. Multiply: $(2 + 6i)(4 + i)$

18. Divide: $\dfrac{-4 + 7i}{7 + 3i}$

In Questions 19 and 20, give an exact answer and an approximation to three decimal places.

19. In a right triangle with $a = 2$ and $b = 6$, find the length of side c.

20. An 11 ft guy wire reaches from the top of a pole to a point on the ground 5 ft from the base of the pole. How tall is the pole?

[✓]──

21. Divide and simplify: $\dfrac{x^2 - 9}{x^2 - 6x + 9} \div \dfrac{2x^2 + 6x}{x^2 - 5x + 6}$

22. Solve: $\dfrac{4a}{2a + 1} = \dfrac{1}{4a - 1}$

23. Complete the square: $a^2 + \dfrac{4}{5}a$

24. The perimeter of a square is two-thirds its area. Find the length of a side.

Δ──

25. Subtract and simplify: $\dfrac{1}{1 - 2i} - \dfrac{2}{3 + 2i}$

Name _____

Class _____ Score _____ Grade _____

1. Divide and write scientific notation for the answer:
$$\frac{1.2 \times 10^{-8}}{6.0 \times 10^{-12}}$$

Simplify. Assume that letters can represent ANY real number.

2. $\sqrt[3]{-8x^3}$

3. $\sqrt{\dfrac{y^2}{9}}$

4. $\sqrt[7]{(-5)^7}$

5. $\sqrt{a^2 + 4a + 4}$

In the remaining questions, assume that ALL expressions under radical signs represent positive numbers.

6. Divide. Then simplify by taking roots, is possible.
$$\frac{\sqrt{32a^7}}{\sqrt{2a^4}}$$

Multiply and simplify.

7. $(\sqrt{5} - \sqrt{2})^2$

8. $\sqrt{15x^3} \ \sqrt{3x}$

Simplify.

9. $(-3a^{-9}b^{-7})(-2a^5b^{-1})$

10. $(\sqrt{3xy^2})^3$

11. $\sqrt{10x^3} - \sqrt{40x^5} + \sqrt{90x}$

12. Rationalize the numerator: $\dfrac{2\sqrt{5} - \sqrt{a}}{\sqrt{5} + \sqrt{a}}$

13. Use fractional exponents to write a single radical expression:
$$\sqrt[3]{2x} \ \sqrt[5]{x - 4}$$

ANSWERS

1._____

2._____

3._____

4._____

5._____

6._____

7._____

8._____

9._____

10._____

11._____

12._____

13._____

Name _____

ANSWERS	

Solve.

14. _____

14. $\sqrt{2x - 3} = 3$ 15. $\sqrt{2x - 5} - 2 = \sqrt{x - 2}$

In Questions 16 and 17, give an exact answer and an approximation to three decimal places.

15. _____

16. In a right triangle with a = 3 and c = 10, find the length of side b.

16. _____

17. Find the length of a diagonal of a rectangle with sides of length 4 cm and 7 cm.

17. _____

18. Subtract: (9 − 4i) − (−2 + i)

19. Divide: $\dfrac{-4 + 5i}{1 - 2i}$

18. _____

20. Multiply: (2 − 7i)(3 − 5i)

19. _____

[✓]─────────────────────────────────────

21. Multiply and simplify: $\dfrac{4x^2 + 4x}{x^2 + 3x + 2} \cdot \dfrac{x^2 - 4}{8x^3}$

20. _____

22. Factor: $4x^2 - 4x + 1 - 81y^2$

21. _____

23. Solve: $\dfrac{3}{x^2 - x - 2} - \dfrac{1}{x + 1} = \dfrac{2}{x - 2}$

22. _____

24. The square of a number is 15 less than 8 times the number. Find the number.

23. _____

Δ───

25. Simplify: $\dfrac{4\sqrt{25a^2b}}{5\sqrt{a^{-4}b^{-1}}} \quad \dfrac{\sqrt{xy^3}}{\sqrt{16x^{-1}y^{-3}}}$

24. _____

25. _____

Name _____

Class _____ Score _____ Grade _____

Solve.

1. $4x^2 - 3 = 0$ 2. $x^2 - 10x + 16 = 0$

3. $2x^2 - x + 1 = 0$ 4. $\dfrac{b}{6} - \dfrac{2}{b} = 1$

5. $y^4 - 4y^2 + 4 = 0$

6. Solve. Approximate the solutions to the nearest tenth: $y^2 + 3y + 1 = 0$

7. Solve for s: $L = \dfrac{Abm}{s^2}$

8. Determine the nature of the solutions:
$$x^2 - 5x - 3 = 0$$

9. Complete the square: $f(x) = 2x^2 + 8x - 7$

10. Find the quadratic function which fits these data points: $(0,0)$, $(1,-3)$, $(4,0)$

11. Find an equation of variation where y varies directly as x and inversely as the square of z and $y = 8$ when $x = 16$ and $z = 6$.

ANSWERS

1. _____

2. _____

3. _____

4. _____

5. _____

6. _____

7. _____

8. _____

9. _____

10. _____

11. _____

Name _____

ANSWERS	

12._____

13._____

14._____

15.___See graph.___

16._____

17._____

18._____

19._____

20._____

12. Find three consecutive integers such that the square of the second integer plus the product of the first and third integers is 127.

13. Joe and Jane work together and paint a room in 6 hours. It would take Jane twice as long as Joe to do the job alone. How long would it take each one to do the job working alone?

14. What is the area of the largest rectangular region that can be enclosed using 160 ft of fencing?

15. a) Graph: $f(x) = -3(x + 1)^2 + 2$

   b) Label the vertex.

   c) Draw the line of symmetry.

   d) Find the maximum or minimum value of the function.

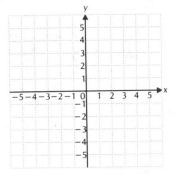

[✓]────────────────────────────

16. Add and simplify: $\dfrac{x}{x^2 - 25} + \dfrac{3}{x^2 + 4x - 5}$

17. Multiply and simplify: $\sqrt[3]{6y^5} \ \sqrt[3]{20x^5y^4}$

18. Solve: $\sqrt{6b} - 2 = \sqrt{3b - 2}$

19. The sum of two numbers is 138, and the difference is 26. Find the numbers.

Δ────────────────────────────

20. Solve: $(2x^3 - 11x^2 - 40x)(6x - 5) = 0$

Name _____

Class _____ Score _____ Grade _____

1. a) Graph: $f(x) = -2(x - 1)^2 + 2$
    b) Label the vertex.
    c) Draw the line of symmetry.
    d) Find the maximum or minimum
       value of the function.

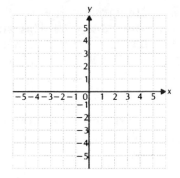

ANSWERS

1.___See graph.___

2._____

3._____

2. Write a quadratic equation whose only solution is –3.

Solve.

3. $2y^2 - 2y + 1 = 0$

4. $r(r - 8) + 16 = 8(r - 6)$

4._____

5._____

5. $3x^2 - 5 = 0$

6. $\dfrac{3x}{2} - \dfrac{2}{3x} = \dfrac{8}{3}$

6._____

7. $4x^{-2} + 4x^{-1} - 3 = 0$

7._____

8. Solve. Approximate the solutions to the nearest tenth.
       $x^2 - 4x - 8 = 0$

8._____

9. Solve for z: $w^2 = y^2 + z^2$

9._____

10. Find the x-intercepts: $f(x) = x^2 + 3x + 5$

10._____

11. Find a quadratic function which fits these data points:
     (0,3), (1,0), (2,–1)

11._____

Name _____

ANSWERS	
12._____	12. The intensity I of light from a light bulb varies inversely as the square of the distance d from the bulb. When the distance is 4 m, I is 100 W/m². Find the intensity at a distance of 8 m.
13._____	13. Find the maximum product of two numbers whose sum is 14.
14._____	14. Airplane A travels 900 miles at a certain speed. Plane B travels 1000 miles at a speed 50 mph slower, and it takes 1 hour longer. Find the speed of each plane.
15._____	15. The product of two numbers is 12. The first number is four times the second. Find the numbers.

[✓]————————————————————————————

16._____   16. Multiply and simplify: $\sqrt[3]{9x^2y^4}$ $\sqrt[3]{6x^2y}$

17._____   17. Add and simplify: $\dfrac{3}{x^2 - 2x} + \dfrac{x + 2}{x^2 - 4}$

18._____   18. Solve: $\sqrt{x + 2} + 1 = \sqrt{3x - 5}$

19._____   19. The length of a rectangle is 7 cm more than the width. The perimeter is 34 cm. Find the width and length.

Δ————————————————————————————

20._____   20. Solve: $x^2 - 2\sqrt{5}\,x + 5 = 0$

Name _____

Class _____ Score _____ Grade _____

1. a) Graph: $f(x) = 4(x - 2)^2 + 1$
    b) Label the vertex.
    c) Draw the line of symmetry.
    d) Find the maximum or minimum
       value of the function.

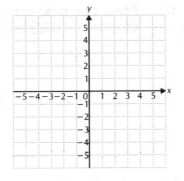

ANSWERS

1.____See graph.____

2._____

3._____

2. Find the x-intercepts: $9x^2 + 6x + 1 = 0$

4._____

3. Write a quadratic equation having solutions $\sqrt{2}$ and
    $3\sqrt{2}$.

5._____

Solve.

4. $9x^2 - 3x = 0$ 5. $3x^2 + 5x - 2 = 0$

6._____

6. $x^2 + 9x + 36 = 0$ 7. $(x^2 - 3)^2 + (x^2 - 3) - 2 = 0$

7._____

8. $\dfrac{2x}{x + 3} + 1 = \dfrac{2x + 1}{x + 1}$

8._____

9. Solve. Approximate the solutions to the nearest tenth.
    $$3y^2 - 8y - 2 = 0$$

9._____

10. Solve for m: $n = pm + 4m^2$

10._____

11. Find an equation of variation where y varies jointly
     as x and the square of z, and y = 16 when x = 8 and
     z = 2.

11._____

Name _____

ANSWERS	
12._____	**12.** Find the quadratic function which fits these data points: (0,2), (1,0), (2,4)
13._____	**13.** Find the maximum product of two numbers whose sum is −20.
14._____	**14.** A boat travels 16 miles upstream and 16 miles back. The time for the roundtrip is 3 hours. The speed of the stream is 4 mph. Find the speed of the boat in still water.
15._____	**15.** A picture frame measures 16 in. by 20 in. and 192 in² of picture shows. Find the width of the frame.

[✓]―――――――――――――――――――――――――――――

16. Multiply and simplify: $\sqrt{14x^3y^4}\ \sqrt{6xy^3}$

16._____

17. Subtract and simplify: $\dfrac{3}{x-4} - \dfrac{2}{x+3}$

17._____

18. Solve: $\sqrt{x+1} - 3 = \sqrt{2x+11}$

18._____

19. The sum of two numbers is 78 and their difference is 44. Find the numbers.

19._____

Δ―――――――――――――――――――――――――――――

20. Solve: $\left(\dfrac{x-1}{3}\right)^2 - 3 = 2\left(\dfrac{x-1}{3}\right)$

20._____

Name _____

Class _____ **Score** _____ **Grade** _____

1. Find the distance between the points $(-3,4)$ and $(6,3)$. Give an exact answer and an approximation to three decimal places.

2. Find the midpoint of the segment with endpoints $(-3,4)$ and $(6,3)$.

3. Find an equation of the circle having center $(3,-2)$ and radius 4.

4. Find the center and radius of the circle $x^2 + y^2 - 4x + 6y + 9 = 0$.

Graph.

5. $\dfrac{x^2}{16} + \dfrac{y^2}{4} = 1$

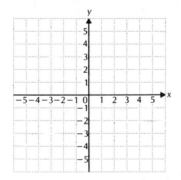

6. $xy = 8$

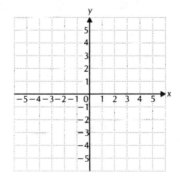

7. $\dfrac{y^2}{4} - \dfrac{x^2}{9} = 1$

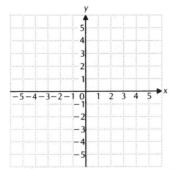

8. $y = x^2 + 3x$

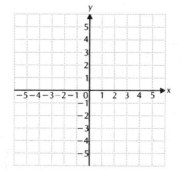

ANSWERS

1. _____

2. _____

3. _____

4. _____

5. ___See graph.___

6. ___See graph.___

7. ___See graph.___

8. ___See graph.___

Name _____

ANSWERS

9.   See graph.

10. _____

11. _____

12. _____

13. _____

14. _____

15. _____

16. _____

17. _____

18. _____

19. _____

20. _____

9.   Graph: $x^2 + y^2 = 5$

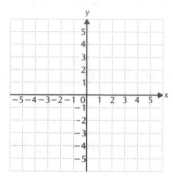

Solve.

10. $x^2 + y^2 = 5$
     $x - y = 3$

11. $x^2 + y^2 = 10$
     $xy = 3$

12. The sum of the areas of two squares is 89 cm². The difference of their areas is 39 cm². Find the length of a side of each square.

13. The sum of two numbers is 4 and the difference of their squares is 56. Find the numbers.

Solve.

14. $x^2 - 3x \leqslant 4$

15. $\dfrac{x - 3}{x + 4} > 2$

[✓]————————————————————————

16. Simplify: $\sqrt{\dfrac{a^2 b^3}{81}}$

17. Rationalize the denominator: $\dfrac{3 + \sqrt{x}}{1 + \sqrt{x}}$

18. Solve: $3x^2 + 2x + 1 = 0$

19. A boat travels 24 miles upstream and 24 miles back in a total time of 5 hours. The speed of the stream is 2 mph. Find the speed of the boat in still water.

Δ————————————————————————

20. If the sides of a triangle have lengths a, b, and c, and $a^2 + b^2 = c^2$ then the triangle is a right triangle. Determine whether the points (-1,3), (3,-1), and (0,-7) are vertices of a right triangle.

Name _____

Class _____ Score _____ Grade _____

Graph.

ANSWERS

1. $xy = 5$

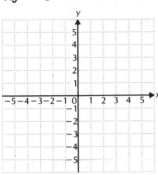

2. $\dfrac{x^2}{9} + \dfrac{y^2}{1} = 1$

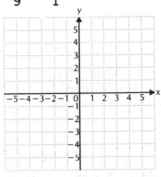

3. $\dfrac{y^2}{16} - \dfrac{x^2}{4} = 1$

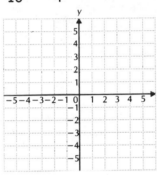

4. $y = 2x^2 - 5x + 3$

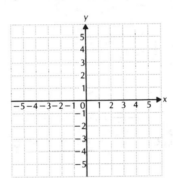

5. $x^2 + y^2 = 6$

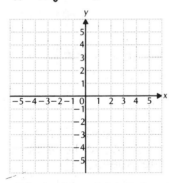

6. Find the midpoint of the segment with endpoints (7,-2) and (3,8).

7. Find the distance between the points (7,-2) and (3,8). Give an exact answer and an approximation to three decimal places.

8. Find the center and radius of the circle $x^2 + y^2 + 2x - 8y + 6 = 0$.

9. Find an equation of the circle having center (-4,7) and radius $\sqrt{3}$.

1.___See graph.___

2.___See graph.___

3.___See graph.___

4.___See graph.___

5.___See graph.___

6._____

7._____

8._____

9._____

Name _____

ANSWERS

Solve.

10. $y^2 = x + 7$

   $2y = x + 4$

11. $x^2 + y^2 = 9$

   $4x^2 - y^2 = 1$

10._____

11._____

12. It will take 190 yd of fencing to enclose a rectangular field. The area of the field is 2200 yd². Find the dimensions.

12._____

13. The product of two numbers is 56. The sum of their squares is 212. Find the numbers.

Solve.

13._____

14. $\dfrac{x - 1}{x + 2} > 0$

15. $x^2 - 9 \leqslant 0$

14._____

[✓]————————————————

16. Solve: $x^2 - 4x + 7 = 0$

15._____

17. Simplify: $-\sqrt[3]{-27}$

16._____

18. Rationalize the numerator: $\dfrac{\sqrt{3} - \sqrt{5}}{\sqrt{2} + \sqrt{3}}$

17._____

19. A car travels 360 miles at a certain speed. If the speed had been 5 mph faster the trip would have been made in 1 hour less time. Find the speed.

18._____

Δ————————————————

20. Find two numbers whose product is 3 and the sum of whose reciprocals is $\dfrac{37}{30}$.

19._____

20._____

Name _____

Class _____ Score _____ Grade _____

1. Find the distance between the points (-1,6) and (2,-1).
   Give an exact answer and an approximation to three
   decimal places.

2. Find the midpoint of the segment with endpoints (-1,6)
   and (2,-1).

3. Find an equation of the circle having center (2,-4)
   and radius $\sqrt{5}$.

4. Find the center and radius of the circle
   $x^2 + y^2 + 6x - 10y + 30 = 0$.

Graph.

5. $\dfrac{y^2}{4} - \dfrac{x^2}{9} = 1$ 6. $xy = 7$

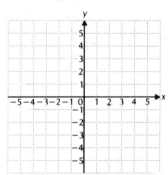   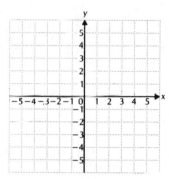

7. $x^2 + y^2 = 11$ 8. $\dfrac{x^2}{4} + \dfrac{y^2}{25} = 1$

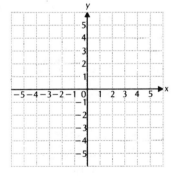   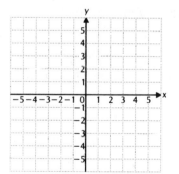

9. $y = x^2 + 2x - 3$

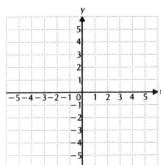

ANSWERS

1._____

2._____

3._____

4._____

5.____See graph.____

6.____See graph.____

7.____See graph.____

8.____See graph.____

9.____See graph.____

Name _____

ANSWERS

Solve.

10. $y = x^2$

    $2x = y - 3$

11. $2xy - y^2 = 8$

    $3xy - 2y^2 = 4$

12. The area of a rectangle is 10 cm². The length of a diagonal is 5 cm. Find the dimensions.

13. The difference of two numbers is 8 and the difference of their squares is 208. Find the numbers.

14. $(x + 2)(x + 1)(x - 4) \geqslant 0$

15. $\dfrac{x - 2}{x + 3} < 0$

[✓]─────────────────────────────────

16. Rationalize the denominator: $\dfrac{2 + \sqrt{x}}{1 - \sqrt{x}}$

17. Simplify: $\sqrt{96x^3}$

18. Solve: $x^2 + 2x + 4 = 0$

19. During the first part of a trip a car travels 75 miles at a certain speed. It travels 60 miles on the second part of the trip at a speed 10 mph slower. The total time for the trip is 3 hours. Find the speed on each part of the trip.

Δ─────────────────────────────────

20. Find an equation of the circle with center (0,2) passing through $(2\sqrt{3}, 3)$.

10. _____

11. _____

12. _____

13. _____

14. _____

15. _____

16. _____

17. _____

18. _____

19. _____

20. _____

Name _____

Class _____ *Score* _____ *Grade* _____

Graph.

ANSWERS

1. $\dfrac{x^2}{9} + \dfrac{y^2}{16} = 1$

2. $xy = 6$

1. ___See graph.___

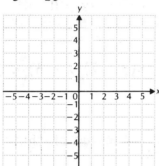

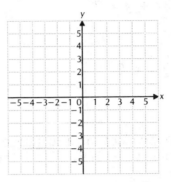

2. ___See graph.___

3. $\dfrac{x^2}{4} - \dfrac{y^2}{25} = 1$

4. $x^2 + y^2 = 4$

3. ___See graph.___

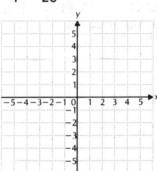

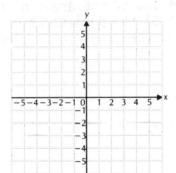

4. ___See graph.___

5. $y = x^2 - 4x + 2$

5. ___See graph.___

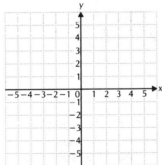

6. _____

6. Find the midpoint of the segment with endpoints (–6,2) and (2,–3).

7. Find the distance between the points (–6,2) and (2,–3). Give an exact answer and an approximation to three decimal places.

7. _____

8. Find the center and radius of the circle $x^2 + y^2 - 8x + 6y - 11 = 0$.

8. _____

9. Find an equation of the circle having center (2,–9) and radius 3.

9. _____

Name _____

ANSWERS

Solve.

10. $6x^2 - y^2 = -10$

    $3x + y = 7$

11. $2x^2 + xy = 5$

    $3x^2 - xy = 0$

10._____

12. $\dfrac{1}{x + 3} \leqslant 0$

13. $x(x - 7)(x + 5) < 0$

11._____

14. The product of two numbers is 60. The sum of their squares is 169. Find the numbers.

12._____

15. The sum of the areas of two squares is 74 ft². The sum of the perimeters of the two squares is 48 ft. Find the length of a side of each square.

13._____

14._____

[✓]

16. Solve: $x^2 + 4x + 6 = 0$

15._____

17. Simplify: $\sqrt[3]{-\dfrac{8}{27}}$

16._____

18. Rationalize the denominator: $\dfrac{\sqrt{2} + \sqrt{5}}{\sqrt{3} - \sqrt{5}}$

17._____

19. Airplane A travels 600 miles at a certain speed. Plane B travels 1250 miles at a speed 100 mph faster but takes 1 hour longer. Find the speed of each plane.

18._____

19._____

20. Solve: $x^2 - y^2 = -10$

    $2xy - 6 = y^2$

20._____

Name _____

Class _____ **Score** _____ **Grade** _____

	ANSWERS

1. Find an equation of the circle with center (−4,5) and diameter $2\sqrt{5}$.

2. Find the center and radius of the circle $x^2 + y^2 + 10x - 2y + 25 = 0$.

3. Find the distance between the points (5,−2) and (−3,2). Give an exact answer and an approximation to three decimal places.

4. Find the midpoint of the segment with endpoints (5,−2) and (−3,4).

Graph.

5. $x^2 + y^2 = 3$

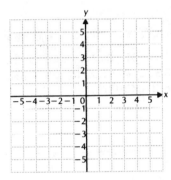

6. $y = -x^2 - 4x - 1$

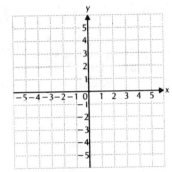

7. $4x^2 - y^2 = 4$

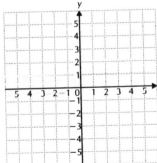

8. $xy = 10$

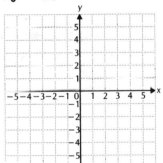

9. $\dfrac{x^2}{25} + \dfrac{y^2}{9} = 1$

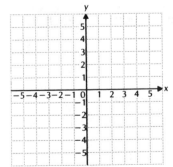

1. _____

2. _____

3. _____

4. _____

5. ___See graph.___

6. ___See graph.___

7. ___See graph.___

8. ___See graph.___

9. ___See graph.___

Name _____

ANSWERS	

Solve.

10. $y^2 - x^2 = 3$
     $2y - 3 = x$

11. $x^2 + 4y^2 = 25$
     $xy = 6$

10. _____

12. $x^2 - 2x - 8 < 0$

13. $\dfrac{x + 5}{x - 5} > 4$

11. _____

14. The sum of two numbers is 6, and the sum of their squares is 50. Find the numbers.

12. _____

15. Two squares are such that the sum of their areas is 97 cm² and the difference of their areas is 65 cm². Find the length of a side of each square.

13. _____

[√]————————————————————————

16. Simplify: $\sqrt{32x^2}$

14. _____

17. Rationalize the numerator: $\dfrac{1 + \sqrt{y}}{3 - \sqrt{y}}$

15. _____

Solve.

18. $y^2 - 6y - 5 = 0$

16. _____

19. A boat travels 9 km upstream and 9 km back. The time for the roundtrip is 4 hours. The speed of the stream is 3 km/h. Find the speed of the boat in still water.

17. _____

18. _____

19. _____

Δ————————————————————————

20. Find the point on the x-axis that is equidistant from (1,4) and (6,3).

20. _____

Name _____

Class _____ Score _____ Grade _____

Graph.

1. $y = x^2 + 4x$

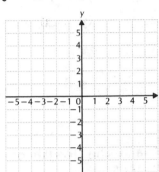

2. $x^2 + y^2 = 8$

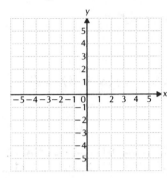

3. $4x^2 - y^2 = 16$

4. $xy = 4$

5. $\dfrac{x^2}{4} + \dfrac{y^2}{9} = 1$

6. Find the center and radius of the circle
   $x^2 + y^2 + 6x - 2y + 6 = 0$.

7. Find an equation of the circle having center $(4, -6)$
   and radius $3\sqrt{2}$.

8. Find the midpoint of the segment with endpoints
   $\left(-\dfrac{2}{5}, \dfrac{3}{4}\right)$ and $\left(\dfrac{1}{5}, \dfrac{5}{4}\right)$.

9. Find the distance between the points $\left(-\dfrac{2}{5}, \dfrac{3}{4}\right)$ and
   $\left(\dfrac{1}{5}, \dfrac{5}{4}\right)$. Give an exact answer and an approximation to
   three decimal places.

ANSWERS

1. ___See graph.___

2. ___See graph.___

3. ___See graph.___

4. ___See graph.___

5. ___See graph.___

6. _____

7. _____

8. _____

9. _____

107

Name _____

ANSWERS	Solve.

10. $2x^2 - y^2 = 2$

     $3x + 2y = -1$

11. $2x^2 - y^2 = 7$

     $xy = 20$

12. $2x(x - 3)(x + 3) \geqslant 0$

13. $\dfrac{x + 9}{x + 11} < 0$

14. The area of a rectangle is 12 m² and the length of a diagonal is 5 m. Find the dimensions.

15. The perimeter of a square is 12 ft more than the perimeter of another square. Its area exceeds the area of the other by 81 ft². Find the perimeter of each square.

[✓]————————————————————————

16. Simplify: $\sqrt[3]{64}$

17. Rationalize the denominator: $\dfrac{4 + \sqrt{a}}{1 - \sqrt{a}}$

Solve.

18. $x^2 - 4x - 1 = 0$

19. A car travels 180 miles at a certain speed. If the speed had been 15 mph faster the trip would have taken 1 hour less time. Find the speed.

Δ————————————————————————

20. Find an equation of the circle that passes through (3,4) and (-2,-1) and whose center is on the line $x + y = 2$.

ANSWERS

10. _____

11. _____

12. _____

13. _____

14. _____

15. _____

16. _____

17. _____

18. _____

19. _____

20. _____

Name _____

Class _____ *Score* _____ *Grade* _____

Graph.

1. $y = 2^{x+1}$ 2. $y = \log_{\frac{1}{3}} x$ ANSWERS

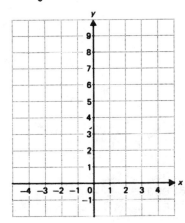   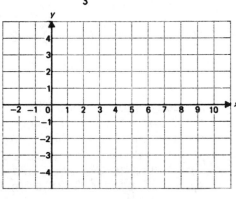

1.___See graph.___

2.___See graph.___

3._____

4._____

3. Convert to an exponential equation: $\log_9 27 = \frac{3}{2}$ 5._____

4. Convert to a logarithmic equation: $\left(\frac{1}{2}\right)^{-2} = 4$ 6._____

5. Express in terms of logarithms of x, y, and z: 7._____

$$\log_a \frac{x^2 y^{\frac{1}{3}}}{z^5}$$

8._____

6. Express as a single logarithm: 9._____

$\frac{1}{4} \log a - 2 \log b - \log c$

10._____

Find each of the following using Table 2.

7. log 339   8. antilog [0.8331 + (-3)]   11._____

Find each of the following using a calculator.

9. log 0.005687   10. antilog 3.8762   12._____

11. ln 12.49   12. antilog$_e$ (-3.876)   13._____

Solve.

14._____

13. $8^{4x-5} = 4$ 14. $6^x = 9.1$

Name _____

ANSWERS	
15._____	15. $\log_x \frac{1}{36} = -2$
	16. $\log_{27} x = \frac{2}{3}$
16._____	17. $\log_2 x + \log_2 (x - 3) = 2$
17._____	18. A study showed that the average walking speed R (in feet per second) of a person living in a city of population P (in thousands) is given by R = 0.85 log P + 0.05. The population of Charlotte, North Carolina, is 324,000. Find the average walking speed of people living in Charlotte.
18._____	[✓]———————————————————————
	19. Add: $(-2 + 3i) + (4 - i)$
19._____	20. Solve for p: $R = \frac{mn}{p^2}$
20._____	Solve.
	21. $y^4 - 6y^2 + 9 = 0$
21._____	22. The sum of two numbers is 3 and the difference of their squares is 21. Find the numbers.
22._____	Δ———————————————————————
	23. Solve: $x \log 4 = \log \frac{1}{4}$
23._____	

Name _____

Class _____ Score _____ Grade _____

1. Convert to a logarithmic equation: $5^{-3} = \frac{1}{125}$

2. Convert to an exponential equation: $\log_2 32 = 5$

3. Express in terms of logarithms of x, y, and z:

$$\log \frac{x^{\frac{1}{3}}}{yz^2}$$

4. Express as a single logarithm:

$$\frac{1}{2}(3 \log a + \log c)$$

Graph.

5. $y = \left(\frac{1}{2}\right)^{x+2}$ 6. $y = \log_4 x$

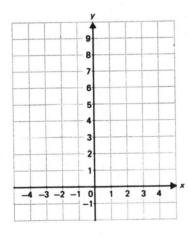   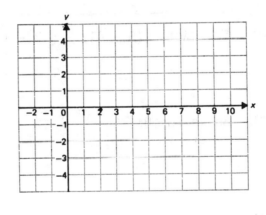

Find each of the following using Table 2.

7. $\log 0.0285$ 8. antilog 2.3345

Find each of the following using a calculator.

9. ln 986.4 10. antilog$_e$ (-6.234)

11. $\log 0.2314$ 12. antilog 4.1898

Solve.

13. $2^x = 1.6$ 14. $9^{x+1} = 27$

ANSWERS

1._____

2._____

3._____

4._____

5.___See graph.___

6.___See graph.___

7._____

8._____

9._____

10._____

11._____

12._____

13._____

14._____

Name _____

ANSWERS
15. _____
16. _____
17. _____
18. _____
19. _____
20. _____
21. _____
22. _____
23. _____

15. $\log_4 x = \dfrac{3}{2}$

16. $\log_x \dfrac{1}{4} = \dfrac{1}{2}$

17. $\log x - \log (x + 9) = -1$

18. The world's population passed 4.0 billion in 1976. The exponential growth rate was 1.9% per year. The equation of world population growth is $P = 4e^{0.019t}$ where P is the population in billions and t is the number of years after 1976. Predict the world's population in 1998.

[✓]─────────────────────────────────

19. Subtract: $(5 - 4i) - (-3 + i)$

20. Solve for Q: $A = \dfrac{Q^2 + 3Q}{2}$

Solve.

21. $2x^{-2} - x^{-1} - 1 = 0$

22. $x^2 + y^2 = 10$
$x - y = 4$

Δ─────────────────────────────────

23. Express as a single logarithm and simplify if possible:
$\log_a (x - 1) + \log_a (x^2 + x + 1)$

Name _____

Class _____ Score _____ Grade _____

Graph.

1. $y = \log_2 x$

2. $y = \left(\frac{1}{3}\right)^{x-1}$

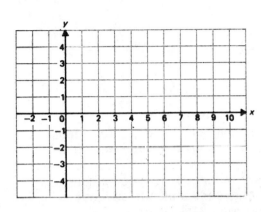 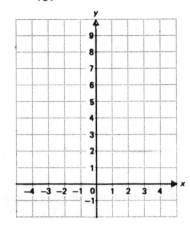

3. Convert to a logarithmic equation: $8^{\frac{2}{3}} = 4$

4. Convert to an exponential equation: $\log_5 \frac{1}{25} = -2$

5. Express in terms of logarithms of x, y, and z:

$$\log_a \sqrt[3]{\frac{xy}{z^2}}$$

6. Express as a single logarithm:
   $\log a + 2 \log b - 3 \log c$

Find each of the following using Table 2.

7. log 29.5

8. antilog [0.4082 + (-2)]

Find each of the following using a calculator.

9. log 0.01846

10. antilog 2.5145

11. ln 2349

12. antilog$_e$ (-11.45)

Solve.

13. $3^{2x+1} = 27$

14. $11^x = 94.2$

ANSWERS

1. ___See graph.___

2. ___See graph.___

3. _____

4. _____

5. _____

6. _____

7. _____

8. _____

9. _____

10. _____

11. _____

12. _____

13. _____

14. _____

ANSWERS

15. _____

16. _____

17. _____

18. _____

19. _____

20. _____

21. _____

22. _____

23. _____

15. $\log_X 2 = -1$ 16. $\log_2 x = -3$

16. $\log_5 (x + 2) + \log_5 (x - 2) = 1$

18. The consumer price index compares the cost of goods and services over various years using $100 worth of goods and services in 1967 as a base. It is given by the equation $P = \$100e^{0.06t}$ where t is the number of years since 1967. Goods and services which cost $100 in 1967 will cost how much in 1990?

[✓]——————————————————————

19. Multiply: $(1 - 3i)(3 + i)$

20. Solve for m: $n = pm^2 + pqm$

Solve.

21. $x^4 - 6x^2 + 8 = 0$ 22. $x^2 = y + 13$
                                          $x = y + 7$

Δ——————————————————————

23. Solve: $16^X = 8^{2X-5}$

Name _____

Class _____ *Score* _____ *Grade* _____

1. Convert to an exponential equation: $\log_8 4 = \frac{2}{3}$

ANSWERS

2. Convert to a logarithmic equation: $32^{\frac{3}{5}} = 8$

1. _____

Graph.

2. _____

3. $y = 3^{2x-3}$ 4. $y = \log_{\frac{1}{2}} x$

3. ___See graph.___

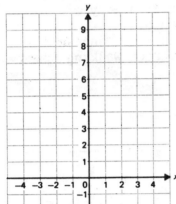

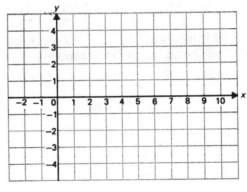

4. ___See graph.___

5. _____

6. _____

Find each of the following using Table 2.

5. log 4130   6. antilog [0.9279 + (−1)]

7. _____

Find each of the following using a calculator.

8. _____

7. log 489,200   8. ln 0.009172

9. _____

9. antilog (−2.3918)   10. antilog$_e$ 3.6896

11. Express in terms of logarithms of x, y, and z:

10. _____

$$\log \sqrt[5]{\frac{xy^2}{z^4}}$$

11. _____

12. Express as a single logarithm:

$2 \log a + \frac{1}{2} \log b - 3 \log c$

12. _____

13. _____

Solve.

13. $\log_x 8 = 2$ 14. $\log_3 x = -2$

14. _____

Name _____

ANSWERS	
15. _____	15. $2^{3x-2} = 4$
	16. $7^x = 11.8$
16. _____	17. $\log_5 (x + 4) - \log_5 x = 1$
17. _____	18. A study showed that the average walking speed R (in feet per second) of a person living in a city of population P (in thousands) is given by $R = 0.85 \log P + 0.05$. The population of Minneapolis, Minnesota, is 370,000. Find the average walking speed of people in Minneapolis.
18. _____	[✓]——————————————————————————
	19. Divide: $\dfrac{2 - 3i}{1 + i}$
19. _____	20. Solve for H: $K = \sqrt{\dfrac{1}{GH}}$
20. _____	Solve.
	21. $x^{-2} + x^{-1} - 12 = 0$
21. _____	22. It will take 44 m of fencing to enclose a garden. The area of the garden is 120 m². Find the dimensions.
22. _____	Δ——————————————————————————
	23. Solve: $\log_2 |3x + 7| = 3$
23. _____	

Name _____

Class _____ Score _____ Grade _____

Graph.

1. $y = \left(\frac{1}{2}\right)^{x-3}$

2. $y = \log_3 x$

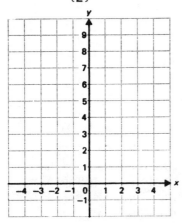

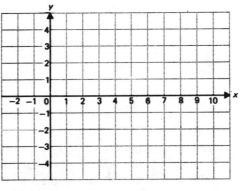

3. Convert to an exponential equation: $\log_2 8 = 3$

4. Convert to a logarithmic equation: $\left(\frac{1}{9}\right)^{-\frac{1}{2}} = 3$

5. Express in terms of logarithms of x, y, and z:

$$\log_a \frac{x^3}{z^2 y}$$

6. Express as a single logarithm:

$\frac{1}{4}(\log a - 3 \log b - 5 \log c)$

Find each of the following using Table 2.
7. log 0.832   8. antilog 4.8007

Find each of the following using a calculator.
9. log 2394   10. antilog (-4.6676)
11. ln 0.01386   12. antilog$_e$ 2.1173

Solve.
13. $4^{x+3} = 8$ 14. $5^x = 2.4$

ANSWERS

1. See graph.

2. See graph.

3. _____

4. _____

5. _____

6. _____

7. _____

8. _____

9. _____

10. _____

11. _____

12. _____

13. _____

14. _____

Name _____

ANSWERS

15. _____

16. _____

17. _____

18. _____

19. _____

20. _____

21. _____

22. _____

23. _____

15. $\log_9 x = \dfrac{1}{2}$

16. $\log_x 81 = 4$

17. $\log_6 x + \log_6 (x - 5) = 1$

18. The world's population passed 4.0 billion in 1976. The exponential growth rate was 1.9% per year. The equation of world population growth is $P = 4e^{0.019t}$ where P is the population in billions and t is the number of years after 1976. Predict the world's population in 2004.

[✓]———————————————————————

19. Express in terms of i and simplify: $\sqrt{-20}$

20. Solve for t: $s^2 = t^2 + w^2$

Solve.

21. $(x^2 - 2)^2 - (x^2 - 2) - 2 = 0$

22. $4x^2 - y^2 = 3$
    $x + 2y = 1$

Δ———————————————————————

23. Solve: $\log_3 \sqrt{x + 2} = 1$

CHAPTER 10

Name _____

Test Form F

Class _____ Score _____ Grade _____

1. Convert to a logarithmic equation: $\left(\frac{1}{3}\right)^{-1} = 3$

ANSWERS

2. Convert to an exponential equation: $\log_{16} 4 = \frac{1}{2}$

1._____

Graph.

2._____

3. $y = \log_{\frac{1}{4}} x$ 4. $y = 2^{x-1}$

3.___See graph.___

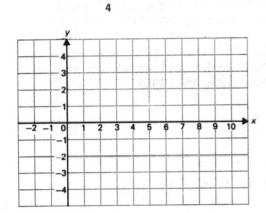
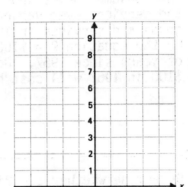

4.___See graph.___

5._____

6._____

Find each of the following using Table 2.

7._____

5. log 648,000   6. antilog [0.6021 + (-2)]

8._____

Find each of the following using a calculator.

9._____

7. log 714   8. ln 0.0008464
9. antilog (-3.4679)   10. antilog$_e$ 4.2024

10._____

11. Express in terms of logarithms of x, y, and z:

$$\log_a \sqrt[4]{\frac{x^3 y}{z^2}}$$

11._____

12. Express as a single logarithm:

$2 \log a + \log b - \frac{1}{3} \log c$

12._____

13._____

Solve.

13. $\log_x 2 = \frac{1}{4}$ 14. $\log_5 x = 2$

14._____

Name _____

ANSWERS	

15. _____

16. _____

17. _____

18. _____

19. _____

20. _____

21. _____

22. _____

23. _____

15. $3^x = 8.6$ 16. $16^{x-3} = 4$

17. $\log (x^2 - 4) - \log (x - 2) = 1$

18. The consumer price index compares the cost of goods and services over various years using $100 worth of goods and services in 1967 as a base. It is given by the equation $P = \$100e^{0.06t}$ where t is the number of years since 1967. Goods and services which cost $100 in 1967 will cost how much in 1995?

[✓]————————————————————

19. Determine whether $1 - 2i$ is a solution of $x^2 - 2x + 5 = 0$.

20. Solve for g: $f = kg + 3g^2$

Solve.

21. $x^4 - 4x^2 + 3 = 0$

22. The sum of the areas of two squares is 34 ft². The sum of the perimeters of the two squares is 32 ft. Find the length of a side of each.

Δ————————————————————

23. Solve: $\log_{12} (x^2 - x) = 1$

	ANSWERS

Chapter 5

22. Subtract:

$(4xy^3 - 3x^2y^2 + 2x^3y^2) - (x^3y^2 + 2xy^3 - 5x^2y^2)$

22._____

23._____

Multiply.

23. $(a - 2b + c)(3a - b - 2c)$ 24. $(3x - y)^2$

24._____

Factor.

25. $4m^2 - n^2$ 26. $3x^2 + 8x - 3$

25._____

26._____

27. $y^3 + 27$

27._____

28. Given the functions $f(x) = x - 4$ and $g(x) = x^2 + 3$, find a) $(f + g)(x)$ b) $(f - g)(x)$ c) $(fg)(x)$ d) $(f/g)(x)$ e) $(ff)(x)$.

28.a)_____

b)_____

29. Given a function f described by $f(x) = x^2 - x - 5$, find $f(-2)$.

c)_____

d)_____

Chapter 6

Perform the indicated operations and simplify.

e)_____

30. $\dfrac{y^2 - 4}{5y - 10} \div \dfrac{y^2 + 4y + 4}{20y^2}$

29._____

31. $(3y^3 - 2y^2 + y - 4) \div (y - 2)$

30._____

32. $\dfrac{3x}{x + 3} - \dfrac{2x}{x - 2} + \dfrac{6x + 8}{x^2 + x - 6}$

31._____

32._____

ANSWERS	Chapter 6 (continued)

33. _____

33. Simplify: $\dfrac{a - \dfrac{1}{2b}}{2a - \dfrac{1}{b}}$

34. _____

Solve.

34. $\dfrac{3}{3x + 1} = \dfrac{1}{3x - 1}$

35. _____

35. A tank can be filled in 8 hours using one pipe. A larger pipe takes 6 hours to fill the tank. How long will it take to fill the tank using the pipes together?

Chapter 7

36. _____

36. Multiply and write scientific notation for the answer: $(5.0 \times 10^{-7})(2.2 \times 10^{12})$

37. _____

37. Simplify. Assume that letters can represent ANY real number.

$$\sqrt{36y^2}$$

38. _____

In the remaining questions assume that ALL expressions under radical signs represent positive numbers.

Perform the indicated operations and simplify.

38. $3\sqrt{12} - \sqrt{27} + 2\sqrt{75}$ 39. $\sqrt{6a^3b} \; \sqrt{30ab^2}$

39. _____

40. $\dfrac{2 - 3i}{1 + 2i}$

40. _____

Chapter 7   (continued)

Solve.

41. $\sqrt{2x - 5} = \sqrt{3x - 5} - 1$

42. In a right triangle with a = 6 and c = 9, find the length b of the remaining side. Give an exact answer and an approximation to three decimal places.

Chapter 8

Solve.

43. $3x^2 = 9x$ 44. $2x^2 + 5 = 4x$

45. $y^{-2} + y^{-1} - 2 = 0$

46. Find three consecutive even integers such that the squares of the second integer plus the product of the other two is 196.

47. Find the maximum product of two numbers whose sum is 10.

Chapter 9

Solve.

48. $x^2 = 2y + 9$ 49. $\dfrac{x + 7}{x - 5} \geqslant 0$
     $x + y = 3$

50. The product of two numbers is 12. The sum of their squares is 25. Find the numbers.

ANSWERS

41._____

42._____

43._____

44._____

45._____

46._____

47._____

48._____

49._____

50._____

ANSWERS	Chapter 9 (continued)

51. _____

51. Find the distance between the points $(2,-5)$ and $(1,-2)$. Give an exact answer and an approximation to three decimal places.

52. Find the center and radius of the circle $x^2 + y^2 - 4x + 6y - 12 = 0$.

52. _____

Graph.

53. $y = x^2 - 2x - 3$ 54. $xy = 3$

53. ___See graph.___

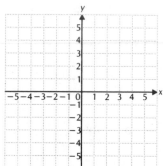

54. ___See graph.___

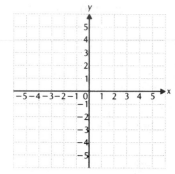

55. ___See graph.___

Chapter 10

Graph.

55. $y = 2^{x-1}$ 56. $y = \log_3 x$

56. ___See graph.___

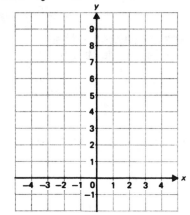

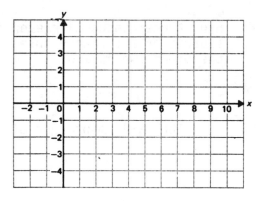

57. _____

57. Convert to a logarithmic equation: $\left(\frac{1}{3}\right)^{-3} = 27$

58. Express as a single logarithm: $\frac{1}{2}(\log a + 3 \log b - \log c)$

58. _____

Solve.

59. _____

59. $4^{x+1} = 8$ 60. $\log_x \frac{1}{5} = -\frac{1}{2}$

60. _____

61. _____

61. Find the value of c so that the graphs of the given lines are perpendicular:
$$3y = cx + 5$$
$$\frac{1}{2}y = 4x - 1$$

62. _____

62. Factor: $x^{3a} + y^{9b}$

Name _____

Class _____ Score _____ Grade _____

Chapter 1

Compute.

1. -4 - (-5)

2. $\frac{2}{9}\left(-\frac{3}{8}\right)$

3. $56 \div 8 - 3^2 + 7$

Simplify.

4. $6(7x + 4) - 8(2x + 9)$

5. $\left(\dfrac{2x^{-4}y^6}{3xy^3}\right)^3$

Chapter 2

6. Solve: $3x - 1 = 5x - 9$

7. Solve for a: $b = \frac{1}{2}c(a + d)$

8. The second angle of a triangle is three times the first, and the third is 20° less than twice the second. Find the measures of the angles.

Graph.

9. $3x - 2y = -6$

10. $y = 3$

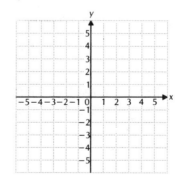

11. Find an equation of the line containing the points (4,-1) and (-2, 2).

ANSWERS

1._____

2._____

3._____

4._____

5._____

6._____

7._____

8._____

9.___See graph.___

10.___See graph.___

11._____

Name _____

ANSWERS	Chapter 3

Solve.

12. _____

12. $2x + 3y = 6$
     $3x - 2y = 9$

13. $x + y + 2z = 1$
     $2x - y + z = -1$
     $x + y + z = 4$

13. _____

14. Solve using Cramer's rule. Show your work.

$$x - 2y = 3$$
$$2x + y = -4$$

14. _____

15. Laura has a total of 247 on three tests. The sum of her second and third test scores exceeds her first score by 69. Her third score is 4 less than her first. Find the three scores.

15. _____

Chapter 4

Solve.

16. _____

16. $5x + 3 > 2x + 6$ 17. $-5 < 3x - 1 \leqslant 2$

18. $|x - 3| \geqslant 4$

17. _____

19. Graph on a number line: $2x + 1 < -3$ <u>or</u> $2x + 1 > 3$

<———+———+———+———+———+———+———+———+———+———+———>
                    0

18. _____

20. Graph on a plane: $x - 2y \geqslant 2$

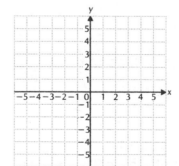

19.   See graph.

20.   See graph.

21. Find the union: $\{1,2,3\} \cup \{1,2,3,4\}$

21. _____

Name _____

Class _____ *Score* _____ *Grade* _____

Chapter 5

Multiply.

22. $(x - 2y)(x + 2y)$

23. $(3x - 1)(2x + 3)$

Factor.

24. $y^2 - 8y + 16$

25. $a^3 + 0.001$

26. $3x^3 + 9x^2 + 3x$

27. $2x^2 - 5x - 3$

28. Given the function g described by $g(x) = 2x^2 - 3x - 3$, find $g(-1)$.

29. Given the functions $f(x) = x - 5$ and $g(x) = x^2 + 2$, find a) $(f + g)(x)$ b) $(f - g)(x)$ c) $(fg)(x)$
    d) $(f/g)(x)$ e) $(ff)(x)$.

Chapter 6

Perform the indicated operations and simplify.

30. $\dfrac{3}{y - 2} - \dfrac{2}{y + 2} + \dfrac{8}{4 - y^2}$

31. $\dfrac{2x^2 + 2x}{x^2 + 3x + 2} \cdot \dfrac{x^2 + 4x + 4}{x^3 - 4x}$

32. Simplify: $\dfrac{\dfrac{1}{a} - 2}{\dfrac{3}{a} - 6}$

ANSWERS

22._____

23._____

24._____

25._____

26._____

27._____

28._____

29.a)_____

b)_____

c)_____

d)_____

e)_____

30._____

31._____

32._____

ANSWERS	Chapter 6 (continued)

Solve.

33. _____

33. $\dfrac{1}{x - 3} = \dfrac{x}{3x - 9}$

34. _____

34. The amount of pay an hourly employee receives is directly proportional to the number of hours worked. The pay for working 25 hours is \$115. Find the pay for working 30 hours.

35. _____

35. The speed of a stream is 2 mph. A boat travels 30 mi downstream in the same time it takes to travel 18 mi upstream. Find the speed of the boat in still water.

Chapter 7

36. _____

Simplify. Assume that letters can represent ANY real number.

36. $\sqrt[3]{-125}$ 37. $\sqrt[8]{y^8}$

37. _____

In the remaining questions assume that ALL expressions under radical signs represent positive numbers.

38. Rationalize the denominator: $\dfrac{\sqrt{3} - \sqrt{2}}{\sqrt{5} + \sqrt{2}}$

38. _____

39. Use fractional exponents to write a single radical expression:

$$\sqrt{y + 1} \ \sqrt[3]{y}$$

39. _____

40. Solve: $\sqrt{x + 2} = 3 - \sqrt{x + 5}$

40. _____

Chapter 7 (continued)

41. Multiply: $(4 - i)(2 + 3i)$

42. Find the length of a guy wire reaching from the top of a 12 ft pole to a point on the ground 8 ft from the base of the pole. Give an exact answer and an approximation to three decimal places.

Chapter 8

Solve.

43. $a^2 + 4 = 4a$

44. $2x^2 - 4x + 1 = 0$

45. $4x^2 = 20$

46. $y^4 - 5y^2 + 4 = 0$

47. The width of a rectangle is 3 m less than the length. The area is 28 m². Find the dimensions.

Chapter 9

48. Find an equation of the circle having center $(-1,4)$ and radius 2.

49. Find the distance between the points $(-4,0)$ and $(3,-5)$. Give an exact answer and an approximation to three decimal places.

Graph.

50. $\dfrac{x^2}{4} + \dfrac{y^2}{9} = 1$

51. $\dfrac{y^2}{16} - \dfrac{x^2}{4} = 1$

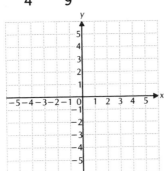

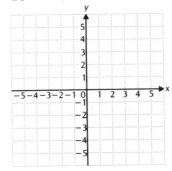

ANSWERS

41._____

42._____

43._____

44._____

45._____

46._____

47._____

48._____

49._____

50.___See graph.___

51.___See graph.___

131

ANSWERS	

Chapter 9   (continued)

Solve.

52. $x^2 + y^2 = 6$
     $xy = 3$

52._____

53. $x^2 - x > 6$

53._____

54. The sum of two numbers is 1 and the difference of their squares is 15. Find the numbers.

54._____

Chapter 10

55. Convert to an exponential equation: $\log_3 81 = 4$

56. Express in terms of logarithms of x, y, and z:

$$\log_a \frac{x^3 y^{\frac{1}{4}}}{z}$$

55._____

56._____

Graph.

57. $y = \log_4 x$

58. $y = \left(\frac{1}{3}\right)^x$

57._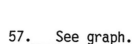 See graph.

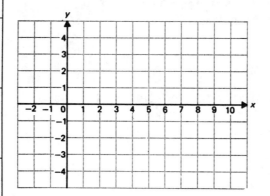

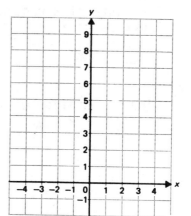

58._ See graph.

59._____

Solve.

59. $5^x = 10$

60. $\log x + \log (x - 3) = 1$

60._____

Solve.

61. $\begin{vmatrix} 1 & -1 & 0 \\ x & -2 & -3 \\ 2 & 3 & 1 \end{vmatrix} = 1$

61._____

62. $\left(\frac{x + 2}{x - 2}\right)^2 + 2 = 3\left(\frac{x + 2}{x - 2}\right)$

62._____

Chapter 1

Compute.

1. $\dfrac{3}{4} - \dfrac{5}{6}$

2. $-3.3 \div -1.1$

Simplify.

3. $3a - [5 - 4(2a - 1)]$

4. $(2x^{-3}y^5z^{-2})(-3xy^{-4}z^5)$

5. $4 \cdot 3 - 2^3 + 5$

Chapter 2

6. Find an equation of the line containing the points $(-3,4)$ and $(2,-6)$.

Graph.

7. $x = -1$

8. $y = 2x$

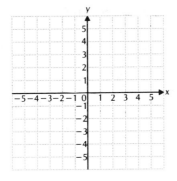

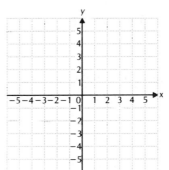

Solve.

9. $x - 4 = 3x + 2$

10. $1 - 2(y - 1) = 3(y + 2) - 6$

11. Find two consecutive even integers whose sum is 70.

ANSWERS

1._____

2._____

3._____

4._____

5._____

6._____

7._____See graph._____

8._____See graph._____

9._____

10._____

11._____

ANSWERS	Chapter 3

Solve.

12. _____

13. _____

14. _____

15. _____

16. _____

17. _____

18. _____

19. _____

20. __See graph.__

21. __See graph.__

Chapter 3

Solve.

12. $2x + y = 3$

   $x + y = -1$

13. $x - 2y + 4z = 3$

   $2x + y + z = 3$

   $x - y + 2z = 3$

14. Jay is 15 years older than Lisa. In three years Jay will be twice as old as Lisa. Find their ages now.

15. Determine whether the system is consistent or inconsistent:

$$2x - y = 3$$
$$4x - 2y = -6$$

Chapter 4

16. Find the union: $\{1,5\} \cup \{3,5\}$

Solve.

17. $-1 \leqslant 2x - 3 < 5$

18. $-6y \leqslant -36$

19. $|x - 4| > 3$

20. Graph on a number line: $x < -1$ or $x \geqslant 2$

<!-- number line from arrow to arrow with 0 marked -->

21. Graph on a plane: $3x - 4y \leqslant 12$

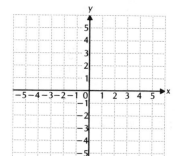

Chapter 5

22. Add: $(2a^3b^4 - 3a^2b^2 - ab^3) + (5a^2b^2 - 2ab^3 + a^3b^4)$

Multiply.

23. $(2x - y)(x + 5y)$ 24. $(a + 3b)^2$

Factor.

25. $3x^2 - 7x - 6$ 26. $y^2 - 4y + 4 - 9z^2$

27. $8y^3 - 1$

28. Complete the square: $x^2 - 5x$

29. Graph: $f(x) = |x| - 3$

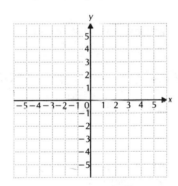

30. Given the functions $f(x) = x - 6$ and $g(x) = x^2 + 1$,
     find a) $(f + g)(x)$ b) $(f - g)(x)$ c) $(fg)(x)$
     d) $(f/g)(x)$ e) $(ff)(x)$.

Chapter 6

Perform the indicated operations and simplify.

31. $\dfrac{x}{x^2 + x} + \dfrac{2}{x^2 - 1}$ 32. $\dfrac{x^2 - 4x + 3}{8x^3} \div \dfrac{x^2 - 2x - 3}{4x^3 + 4x^2}$

ANSWERS

22._____

23._____

24._____

25._____

26._____

27._____

28._____

29.___See graph.___

30.a)_____

   b)_____

   c)_____

   d)_____

   e)_____

31._____

32._____

ANSWERS	Chapter 6 (continued)

33. _____

33. Divide using synthetic division. Show your work.

$$(3x^3 - 4x^2 + 5) \div (x + 1)$$

34. _____

Solve.

34. $\dfrac{3}{y} + \dfrac{12}{y^2 - 2y} = \dfrac{y + 4}{y - 2}$

35. _____

35. The speed of train A is 20 mph slower than the speed of train B. Train A travels 400 miles in the same time it takes train B to travel 500 miles. Find the speed of each train.

36. _____

Chapter 7

Simplify. Assume that letters can represent ANY real number.

37. _____

36. $\sqrt[3]{-\dfrac{1}{64}}$ **37.** $\sqrt{x^2 - 2x + 1}$ **38.** $\sqrt[4]{(-5)^4}$

38. _____

In the remaining questions assume that ALL expressions under radical signs represent positive numbers.

Perform the indicated operations and simplify.

39. _____

39. $(2\sqrt{3} - \sqrt{2})(\sqrt{3} - 3\sqrt{2})$ **40.** $\dfrac{\sqrt{75a^3b^5}}{\sqrt{3ab^2}}$

40. _____

41. $(8 - 5i) - (-4 + 3i)$

41. _____

Name _____

Class _____ *Score* _____ *Grade* _____

	ANSWERS

Chapter 7 (continued)

42. Solve: $\sqrt{4x - 2} = 1 - \sqrt{8x - 2}$

42._____

Chapter 8

Solve.

43. $2x = 8x^2$ 44. $x^2 + 4x - 4 = 0$

43._____

45. Solve for T: $Q = \dfrac{T^2 - 3T}{2}$

44._____

46. Find an equation of variation where y varies jointly as x and z and inversely as the square of w, and y = 8 when x = 4, z = 18, and w = 3.

45._____

47. The product of two numbers is 36. The first is six times the second. Find the numbers.

46._____

Chapter 9

Graph.

48. $x^2 + y^2 = 9$ 49. $\dfrac{x^2}{1} + \dfrac{y^2}{4} = 1$

47._____

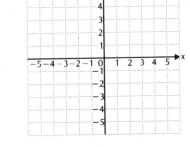   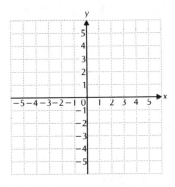

48.___See graph.___

49.___See graph.___

50. Find the midpoint of the segment with endpoints (5,-7) and (-3,4).

50._____

51. Find an equation of the circle having center (0,-2) and radius 5.

51._____

ANSWERS	

<u>Chapter 9</u>   (continued)

Solve.

52. $y = 3x^2$

     $2x + y = 1$

53. $\dfrac{x + 2}{x - 2} \geqslant 0$

54. The product of two numbers is 36. The sum of their squares is 153. Find the numbers.

<u>Chapter 10</u>

Graph.

55. $y = \log_{\frac{1}{2}} x$

56. $y = 3^{x-2}$

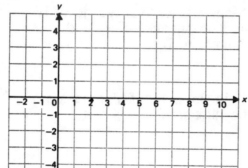

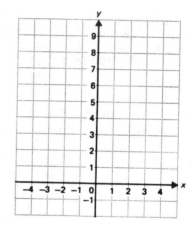

57. Express as a single logarithm:

    $\dfrac{1}{2} \log a + 3 \log b - 2 \log c$

58. Convert to an exponential equation:

    $\log_6 1 = 0$

Solve.

59. $\log_x 27 = -3$

60. $2^{x-4} = 8$

Δ———————————————————————————

61. Solve: $\log_3 |4x - 5| = 2$

62. Find the reciprocal and simplify:

    $\dfrac{x - \dfrac{1}{x}}{1 - \dfrac{1}{x}}$

52. _____

53. _____

54. _____

55. __See graph.__

56. __See graph.__

57. _____

58. _____

59. _____

60. _____

61. _____

62. _____

Name _____

Class _____ Score _____ Grade _____

ANSWERS

45. $y = \left(\frac{1}{2}\right)^x$

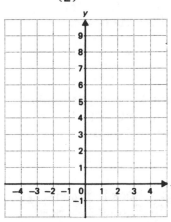

46. $y = \log_2 x$

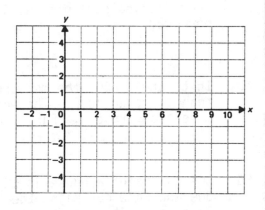

47. $2x + 5y \geqslant 10$

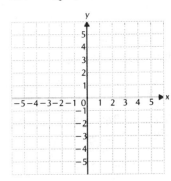

48. Find an equation of the line having slope -2 and containing the point (3,-1).

49. Find the center and radius of the circle $x^2 + y^2 + 8x - 2y + 4 = 0$.

50. Find the distance between the points (0,5) and (-4,-3). Give an exact answer and an approximation to three decimal places.

51. Given the functions $f(x) = x + 3$ and $g(x) = x^2$, find
a) $(f + g)(x)$ b) $(f - g)(x)$ c) $(fg)(x)$ d) $(f/g)(x)$
e) $(ff)(x)$.

52. Convert to a logarithmic equation: $16^{\frac{1}{4}} = 2$

53. Express in terms of logarithms of x, y, and z:

$$\log_a \sqrt[3]{\frac{x^2 y}{z^2}}$$

45. ___See graph.___

46. ___See graph.___

47. ___See graph.___

48. _____

49. _____

50. _____

51. a)_____

    b)_____

    c)_____

    d)_____

    e)_____

52. _____

53. _____

143

Name _____

ANSWERS	

Solve.

54. _____

54. Money is borrowed at 11% simple interest. After one year $721.50 pays off the loan. How much was borrowed?

55. _____

55. In triangle ABC, the measure of angle B is 5° more than twice angle C. The measure of angle B is 5° more than angle A. Find the angle measures.

56. _____

56. Joe can paint a house in 12 hours. Working together, Joe and Jane can paint the house in 8 hours. How long would it take Jane to paint the house by herself?

57. _____

57. In a right triangle with a = 4 and b = 7, find the length c of the remaining side. Give an exact answer and an approximation to three decimal places.

58. _____

58. Find the area of the largest rectangular region that can be enclosed using 220 m of fencing.

59. _____

59. A picture frame measures 12 in. by 15 in. and 108 in² of picture shows. Find the width of the frame.

60. _____

60. The sum of the areas of two squares is 53 cm². The sum of the perimeters of the two squares is 36 cm. Find the length of a side of each square.

Δ————————————————————————

61. _____

61. Subtract and simplify: $\dfrac{2}{2-i} - \dfrac{3}{1+3i}$

62. Solve: $|x + 3| < |x - 4|$

62. _____

		ANSWERS

46. $y = x^2 - 2x + 1$

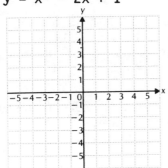

47. $y = \log_{\frac{1}{3}} x$

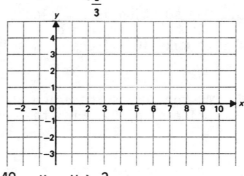

46. **See graph.**

47. **See graph.**

48. $y = 3^{x+1}$

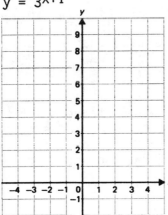

49. $x - y \geqslant 3$

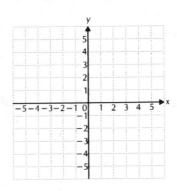

48. **See graph.**

49. **See graph.**

50. $y < 2$

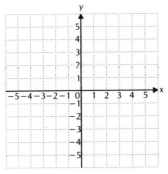

50. **See graph.**

51. Use fractional exponents to write a single radical expression:
$$\sqrt[3]{x + 2} \quad \sqrt[4]{x}$$

52. Find an equation of the circle having center (5,-1) and radius 3.

53. Express as a single logarithm:
$$\frac{1}{5}(2 \log a - \log b)$$

54. Convert to a logarithmic equation: $\left(\frac{1}{4}\right)^{-2} = 16$

51. _____

52. _____

53. _____

54. _____

149

ANSWERS	Solve.
55._____	55. One solution is 70% alcohol and a second is 55% alcohol. How much of each should be mixed together to make 100 liters of a solution that is 58% alcohol?
56._____	56. A store drops the price of a dishwasher 20% to a sale price of $336. Find the original price.
57._____	57. The amount of tread left on a tire varies inversely as the number of miles the tire has traveled. A tire that has traveled 15,000 miles has $\frac{1}{4}$ in. of tread left. How much tread will be left on a tire that has traveled 20,000 miles?
58._____	58. During the first part of a trip a car travels 125 km at a certain speed. It travels 90 km on the second part of the trip at a speed 10 km/h faster. The total time for the trip is 4 hours. Find the speed on each part of the trip.
59._____	59. The area of a rectangle is 48 m². The length of a diagonal is $4\sqrt{10}$ m. Find the dimensions.
60._____	60. A boat can travel at a speed of 9 km/h in still water. The boat travels 18 km downstream in a river in the same time it takes to travel 9 km upstream. Find the speed of the river current.
	Δ———————————————
61._____	61. Find the point on the y-axis that is equidistant from (2,3) and (-5,1).
62._____	62. Find k so that when $x^3 - kx^2 - 5x + 6k$ is divided by $x + 2$ the remainder is 0.

Name _____

Class _____ Score _____ Grade _____

---

1. Evaluate $\dfrac{m - n}{3}$ when m = -6 and n = 3.

2. Find percent notation: $\dfrac{9}{8}$

Performe the indicated operations and simplify.

3. 8(-6)

4. $-\dfrac{3}{4} - \left(-\dfrac{3}{10}\right)$

5. $(-3x^{-2}y^3z^{-4})(-4xy^{-1}z^7)$

6. $2[4 - (2x + 3)]$

7. $(3xy^3 + 2x^2y - 4x^3y^4) + (2x^2y + 3x^3y^4 - xy^3)$

8. $(2a - 3)(3a - 2)$

9. $(3y - 2z^2)^2$

10. $\dfrac{3x + 15}{x^2 + 6x + 5} \cdot \dfrac{x^2 + 4x + 3}{6x - 18}$

11. $\dfrac{2x - 16}{x^2 - 16} - \dfrac{2}{x + 4} + \dfrac{1}{x - 4}$

12. $\dfrac{y^2 - \dfrac{b^3}{y}}{1 - \dfrac{b}{y}}$

13. $(8x^3 - 6x + 3) \div (x - 1)$

14. $4 \cdot 9 - 3^2 + 5$

15. $\sqrt{20} + 3\sqrt{80} - 5\sqrt{45}$

ANSWERS

1._____

2._____

3._____

4._____

5._____

6._____

7._____

8._____

9._____

10._____

11._____

12._____

13._____

14._____

15._____

ANSWERS	
16._____	16. $(4 - 5i) - (-2 - 6i)$
	17. For the function f described by $f(x) = 2x^3 + x^2 - 3x$, find $f(-2)$.
17._____	
	18. Find an equation of the line containing the points $(5,-7)$ and $(-4,2)$.
18._____	
	19. Find the center and radius of the circle $x^2 + y^2 + 2x - 10y - 10 = 0$.
19._____	
	20. Convert to an exponential equation: $\log_9 \frac{1}{3} = -\frac{1}{2}$
20._____	
	21. Express in terms of logarithms of x, y, and z: $$\log_a \frac{xy^3}{z^{\frac{1}{2}}}$$
21._____	
	22. Find the intersection: $\{5,7,10,14\} \cap \{2,5,8,11,14\}$
22._____	Simplify. Assume that letters can represent ANY real number.
	23. $\sqrt{x^2 - 6x + 9}$ 24. $\sqrt[3]{-\frac{1}{27}}$
23._____	
	25. Rationalize the denominator. Assume that ALL expressions under radical signs represent positive numbers. $$\frac{2 - \sqrt{a}}{1 + \sqrt{a}}$$
24._____	
25._____	

Factor.

26. $16x^4 - 25$ 27. $4x^2 - 11x - 3$ 28. $125a^3 - 1$

Evaluate.

29. $\begin{vmatrix} -3 & 4 & 2 \\ 1 & -1 & 0 \\ 5 & -2 & 1 \end{vmatrix}$

Solve.

30. $4 - (2x + 1) = 3(x - 3) + 5$ 31. $8x - 10 = 5x + 2$

32. $x^2 + 10 = 6x$ 33. $5x = 4x^2$

34. $\dfrac{2x}{x + 4} = \dfrac{x}{x + 6}$ 35. $\sqrt{2x - 2} = 2 + \sqrt{x - 5}$

36. $\begin{aligned} x + 2y &= 3 \\ 2x + 3y &= 2 \end{aligned}$ 37. $\begin{aligned} x + 2y + z &= -2 \\ x - y - z &= -6 \\ 2x + 3y + 2z &= 0 \end{aligned}$

ANSWERS

26._____

27._____

28._____

29._____

30._____

31._____

32._____

33._____

34._____

35._____

36._____

37._____

ANSWERS	
38._____	
39._____	
40._____	
41._____	
42._____	
43._____	
44._____	
45. See graph.	
46. See graph.	
47. See graph.	

38. $y^2 - xy = 12$
     $3y^2 + 2xy = 6$

39. $3^{x-3} = 27$

40. $\log (x + 5) - \log x = 1$

41. $x - 1 \leqslant 4x + 5$

42. $|2x - 3| > 5$

43. $\dfrac{x - 3}{x + 6} \geqslant 2$

44. Solve for q: $m^2 = p^2 - q^2$

45. Graph on a number line: $-3 < x - 1 \leqslant 2$

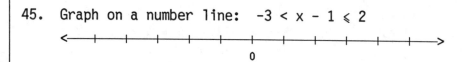

Graph.

46. $y = 1$

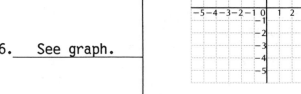

47. $4x + 3y = -12$

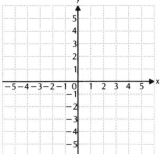

Name _____

Class _____ Score _____ Grade _____

48. a) Graph $f(x) = 2(x + 1)^2 - 1$
     b) Label the vertex.
     c) Draw the line of symmetry.
     d) Find the maximum or minimum
        value of the function.

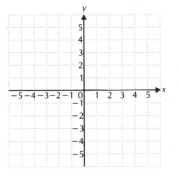

Graph.

49. $\dfrac{x^2}{4} - \dfrac{y^2}{16} = 1$ 50. $\dfrac{x^2}{16} + \dfrac{y^2}{4} = 1$

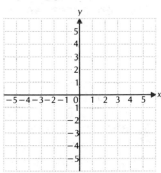   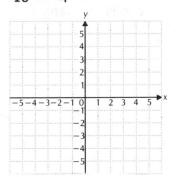

51. $y = \log_{\frac{1}{4}} x$ 52. $y = 3^{x+2}$ 53. $x - y \leqslant 2$

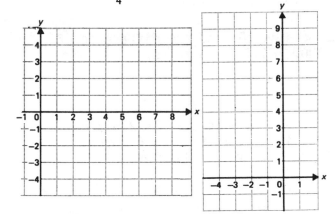

54. The centripetal force F of an object moving in a circle
     varies directly as the square of the velocity v and
     inversely as the radius r of the circle. If F = 5
     when v = 2 and r = 4, find F when v = 3 and r = 10.

ANSWERS

48. ___See graph.___

49. ___See graph.___

50. ___See graph.___

51. ___See graph.___

52. ___See graph.___

53. ___See graph.___

54. _____

Name _____

ANSWERS	Solve.

55. _____

55. Mark can type a report in 5 hours. Working together, Mark and Martha can type the report in 3 hours. How long would it take Martha to type the report by herself?

56. _____

56. The perimeter of a rectangle is 30 m. The length is twice the width. Find the dimensions.

57. _____

57. Find the length of a diagonal of a rectangle with sides of length 5 cm and 9 cm. Give an exact answer and an approximation to three decimal places.

58. _____

58. An investment of $80,000 was split into three parts and lasted one year. The first part of the investment earned 6% interest, the second 8%, and the third 10%. Total interest from the investment was $6200. The interest from the second part of the investment was $200 more than twice the interest from the first. Find the amount of each part of the investment.

59. _____

59. The sum of two numbers is 10, and the difference of their squares is 300. Find the numbers.

60. _____

60. A stream flows at 2 mph. A boat travels 24 miles upstream and returns in a total time of 5 hours. Find the speed of the boat in still water.

61. _____

Δ ———————————————————————

Solve.

61. $2a - 3 < a + 1 < 3a + 4$ 62. $4^{x^2} = 8$

62. _____

ANSWER KEYS FOR ALTERNATE TEST FORMS

Chapter 1, Test Form A

1. 6   **2.** -1.8   **3.** 0.492   **4.** $\frac{56}{100}$ **5.** $\frac{47}{1000}$ **6.** 220%   **7.** 22.6%   **8.** 34

9. 2   **10.** -8.1   **11.** $-\frac{1}{12}$ **12.** -11   **13.** -16   **14.** 11.76   **15.** $-\frac{5}{3}$

16. -3   **17.** <   **18.** $6a + 3b$ **19.** $6rst - 2rs$ **20.** $4(x - 2y + 3z)$

21. $ab(c + d)$ **22.** $3a - 2b$ **23.** $8a + 6b - 3c$ **24.** $11a + 6$ **25.** $4x - 5$

26. -13   **27.** $\frac{27y^{15}}{8x^{15}}$ or $\frac{27}{8}x^{-15}y^{15}$ **28.** $-15x^{-1}y^5$ **29.** $-\frac{4a^8b^{-5}}{9}$ or $-\frac{4a^8}{9b^5}$

30. $\frac{15}{8}$

Chapter 1, Test Form B

1. $y + 3$ **2.** >   **3.** $\frac{7}{10}$ **4.** -4   **5.** -9   **6.** -7.5   **7.** $\frac{3}{4}$ **8.** -90   **9.** -7

10. -11   **11.** $\frac{180}{100}$ **12.** $\frac{323}{1000}$ **13.** $0.\overline{4}$ **14.** 0.143   **15.** 1.4%   **16.** 35%

17. $-\frac{3}{4}$ **18.** $\frac{8}{7}$ **19.** $4a - 5b$ **20.** $-6x + 30y$ **21.** $2abc + 2abd$

22. $3(6m - 3n - 2p)$ **23.** $x(y + 2 - z)$ **24.** $-4x - 15$ **25.** $8a + 17$

26. 90   **27.** $\frac{x^{-6}y^2b^{10}}{16}$ or $\frac{y^2b^{10}}{16x^6}$ **28.** $-20x^3y^{-9}$ or $-\frac{20x^3}{y^9}$ **29.** $-\frac{7a^{-8}b}{2}$ or $-\frac{7b}{2a^8}$

30. 27

Chapter 1, Test Form C

1. 29.8%   **2.** 120%   **3.** 0.3125   **4.** 0.0367   **5.** $\frac{517}{1000}$ **6.** $\frac{119}{100}$ **7.** 3

8. >   **9.** -2.8   **10.** -12   **11.** -6   **12.** $-\frac{35}{36}$ **13.** -14.62   **14.** 54   **15.** 9

16. $-\frac{3}{2}$ **17.** 0   **18.** $\frac{18}{7}$ **19.** $12x - 4y$ **20.** $2mns + 3mn$ **21.** $-3m + 4n$

22. $5(3a + b - 4c)$ **23.** $2\pi(2r - 1)$ **24.** $-6m + 5n + 2p$ **25.** 13

26. $\frac{4x^{-6}y^4}{25}$ or $\frac{4y^4}{25x^6}$ **27.** $15a + 1$ **28.** $-8x^{-1}y^{-6}$ or $-\frac{8}{xy^6}$ **29.** $-\frac{3a^{-2}b^{-1}}{4}$ or $-\frac{3}{4a^2b}$ **30.** 3^{a-4}

Chapter 1, Test Form D

1. $d - 5$ 2. $>$ 3. -1 4. $-\frac{29}{15}$ 5. -0.8 6. 12 7. $-\frac{3}{4}$ 8. 24

9. -4 10. -2.1 11. 96% 12. 320% 13. $\frac{4155}{10,000}$ 14. $\frac{1}{1000}$ 15. 1.375

16. 0.08 17. 3.23 18. $\frac{9}{10}$ 19. $8x + 6y$ 20. $3x - 4y + z$ 21. $m - 8n$

22. $3(4m - 2n - 3p)$ 23. $2x(y + 2)$ 24. 0 25. $4x$ 26. $13a - 5$

27. $\frac{16x^{-2}y^{-4}}{25}$ or $\frac{16}{25x^2y^4}$ 28. $-21x^3y^{-4}$ or $-\frac{21x^3}{y^4}$ 29. $-\frac{4a^{-2}b^4}{3}$ or $-\frac{4b^4}{3a^2}$

30. $\frac{153}{16}$

Chapter 1, Test Form E

1. $>$ 2. 2 3. 7.5% 4. 500% 5. 0.054 6. -1.5 7. $\frac{47}{100}$ 8. $\frac{623}{1000}$

9. $\frac{1}{6}$ 10. -3 11. -7 12. -10.9 13. -28 14. $-\frac{5}{8}$ 15. $-\frac{7}{6}$ 16. 4

17. 5 18. $5m + 3n - 6p$ 19. $x + 3y$ 20. $-8x + 6y$ 21. $4abc - 8abd$

22. $4(4a + 2b - c)$ 23. $p(n + 1)$ 24. $6a + 3$ 25. $-x - 8$ 26. -2

27. $\frac{x^4y^{-2}z^{-6}}{9}$ or $\frac{x^4}{9y^2z^6}$ 28. $-12x^6y^{-2}$ or $-\frac{12x^6}{y^2}$ 29. $-\frac{9a^{10}b^{-5}}{5}$ or $-\frac{9a^{10}}{5b^5}$

30. $-x^9y^{-15}$ or $-\frac{x^9}{y^{15}}$

Chapter 1, Test Form F

1. 4.7 2. 7.6 3. $b - a$ 4. $<$ 5. -11 6. -1.4 7. -7 8. $\frac{19}{12}$

9. -7.98 10. -48 11. -2 12. $\frac{3}{5}$ 13. $-3.\overline{6}$ 14. 0.453 15. $\frac{862}{10,000}$

16. $\frac{226}{100}$ 17. 90% 18. 0.9% 19. $-2x + 4y + 5z$ 20. $-5m + 5n$

21. $15xyz - 10xy$ 22. $3(x - 2y + 3z)$ 23. $a(b + 3c - d)$ 24. $-3x - y$

25. $x - 7$ 26. -18 27. $-\frac{x^{-15}y^6z^9}{8}$ or $-\frac{y^6z^9}{8x^{15}}$ 28. $-18x^2y^{-2}$ or $-\frac{18x^2}{y^2}$

29. $-a^{-9}b^2$ or $-\frac{b^2}{a^9}$ 30. $\frac{11x^2y^2}{16}$

1. $\frac{19}{3}$ 2. $\frac{2}{5}$ 3. $\frac{1}{2}$, -5   4. $p = \frac{4}{3}(m + 5)$ 5. Slope is 4; y-intercept is

(0,-3)   6. $\frac{4}{5}$ 7. $y = 2x - 8$ 8. $y = -\frac{2}{5}x + \frac{6}{5}$ 9. $y = -\frac{4}{3}x - \frac{13}{3}$

10.
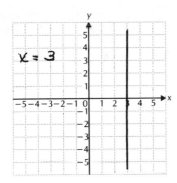

11.
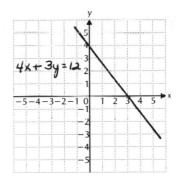

12.
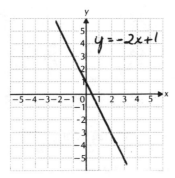

13.
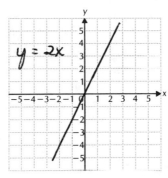

14. 16, 18   15. $450   16. -8.2   17. $-\frac{3}{20}$ 18. $3(x - 6)$

19. $-15xy^{-5}$ or $-\frac{15x}{y^5}$ 20. $\frac{1}{30}$

1. -1   2. $\frac{1}{2}$ 3. 0, 1   4. $D = \frac{3B + AE}{A}$ 5. Slope is -3; y-intercept is

(0, 5)   6.
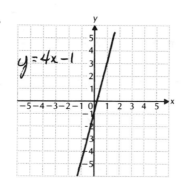

7.
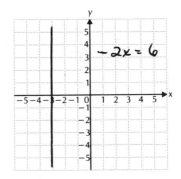

8.
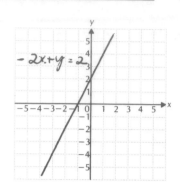
$-2x + y = 2$

9.
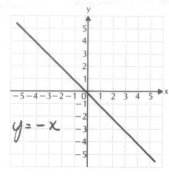
$y = -x$

10. 2

11. $y = -3x - 8$

12. $y = -\frac{1}{3}x + \frac{10}{3}$

13. $y = -\frac{2}{5}x - \frac{7}{5}$

14. 25°, 50°, 105°

15. \$15,500   16. $-\frac{1}{6}$

17. 24   18. $-3x + 5y$ 19. $-\frac{a^{15}b^{-3}c^{-6}}{8}$ or $-\frac{a^{15}}{8b^3c^6}$ 20. $-\frac{16}{3}$

Chapter 2, Test Form C

1. Slope is -16; y-intercept is (0, 10)   2. -1   3. $y = -\frac{9}{10}x - \frac{13}{10}$

4. $y = -4x - 11$ 5. $y = -\frac{1}{4}x + \frac{9}{2}$ 6.

$y = -x + 2$

7.
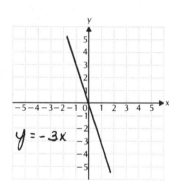
$y = -3x$

8.
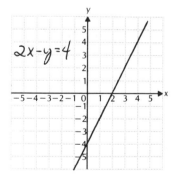
$2x - y = 4$

9.
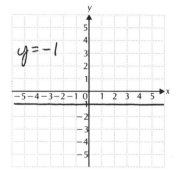
$y = -1$

10. $k = \frac{5h - G}{3}$

11. $\frac{3}{7}$ 12. -2

13. $\frac{4}{3}$, -1   14. \$750

15. 40 m × 45 m

16. $\frac{5}{6}$ 17. $-\frac{25}{6}$

18. $-3y + 21$

19. $-\frac{2m^{-6}n^3}{5}$ or $-\frac{2n^3}{5m^6}$ 20. 99%

Chapter 2, Test Form D

1. $-4, \frac{2}{3}$ **2.** -1 **3.** $\frac{14}{5}$ **4.** $s^2 = \frac{P}{r}$ **5.**

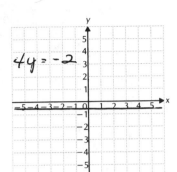

6.

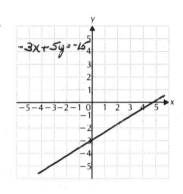

7.

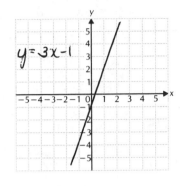

8.

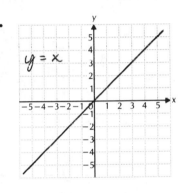

9. Slope is -11; y-intercept is $(0, 4)$

10. $-\frac{2}{3}$ **11.** $y = -6$

12. $y = -2x - 1$

13. $y = \frac{1}{5}x - \frac{17}{5}$

14. $415, 417$

15. $1050   **16.** 3 **17.** $-\frac{15}{4}$ **18.** $-3a + b$ **19.** $-12x^6y^{-1}z^{-2}$ or $-\frac{12x^6}{yz^2}$

20. $-\frac{5}{3}$

Chapter 2, Test Form E

1. 1 **2.** $2, -\frac{7}{6}$ **3.** 1 **4.** $p^2 = m^2 - n^2$ **5.** Slope is 5; y-intercept is $(0, -3)$ **6.** 0 **7.**

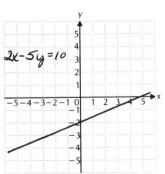

8.

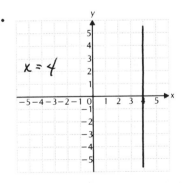

9.
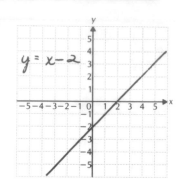

10.
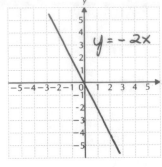

11. $y = x + 10$

12. $y = 6x + 23$

13. $y = -\frac{7}{2}x + 12$

14. 11 m × 22 m

15. $140   16. 5.79

17. $\frac{7}{3}$

18. $-4x + 12$ 19. $\frac{a^4b^{-2}c^{-6}}{9}$ or $\frac{a^4}{9b^2c^6}$ 20. $-\frac{d}{a}$

Chapter 2, Test Form F

1.
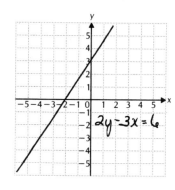

2.
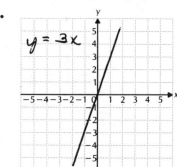

3.
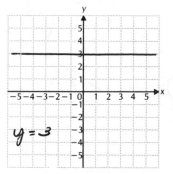

4.
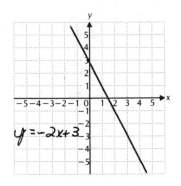

5. Slope is 4; y-intercept is (0, 2)

6. No slope   7. $y = -4x - 42$ 8. $y = x + 3$

9. $y = 2x + 10$ 10. $a = \frac{T}{1 + bc}$ 11. 2

12. $\frac{3}{5}$, -6   13. $\frac{7}{5}$ 14. 3   15. $2705   16. $\frac{7}{18}$

17. $3(2y - 3)$ 18. -3   19. $-4a^{-1}bc^2$ or $-\frac{4bc^2}{a}$

20. $\frac{405}{11}$

Chapter 3, Test Form A

1.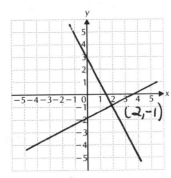

2. (-2, -3)   3. (1, 2)   4. (-3, -2, 0)   5. -5

6. -12   7. (4, -3)   8. a) P = 45x - 45,000

b) 1000 units   9. Inconsistent   10. Independent

11. 40 liters of 65% solution, 60 liters of 40%

solution   12. Monday: $40; Tuesday: $55;

Wednesday: $65   13. 2x - 26   14. 3

15. $t^2 = p^2 - m^2$ 16. 35°, 40°, 105°   17. -4

Chapter 3, Test Form B

1. (3, -1)   2. (-2 ,-3)   3.

4. -14   5. 10

6. (1, 2)   7. (-1, 4, -2)

8. a) P = 350x - 105,000

b) 300 units

9. Dependent

10. Consistent

11. 10 cm × 15 cm

12. 25°, 105°, 50°

13. 7x - 34   14. -2   15. $a = \frac{5}{2}(b - 3)$ 16. $2500   17. m = 3, b = -5

Chapter 3, Test Form C

1. (1, -1)   2. (1, 5)   3.

4. (-1, 2, 3)

5. 25 and -16

6. Student: 60;

adult: 80;

children: 50   7. 2

8. 15   9. (2, -1)

10. Inconsistent

11. Dependent

12. a) P = 25x - 30,000

b) 1200 units   13. 3x + 7   14. -3

15. $m = \dfrac{2p + rn}{n}$ 16. 151, 153   17. 5 mL

Chapter 3, Test Form D

1.

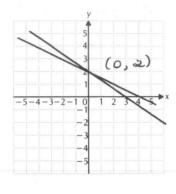

(0, 2)

2. (-3, -4)   3. (1, -1)   4. (-2, -1, 4)   5. 22

6. -9   7. (2, 0, -4)   8. a) P = 50x - 200,000

b) 4000 units   9. Independent   10. Consistent

11. 125 dimes, 80 quarters   12. 29, 46, 134

13. 13a - 2   14. -3   15. $R = \dfrac{4Q - T}{7}$ 16. $85

17. 193

Chapter 3, Test Form E

1. (4, -5)   2. (-3, 2)   3.

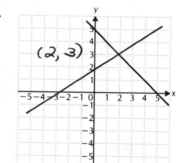

(2, 3)

4. (1, 2, 3)   5. -17

6. -5   7. (3, -1, 2)

David: 12 years

$35,000 at 9%,

8. Toni: 16 years;

9. $25,000 at 8%,

$40,000 at 10%

10. Inconsistent

11. Dependent

12. a) P = 23x - 46,000 b) 2000 units   13. -a + 6   14. 2   15. $b^2 = \dfrac{A}{c}$

16. 2   17. $\dfrac{9}{16}$

Chapter 3, Test Form F

1. -1   2. -40   3. (1, 2, -1)   4. a) P = 8x + 16,000 b) 2000 units

Chapter 3, Test Form F   (continued)

5.

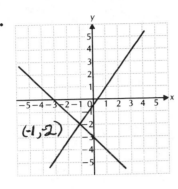

(-1,2)

6. (5, 4)   7. (3, -3)   8. $3000 at 8%,

$4500 at 10%   9. 87, 80, 75   10. (1, -2, 2)

11. Independent   12. Consistent   13. 2y - 14

14. 4   15. $P = \frac{R + Q}{3}$ 16. 102, 104   17. $\frac{17}{2}$

Chapter 4, Test Form A

1. $\{x \mid x > 17\}$ 2. $\{y \mid y \geqslant -6\}$ 3. $\{x \mid x < 3\}$ 4. $\{y \mid -2 < y \leqslant 1\}$

5. $\left\{x \mid x < \frac{1}{5} \text{ or } x > 1\right\}$ 6. $\{5,2\}$ 7. $\left\{a \mid a \geqslant 1 \text{ or } a \leqslant -\frac{3}{2}\right\}$ 8. $\{0,10\}$

9. $\{1,2,3,4,6,8\}$ 10. ⟨——————⊕—⊕————⟩
                              −1 0 1

11. ⟨————•————⊕———⟩   12. False   13. True
         −2   0   3

14.

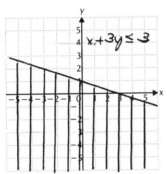

15.

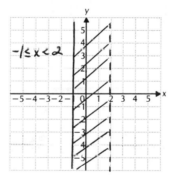

16.

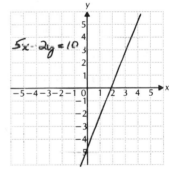

17. 3, $-\frac{1}{2}$ 18. (6, -2)   19. 40 nickels, 55 dimes   20. $\left\{\frac{5}{2}, \frac{3}{4}\right\}$

Chapter 4, Test Form B

1. $\{-7,-3,-1,0,3,9\}$ 2. $\{1,5,6,9\}$ 3. True   4. True

5. ⟨——⊕—⊕——————————⟩   6. ⟨———•———————•———⟩
      −3−2 0   −3   0   2

7.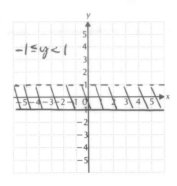

8.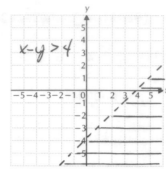

9. $\{y \mid y < 4\}$

10. $\{y \mid y \geqslant 6\}$

11. $\{x \mid x > 4\}$

12. $\{y \mid 1 < y \leqslant 2\}$

13. $\{a \mid -3 < a < 4\}$

14. $\left\{\dfrac{1}{2}, -\dfrac{3}{2}\right\}$

15. $\left\{y \mid y < -1 \text{ or } y > -\dfrac{1}{3}\right\}$ 16. 4   17. (2,−1)   18.

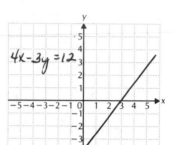

19. 600 L of 80% solution, 400 L of 65% solution

20. $\{a \mid -2 < a < 5\}$

Chapter 4, Test Form C

1. 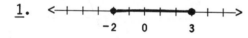   2. 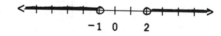   3. ∅

4. $\{-2,-1,1,4\}$ 5. $\left\{x \mid x > -\dfrac{1}{3}\right\}$ 6. $\{y \mid y > -3\}$ 7. $\{y \mid -1 < y < 5\}$

8. $\{x \mid x \geqslant 14\}$ 9. $\left\{y \mid -1 < y < \dfrac{13}{3}\right\}$ 10. $\left\{1, -\dfrac{9}{5}\right\}$ 11. $\{a \mid a \leqslant -4 \text{ or } a \geqslant 1\}$

12. 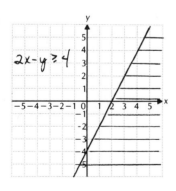   13. 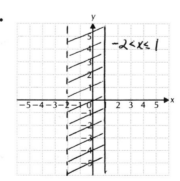   14. True   15. True   16.

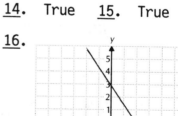

17. $\frac{1}{4}$, -5   18. (3, -2)   19. 17, 35   20. All real numbers

Chapter 4, Test Form D

1. {x|x ≤ -6}   2. {x|x ≤ 2}   3. {y|y < -9}   4. {y|-1 ≤ y < 6}

5. $\left\{1, -\frac{5}{2}\right\}$ 6. {a|a > 3 or a < -7}   7. $\left\{a \,\middle|\, a \leq 0 \text{ or } a \geq \frac{8}{3}\right\}$

8.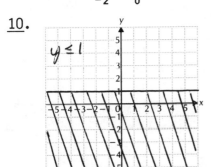

9.

10.

$y \leq 1$

11.

$x + y > 2$

12. False

13. True

14. {1,5,10,12}

15. {1,2,3}

16. -7   17. (-1, 3)

18.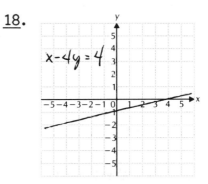

$x - 4y = 4$

19. 28 m × 39 m   20. $\left\{x \,\middle|\, x \geq \frac{1}{2}\right\}$

Chapter 4, Test Form E

1. True   2. False   3. {-3,4}   4. {-1,0,1}   5.

6.

7.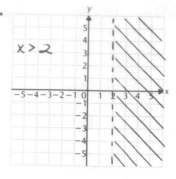

8.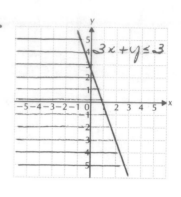

9. {x|x < 3}   10. {x|x ⩾ -3}

11. {y|y ⩾ -1}

12. $\left\{x \,\middle|\, -1 < x \leqslant \frac{2}{3}\right\}$ 13. {8,-1}

14. $\left\{a \,\middle|\, a > -\frac{4}{3} \text{ or } a < -2\right\}$

15. $\left\{a \,\middle|\, a < -2 \text{ or } a > -\frac{1}{2}\right\}$ 16.

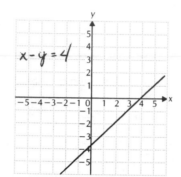

17. $7, \, -\frac{5}{2}$

18. (3, -4)   19. Fred: 36,

Sue: 12

20.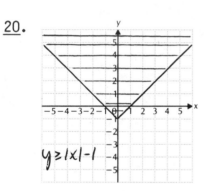

1. {z|z < -10}   2. {x|x ⩽ 1}   3. {x|1 < x < 3}   4. {x|x ⩽ 7}

5. $\left\{y \,\middle|\, y < -\frac{13}{5} \text{ or } y > 1\right\}$ 6. $\left\{1, \, -\frac{11}{3}\right\}$ 7. {y|y > 4 or y < -1}

8.

9.

10. Ø   11. {1,2,3,5}   12. False   13. True

<u>14.</u>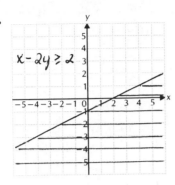

<u>15.</u>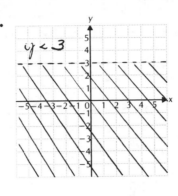

<u>16.</u>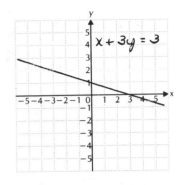

<u>17.</u> $\frac{8}{7}$ <u>18.</u> (3, -3)   <u>19.</u> $4000 at 8%, $8000 at 9%   <u>20.</u> False. Let a = -1, b = 2, c = -3, d = 0.

Chapter 5, Test Form A

<u>1.</u> -20   <u>2.</u> $9x^3 - 12x^2 + 10x - 2$ <u>3.</u> $6x^2 - 9xy + 3y^2$ <u>4.</u> $-12x^4y^9z^4$

<u>5.</u> $x^2 - 4xy + 4y^2$ <u>6.</u> $4a^2 - 9$ <u>7.</u> $2x(2x^2 + 3x + 6)$ <u>8.</u> $(y^3 - 2)(y + 3)$

<u>9.</u> $(3a + 4)(3a - 4)$ <u>10.</u> $(3m + 5)(2m + 3)$ <u>11.</u> $(b - 0.3)(b^2 + 0.3b + 0.09)$

<u>12.</u> $(x + 19)(x + 9)$ <u>13.</u> 5, 1   <u>14.</u> 14 and 16   <u>15.</u> 3   <u>16.</u> a) $x + 1 + x^2$
b) $x + 1 - x^2$ c) $x^3 + x^2$ d) $\frac{x + 1}{x^2}$ e) $x^2 + 2x + 1$ <u>17.</u>

<u>18.</u> $\{x \mid x \geqslant 1\}$ <u>19.</u> $\left\{ b \mid -\frac{7}{3} < b < 3 \right\}$

<u>20.</u> (-2, 3, 1)   <u>21.</u> 35°, 25°, 120°   <u>22.</u> $\frac{1}{2}\left(p - \frac{4}{5} \right)^2$

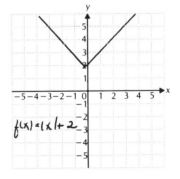

Chapter 5, Test Form B

<u>1.</u> $-6xy + 10y^2$ <u>2.</u> $4x^2y - 5xy - 4xy^2$ <u>3.</u> 5,4,6,8; 8   <u>4.</u> $6x^2 - 11xy + 3y^2$

<u>5.</u> $-21m^4n^3 + 28m^5n^5$ <u>6.</u> $6a^2 - 25ab + 15a + 4b^2 - 14b + 6$ <u>7.</u> $(x - 4)(x - 3)$

8. $(a + 3b)(a - 3b)$ 9. $4(2m + 3)^2$ 10. $(2y - 5)(4y^2 + 10y + 25)$

11. $(x + 2 + 3y)(x + 2 - 3y)$ 12. $-\frac{1}{4}, \frac{1}{3}$ 13. $x^2 - 7x + \frac{49}{4}$

14. 4 ft, 12 ft   15. -9   16. a) $x - 2 + x^2$ b) $x - 4 - x^2$

c) $x^3 - 3x^2 + x - 3$ d) $\frac{x - 3}{x^2 + 1}$ e) $x^2 - 6x + 9$ 17.

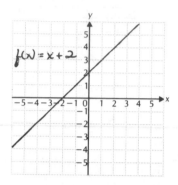

18. $(3, 0, -5)$ 19. $\left\{2, -\frac{14}{5}\right\}$ 20. $\{y \mid y > -1\}$

21. Senior citizen: 70; adult: 175; children: 80

22. $-9(2y + 3)$

Chapter 5, Test Form C

1. $9a^2b^2 - c^2$ 2. $4x^2 + 5xy - 6y^2$ 3. $10x^3 - 9x^2 + 4x - 1$

4. $(2m + 1)(3m + 4)$ 5. $(2y + 3)(2y - 3)$ 6. $3(y - 1)(y^2 + y + 1)$

7. $4x(3x + 4)$ 8. $(7a + 4)^2$ 9. $(x - 10)(x - 20)$

10. $-2ab^4 + 3a^2b^3 - a^5b^2 + 5a^3b$ 11. $-14x^3 + 5x - 1$ 12. $12xy - 7x^2y$

13. $-4, -8$ 14. 8   15. 13   16. a) $x + 1 + x^2$ b) $x + 3 - x^2$

c) $x^3 + 2x^2 - x - 2$ d) $\frac{x + 2}{x^2 - 1}$ e) $x^2 + 4x + 4$ 17.

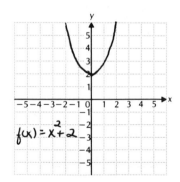

18. $\{y \mid y < 2\}$ 19. $\{x \mid x \geq 1 \text{ or } x \leq -4\}$

20. $(4, -1, 1)$ 21. 92, 89, 83   22. 9 and 15

Chapter 5, Test Form D

1. -44   2. $7xy^2 + xy - 2x^2y$ 3. $a^2 - 3ab + 6b^2$ 4. $4x^2 + 4xy + y^2$

5. $-20y^5z^{10}$ 6. $12x^2 + 5x - 25$ 7. $(3x + 2)(x - 4)$ 8. $(3m - 8)^2$

9. $(y^2 + 4)(y + 2)(y - 2)$ 10. $2(x + 5)(x^2 - 5x + 25)$ 11. $(2x^2 - 3)(x + 2)$

12. $x^2 - \frac{2}{3}x + \frac{1}{9}$ 13. $-\frac{4}{3}, 1$ 14. 9 cm, 6 cm   15.

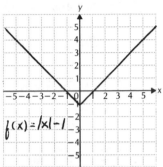

16. a) $x^2 - 1 + x$ b) $x^2 + 7 - x$

c) $x^3 - 4x^2 + 3x - 12$ d) $\frac{x^2 + 3}{x - 4}$ e) $x^2 - 8x + 16$

17. -28   18. $\{4, -1\}$ 19. $\{y \mid y \leqslant -3\}$

20. $(-2, 2, 3)$ 21. 15, 32, 66

22. $(x + y + a - 2b)(x + y - a + 2b)$

Chapter 5, Test Form E

1. $6x^2y + xy$ 2. $m^3 - 2m^2 + 12$ 3. $-3x^6y^2 + x^2y^3 + 4xy^5 - 2y$

4. $x^4 - 2x^3 + 2x - 1$ 5. $8y^2 + 18yz - 5z^2$ 6. $a^2 - 9b^2$ 7. $(2x - 1)(2x + 3)$

8. $2(5m + 2)^2$ 9. $4y^3(y + 1)(y^2 - y + 1)$ 10. $(a + 2)(a + 4)$

11. $(x - 3 + 7y)(x - 3 - 7y)$ 12. $(x - 17)(x + 13)$ 13. $-\frac{2}{3}, \frac{4}{3}$ 14. 7 or -5

15. a) $x + 2 + x^2$ b) $x - 6 - x^2$ c) $x^3 - 2x^2 + 4x - 8$ d) $\frac{x - 2}{x^2 + 4}$ e) $x^2 - 4x + 4$

16. 6   17.

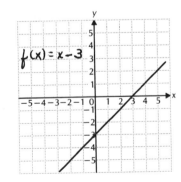

18. $\{y \mid y \leqslant 5\}$ 19. $\left\{x \mid -\frac{1}{3} < x < 3\right\}$

20. $(-1, 1, -3)$ 21. Monday: 15 bushels, Tuesday: 22 bushels, Wednesday: 27 bushels

22. $(x^{3a} - y^{2b})(x^{6a} + x^{3a}y^{2b} + y^{4b})$

Chapter 5, Test Form F

1. $4x^2 - y^2$ 2. $3a^2 - 11ab + 6b^2$ 3. $9m^2 - 12mn + 4n^2$ 4. $(x - 5)^2$

5. $3(3m + 4)(m - 4)$ 6. $(x^2 + 9)(x + 3)(x - 3)$ 7. $(2y^3 - 1)(y - 3)$

8. $(a - 3)(a^2 + 3a + 9)$ 9. $2(b^2 - 8b + 16)$ 10. 4,6,3,4; 6   11. $5ab + 10b^2$

12. $13x^2y - 19xy^2$ 13. $-\frac{4}{3}, \frac{3}{2}$ 14. 8 m, 5 m   15.

16. a) $x^2 - 2 + x$ b) $x^2 + 8 - x$

c) $x^3 - 5x^2 + 3x - 15$ d) $\frac{x^2 + 3}{x - 5}$ e) $x^4 + 6x^2 + 9$

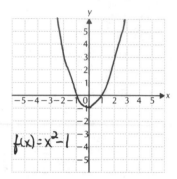

17. 2   18. $\{x \mid x \geqslant 5 \text{ or } x \leqslant 3\}$ 19. $\{y \mid y < 2\}$

20. $(4, -3, 2)$ 21. $40°, 50°, 90°$

22. $(x^a + 13)(x^a - 9)$

Chapter 6, Test Form A

1. $(x + 2)(x - 1)(x - 4)$ 2. $\frac{y + 1}{2}$ 3. $\frac{x^2 - 4x + 16}{x - 7}$ 4. $\frac{6a^2b}{(a + b)(a - b)}$

5. $\frac{x + 33}{(x + 3)^2(x - 3)}$ 6. $\frac{1}{y - 4}$ 7. $\frac{3}{5}$ 8. No solution   9. $\frac{(y + 3)(y - 5)}{(y + 1)^2}$

10. $y - 11$, R -5 11. $3y^2 - 6y + 10$, R -19 12. $d = bcy - a$ 13. $y = \frac{36}{x}$

14. 80,000 BTU   15. $\frac{12}{5}$ days   16. 9 mph   17. $4(x^2 - 10xy + y^2)$

18. $(2a + 3b)(4a^2 - 6ab + 9b^2)$ 19. $\frac{2}{5}, -3$ 20.

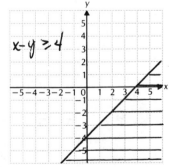

21. -1

Chapter 6, Test Form B

1. $\frac{a^2 + 2a - 2}{(a + 2)(a - 2)}$ 2. $\frac{-3x + 8}{(x - 2)(x^2 + 2x + 4)}$ 3. $\frac{3}{y + 1}$ 4. $y - 4$, R 7

172

5. $\dfrac{(x^2 - 3x + 9)(x + 1)}{(x - 8)(x + 3)}$ 6. $\dfrac{y^2 + 2}{2y - 3}$ 7. $4x^3 - 8x^2 + 19x - 40$, R 81

8. $(2x + 1)(x - 2)(x + 3)$ 9. $\dfrac{1}{3}$ 10. 36   11. 7   12. $r = \dfrac{sT}{s - T}$

13. $y = \dfrac{2}{3}x$ 14. 28.75 miles per gallon   15. $\dfrac{117}{22}$ hours   16. 1080 km

17.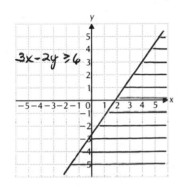
$-3x - 2y \geq 6$

18. $(a - 4)(a^2 + 4a + 16)$ 19. $(6x - 5)(x + 1)$

20. $\dfrac{7}{2}, -\dfrac{7}{2}$ 21. 2 mph

Chapter 6, Test Form C

1. $4(x - 1)^2$ 2. $4y^3 + 3y^2 - 12y - 3$, R $12y + 6$ 3. $\dfrac{3}{2(y - 6)}$

4. $\dfrac{x^2 - 2x + 4}{x + 8}$ 5. $\dfrac{-x - 2}{(x + 4)(x - 4)}$ 6. $\dfrac{5x - 4}{3(x + 2)(x - 2)}$ 7. $\dfrac{y^2 + 1}{(y + 1)(y - 1)}$

8. $y - 12$, R 64   9. 10   10. No solution   11. $\dfrac{y - 1}{y + 1}$ 12. $p = \dfrac{mn}{nR + 1}$

13. $y = \dfrac{0.16}{x}$ 14. 60,000   15. Train A: 105 mph, train B: 90 mph

16. 3 hours   17. $3(x + 3)(x + 1)$ 18. $(3b - 1)(9b^2 + 3b + 1)$ 19. 0, 6

20.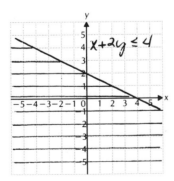
$x + 2y \leq 4$

21. $\dfrac{1}{x}$

1. $6x^3(x + 2)$ 2. $\dfrac{y - 35}{(y + 5)^2(y - 5)}$ 3. $\dfrac{a}{a - b}$ 4. $\dfrac{-4y - 6}{(y + 6)(y - 6)(y + 1)}$

5. $\dfrac{(y - 1)(y - 3)}{9}$ 6. $\dfrac{x + 6}{x^2 + 2x + 4}$ 7. $y - 12$, R 44 8. $\dfrac{y + 10}{y - 7}$

9. $a = \dfrac{b}{bF - 1}$ 10. $\dfrac{56}{15}$ 11. $\dfrac{6}{5}$, -2 12. $4x^3 + 8x^2 + 10x + 15$, R 34

13. $y = 3x$ 14. 80.5% 15. 8 km/h 16. $\dfrac{10}{3}$ hours

17.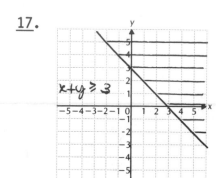

18. $(a + 5)(a^2 - 5a + 25)$ 19. $(3x - 2)(2x + 5)$

20. -5, -1 21. $\dfrac{y + z}{y - z + 1}$

1. $4(y + 6)^2$ 2. $\dfrac{1}{8}$ 3. $y - 4$, R 5 4. $\dfrac{2(x - 7)}{x + 10}$ 5. $\dfrac{2a^2 + 2b^2}{(a + b)(a - b)}$

6. $\dfrac{-2y + 10}{(y - 4)(y^2 + 4y + 16)}$ 7. $\dfrac{7y + 25}{(y + 5)(y - 5)(y + 1)}$ 8. $3y^2 - 9y + 25$, R -70

9. $\dfrac{a}{b}$ 10. -13 11. No solution 12. $a = \dfrac{P}{B(c - d)}$ 13. $y = 0.015625x$ or

$y = \dfrac{1}{64}x$ 14. $\dfrac{5}{32}$ in. 15. 2 hours 16. 18 mph 17. $8(y - 2)(y^2 + 2y + 4)$

18. $(2x - 3y)^2$ 19. 0, $\dfrac{4}{3}$ 20.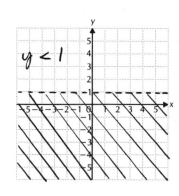

21. $\dfrac{x^2 + 2x + 2}{x^2 + x + 1}$

Chapter 6, Test Form F

1. $2x^2(x - 2)(x - 1)$ 2. $\dfrac{y + 9}{(y + 4)^2(y + 5)}$ 3. $\dfrac{-a + 4}{a - 1}$ 4. $\dfrac{1}{2(y + 8)}$

5. $\dfrac{(y - 11)^2}{(y - 2)^2}$ 6. $3y^2 - 6y + 9$, R $-12y - 8$ 7. $\dfrac{2}{3(y + 1)}$ 8. $\dfrac{2(y - 8)}{y + 4}$

9. $y - 8$, R 46   10. $\dfrac{132}{17}$ 11. -25 12. $b = \dfrac{c}{aM - a}$ 13. $y = \dfrac{15}{x}$

14. 5.625 yd^3 15. Train A: 250 km/h, train B: 200 km/h   16. $\dfrac{12}{7}$ hours

17.

18. $4(x - 4)(x + 3)$ 19. $(y - 2)(y^2 + 2y + 4)$

20. $-\dfrac{3}{2}$, 2   21. $\dfrac{x^2}{x + 1}$

Chapter 7, Test Form A

1. $-10x^{-2}y^{-3}$ 2. $8|x|$ 3. -3 4. $|y|$ 5. 5.0×10^{-6} 6. 12.166

7. $19\sqrt{2}$ 8. $16xy^2\sqrt{x}$ 9. -23 10. $2y\sqrt{2xy}$ 11. $\dfrac{\sqrt{6} - \sqrt{2a} + \sqrt{3a} - a}{3 - a}$

12. $(2x^2y)^{5/3}$ 13. $\sqrt[12]{x^7}$ 14. 2 15. $\sqrt{34} \approx 5.831$ 16. $\sqrt{149} \approx 12.207$

17. $2\sqrt{3}i$ 18. $8 + 3i$ 19. $17 + 11i$ 20. $-\dfrac{2}{5} + \dfrac{11}{5}i$ 21. $\dfrac{x + 1}{2}$

22. $-\dfrac{2}{3}$, 4   23. $\left(x - \dfrac{3}{2}\right)^2$ 24. 12 and 14; -14 and -12 25. $2\sqrt{21}$

Chapter 7, Test Form B

1. $|x - 4|$ 2. 3   3. $-\dfrac{1}{2}$ 4. 11.619 5. $\dfrac{8a^6}{9b^6}$ 6. $9\sqrt{3}$ 7. 1.085×10^7

8. $27 - 7\sqrt{5}$ 9. $3ab^4\sqrt{2a}$ 10. $5a^2\sqrt{b}$ 11. $\left(\sqrt[3]{4x}\right)^2$ or $\sqrt[3]{(4x)^2}$

12. $\sqrt[12]{(3x)^3(x - 2)^2}$ 13. $\dfrac{6 + 2\sqrt{2} + 3\sqrt{3} + \sqrt{6}}{7}$ 14. -3 15. $-5 + 5i$

16. $\dfrac{24}{13} + \dfrac{3}{13}i$ 17. $26 - 2i$ 18. Yes   19. $\sqrt{65} \approx 8.062$ 20. $\dfrac{5\sqrt{2}}{2} \approx 3.536$ m

21. $\dfrac{6}{(y-1)^2}$ 22. $(x+13)(x-7)$ 23. No solution   24. 7 cm, 12 cm

25. $a^2 b^3 y^2 \sqrt{xy}$

Chapter 7, Test Form C

1. 2.5×10^{10} 2. -4 3. $10|a|$ 4. x 5. $mn\sqrt[4]{n}$ 6. $14 - 6\sqrt{5}$

7. $a^3\sqrt{3}$ 8. $-12x^{-1}y^5$ 9. $15\sqrt{2}$ 10. $\sqrt{12} - \sqrt{10} + \sqrt{18} - \sqrt{15}$ 11. $\dfrac{11}{3}$

12. 5 13. $(2a^2 b)^{7/3}$ 14. $\sqrt[24]{a^4(a-3)^3}$ 15. $\sqrt{84} \approx 9.165$

16. $4\sqrt{2}$ cm ≈ 5.657 cm   17. $6 - 3i$ 18. $-41 + i$ 19. $-\dfrac{1}{3} - 3i$ 20. $-3\sqrt{3}i$

21. $(y - 6 + 4z)(y - 6 - 4z)$ 22. $\dfrac{x}{x-1}$ 23. No solution   24. 9, 10, 11

25. $\dfrac{11}{19} + \dfrac{4\sqrt{15}}{19}i$

Chapter 7, Test Form D

1. $|x - 1|$ 2. -1 3. $|y|$ 4. 10.198 5. 1.05×10^{-5} 6. $9x\sqrt{x}$

7. $-13 - 2\sqrt{2}$ 8. $\dfrac{4y^5}{3x^{10}}$ 9. $11\sqrt{6}$ 10. $x\sqrt{7x}$ 11. $\dfrac{12 - \sqrt{a} - a}{9 - a}$

12. $\sqrt[5]{4ab^3}$ 13. $\sqrt[10]{y^5(y+1)^2}$ 14. 4 15. $-5i$ 16. $9 - 2i$ 17. $2 + 26i$

18. $-\dfrac{7}{58} + \dfrac{61}{58}i$ 19. $\sqrt{40} \approx 6.325$ 20. $\sqrt{96}$ ft ≈ 9.798 ft   21. $\dfrac{x-2}{2x}$

22. $\dfrac{1}{2}, -\dfrac{1}{8}$ 23. $\left(a + \dfrac{2}{5}\right)^2$ 24. 6 units   25. $-\dfrac{17}{65} + \dfrac{46}{65}i$

Chapter 7, Test Form E

1. 2.0×10^3 2. $-2x$ 3. $\dfrac{|y|}{3}$ 4. -5 5. $|a + 2|$ 6. $4a\sqrt{a}$

7. $7 - 2\sqrt{10}$ 8. $3x^2\sqrt{5}$ 9. $6a^{-4}b^{-8}$ 10. $3xy^3\sqrt{3x}$ 11. $(x - 2x^2 + 3)\sqrt{10x}$

12. $\dfrac{20 - a}{10 + 3\sqrt{5a} + a}$ 13. $\sqrt[15]{(2x^5)(x-4)^3}$ 14. 6 15. 27 16. $\sqrt{91} \approx 9.539$

17. $\sqrt{65}$ cm ≈ 8.062 cm   18. $11 - 5i$ 19. $-\dfrac{14}{5} - \dfrac{3}{5}i$ 20. $-29 - 31i$

21. $\dfrac{x-2}{2x^2}$ 22. $(2x - 1 + 9y)(2x - 1 - 9y)$ 23. 1   24. 3, 5   25. $a^3 bxy^3$

Chapter 7, Test Form F

__1.__ $\dfrac{125x^7y^{-2}}{4}$ __2.__ $8|b|$ __3.__ 4   __4.__ $|y|$ __5.__ $3a\sqrt[3]{3ab^2}$ __6.__ $4\sqrt{5}$

__7.__ 1.302×10^8 __8.__ $12x^2\sqrt{x}$ __9.__ $25 - 4\sqrt{6}$ __10.__ $2\sqrt{a}$ __11.__ $\dfrac{x^2 - z}{3x^2 + 4x\sqrt{z} + z}$

__12.__ $-\dfrac{1}{2}$ __13.__ 0, 8   __14.__ $\sqrt[6]{x^3(x - 4)^2}$ __15.__ $\sqrt{39} \approx 6.245$ __16.__ $\sqrt{32}$ ft ≈ 5.657

__17.__ No   __18.__ $-5 + 13i$ __19.__ $24 - 7i$ __20.__ $-\dfrac{14}{13} - \dfrac{5}{13}i$ __21.__ $\dfrac{3(x - 1)}{x - 2}$

__22.__ $(x + 15)(x - 9)$ __23.__ No solution   __24.__ 5 ft, 8 ft   __25.__ $1 + 2\sqrt{30}$

Chapter 8, Test Form A

__1.__ $\dfrac{\sqrt{3}}{2}, -\dfrac{\sqrt{3}}{2}$ __2.__ 2, 8   __3.__ $\dfrac{1 \pm i\sqrt{7}}{4}$ __4.__ $3 \pm \sqrt{21}$ __5.__ $\sqrt{2}, -\sqrt{2}$

__6.__ $-0.4, -2.6$ __7.__ $s = \sqrt{\dfrac{Abm}{L}}$ __8.__ Two real   __9.__ $f(x) = 2(x + 2)^2 - 15$

__10.__ $f(x) = x^2 - 4x$ __11.__ $y = \dfrac{18x}{z^2}$ __12.__ 7, 8, 9; -9, -8, -7

__13.__ Joe: 9 hours, Jane: 18 hours   __14.__ 1600 ft²   __15.__

__16.__ $\dfrac{x - 3}{(x - 5)(x - 1)}$ __17.__ $2xy^3\sqrt[3]{15x^2}$ __18.__ $\dfrac{2}{3}, 6$

__19.__ 82, 56   __20.__ $0, -\dfrac{5}{2}, 8, \dfrac{5}{6}$

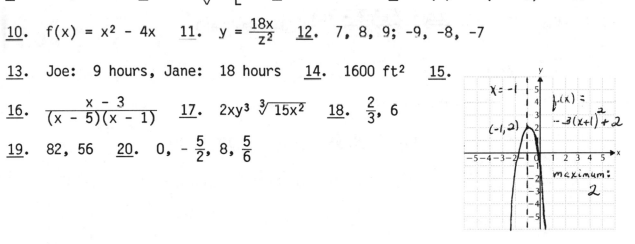

Chapter 8, Test Form B

__1.__ Two nonreal   __2.__ $f(x) = 3(x - 2)^2 - 5$ __3.__ 3, -10   __4.__ $1 \pm 2i$ __5.__ $0, \dfrac{1}{2}$

__6.__ $\sqrt{2}, -\sqrt{2}, \sqrt{7}, -\sqrt{7}$ __7.__ -3, 11   __8.__ 0.7, -6.7   __9.__ $R = -1 \pm \sqrt{1 + 3M}$

<u>10.</u>

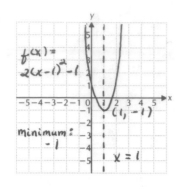

<u>11.</u> $f(x) = 2x^2 - 3x - 1$ <u>12.</u> 9 yd × 13 yd

<u>13.</u> 180 cm³   <u>14.</u> 12 mph   <u>15.</u> 64

<u>16.</u> $\dfrac{x^2 - 3x - 5}{(x + 5)(x + 4)(x - 2)}$ <u>17.</u> $5x^3y\sqrt{6y}$ <u>18.</u> 5

<u>19.</u> 22 dimes, 24 quarters   <u>20.</u> $\sqrt{5}, -\sqrt{5}$

Chapter 8, Test Form C

<u>1.</u> 11, -3   <u>2.</u> $\dfrac{1 \pm 2\sqrt{2}i}{3}$ <u>3.</u> $\dfrac{2}{3}, -\dfrac{2}{3}$ <u>4.</u> -2, -3   <u>5.</u> $\sqrt{2}, -\sqrt{2}, \sqrt{3}, -\sqrt{3}$

<u>6.</u> -0.4, -5.6   <u>7.</u> $b = \dfrac{-ac \pm \sqrt{a^2c^2 + 4aA}}{2a}$ <u>8.</u> One real

<u>9.</u> $f(x) = 2\left(x - \dfrac{3}{2}\right)^2 + \dfrac{9}{2}$ <u>10.</u> $f(x) = x^2 - 2x + 3$ <u>11.</u> 73.5 cm²

<u>12.</u> Legs: $3\sqrt{2}, 4\sqrt{2}$; hypotenuse: $5\sqrt{2}$ <u>13.</u> 40 mph   <u>14.</u> 144

<u>15.</u>

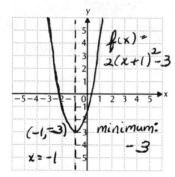

<u>16.</u> $6xy\sqrt[3]{y^2}$ <u>17.</u> 1   <u>18.</u> -4

<u>19.</u> Peanuts: 6 pounds; cashews: 4 pounds

<u>20.</u> 1, $\dfrac{3}{2}$

Chapter 8, Test Form D

<u>1.</u> 0, -3   <u>2.</u> -2 ± 2i   <u>3.</u> 5   <u>4.</u> $-\dfrac{1}{2}$, -3   <u>5.</u> $\dfrac{7}{2}$, -1   <u>6.</u> 0.2, -2.2

7. $T = \frac{1}{RW^2}$ 8. $3x^2 + 4x - 4 = 0$ 9.

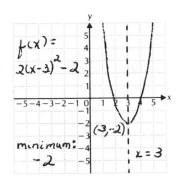

10. $(3 + \sqrt{5}, 0), (3 - \sqrt{5}, 0)$

11. $f(x) = 4x^2 - 5x + 1$ 12. $y = \frac{xz^2}{4w}$

13. 6, 8, 10   14. First part: 40 mph;

second part: 48 mph   15. 5625 ft^2

16. $\frac{4x + 2}{(x - 1)^2(x + 1)}$ 17. $3a^3b^2\sqrt{14b}$

18. 0   19. Bill: 45 years; Bess: 15 years   20. $\sqrt[3]{9}$

Chapter 8, Test Form E

1.

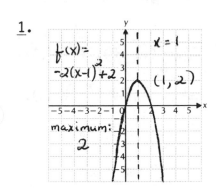

2. $x^2 + 6x + 9 = 0$ 3. $\frac{1 \pm i}{2}$ 4. 8

5. $\frac{\sqrt{15}}{3}, -\frac{\sqrt{15}}{3}$ 6. $2, -\frac{2}{9}$ 7. $2, -\frac{2}{3}$

8. 5.5, −1.5   9. $z = \sqrt{w^2 - y^2}$ 10. None

11. $f(x) = x^2 - 4x + 3$ 12. 25 W/m^2 13. 49

14. Airplane A: 300 mph; airplane B: 250 mph

15. $4\sqrt{3}, \sqrt{3}; -4\sqrt{3}, -\sqrt{3}$ 16. $3xy\sqrt[3]{2xy^2}$

17. $\frac{x + 3}{x(x - 2)}$ 18. 7   19. 5 cm, 12 cm   20. $\sqrt{5}$

Chapter 8, Test Form F

1.

2. $\left[-\frac{1}{3}, 0\right]$ 3. $x^2 - 4\sqrt{2}x + 6 = 0$ 4. $0, \frac{1}{3}$

5. $\frac{1}{3}, -2$ 6. $\frac{-9 \pm 3\sqrt{7}i}{2}$ 7. 1, −1, 2, −2

8. 0, 1   9. 2.9, −0.2   10. $m = \frac{-p \pm \sqrt{p^2 + 16n}}{8}$

11. $y = \frac{1}{2}xz^2$ 12. $f(x) = 3x^2 - 5x + 2$ 13. 100

14. 12 mph   15. 2 in.   16. $2x^2y^3\sqrt{21y}$

17. $\dfrac{x + 17}{(x - 4)(x + 3)}$ 18. No solution   19. 61, 17   20. 10, -2

Chapter 9, Test Form A

1. $\sqrt{82} \approx 9.055$ 2. $\left(\dfrac{3}{2}, \dfrac{7}{2}\right)$ 3. $(x - 3)^2 + (y + 2)^2 = 16$ 4. $(2, -3)$; 2

5.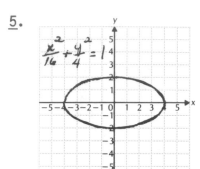

6.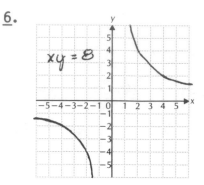

7.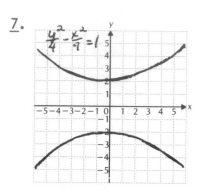

8.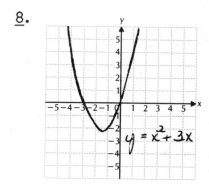

9.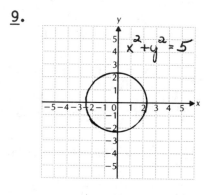

10. $(1, -2)$, $(2, -1)$

11. $(3, 1)$, $(-3, -1)$,

$(1, 3)$, $(-1, -3)$

12. 8 cm, 5 cm

13. 9, -5

14. $\{x \mid -1 \leqslant x \leqslant 4\}$

15. $\{x \mid -11 < x < -4\}$ 16. $\dfrac{ab\sqrt{b}}{9}$ 17. $\dfrac{3 - 2\sqrt{x} - x}{1 - x}$ 18. $\dfrac{-1 \pm \sqrt{2}\,i}{3}$

19. 10 mph   20. No

1.

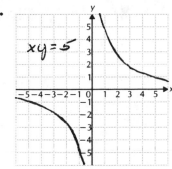

$xy = 5$

2.

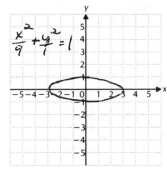

$\frac{x^2}{9} + \frac{y^2}{1} = 1$

3.

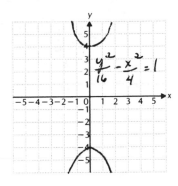

$\frac{y^2}{16} - \frac{x^2}{4} = 1$

4.

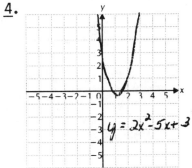

$y = 2x^2 - 5x + 3$

5.

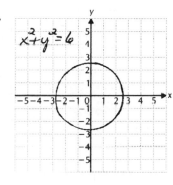

$x^2 + y^2 = 6$

6. (5, 3)

7. $\sqrt{116} \approx 10.770$

8. (-1, 4); $\sqrt{11}$

9. $(x + 4)^2 + (y - 7)^2 = 3$

10. (2, 3), (-6, -1)

11. $(\sqrt{2}, \sqrt{7})$,

$(\sqrt{2}, -\sqrt{7})$, $(-\sqrt{2}, \sqrt{7})$, $(-\sqrt{2}, -\sqrt{7})$ **12.** 40 yd × 55 yd **13.** 14 and 4;

-14 and -4 **14.** {x|x < -2 or x > 1} **15.** {x|-3 ⩽ x ⩽ 3} **16.** $2 \pm 2\sqrt{3}i$

17. 3 **18.** $\dfrac{-2}{\sqrt{6} + \sqrt{10} + 3 + \sqrt{15}}$ **19.** 40 mph **20.** $\dfrac{5}{2}, \dfrac{6}{5}$

Chapter 9, Test Form C

1. $\sqrt{58} \approx 7.616$ **2.** $\left(\dfrac{1}{2}, \dfrac{5}{2}\right)$ **3.** $(x - 2)^2 + (y + 4)^2 = 5$ **4.** (-3, 5); 2

5.

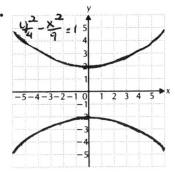

$\frac{y^2}{4} - \frac{x^2}{9} = 1$

6.

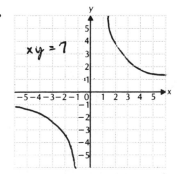

$xy = 7$

7.

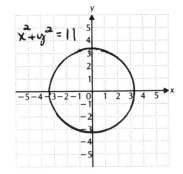

$x^2 + y^2 = 11$

8.
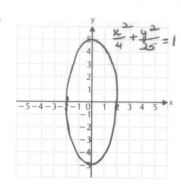
$\frac{x^2}{4} + \frac{y^2}{25} = 1$

9.
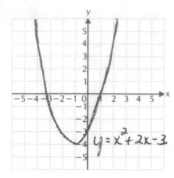
$y = x^2 + 2x - 3$

10. (3, 9), (-1, 1)

11. (3, 4), (-3, -4)

12. $\sqrt{5}$ cm $\times$ $2\sqrt{5}$ cm

13. 17, 9

14. $\{x | -2 \leqslant x \leqslant -1$ or

$x \geqslant 4\}$ 15. $\{x | -3 < x < 2\}$

16. $\dfrac{2 + 3\sqrt{x} + x}{1 - x}$ 17. $4x\sqrt{6x}$ 18. $-1 \pm \sqrt{3}i$ 19. First part: 50 mph;

second part: 40 mph   20. $x^2 + (y - 2)^2 = 13$

Chapter 9, Test Form D

1.
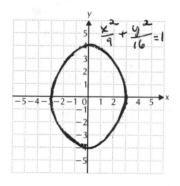
$\frac{x^2}{9} + \frac{y^2}{16} = 1$

2.
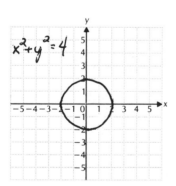
$xy = 6$

3.
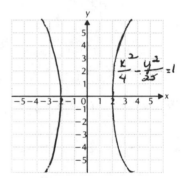
$\frac{x^2}{4} - \frac{y^2}{25} = 1$

4.
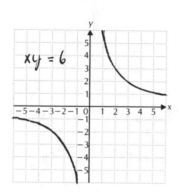
$x^2 + y^2 = 4$

5.
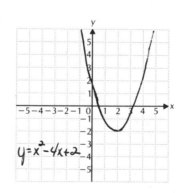
$y = x^2 - 4x + 2$

6. $\left[-2, -\dfrac{1}{2}\right]$

7. $\sqrt{89} \approx 9.434$

8. (4, -3); 6

9. $(x - 2)^2 + (y + 9)^2 = 9$

10. (13, -32), (1, 4)

11. (1, 3), (-1, -3)

12. $\{x | x < -3\}$ 13. $\{x | x < -5$ or $0 < x < 7\}$ 14. (5, 12), (-5, -12), (12, 5),

(-12, -5)   <u>15.</u> 5 ft, 7 ft   <u>16.</u> $-2 \pm \sqrt{2}i$ <u>17.</u> $-\frac{2}{3}$

<u>18.</u> $\frac{\sqrt{6} + \sqrt{10} + \sqrt{15} + 5}{-2}$ <u>19.</u> Airplane A: 400 mph; airplane B: 500 mph or

airplane A: 150 mph; airplane B: 250 mph   <u>20.</u> $(2\sqrt{2}, 3\sqrt{2})$

Chapter 9, Test Form E

<u>1.</u> $(x + 4)^2 + (y - 5)^2 = 5$ <u>2.</u> (-5, 1); 1   <u>3.</u> $\sqrt{80} \approx 8.944$ <u>4.</u> (1, 1)

<u>5.</u>
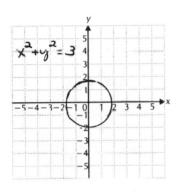

<u>6.</u>
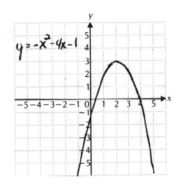

<u>7.</u>
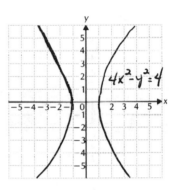

<u>8.</u>
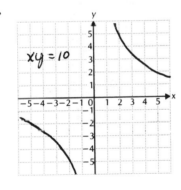

<u>9.</u>
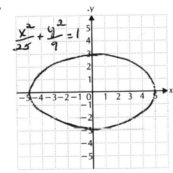

<u>10.</u> (1, 2)   <u>11.</u> (3, 2),

(-3, -2), $\left[4, \frac{3}{2}\right]$, $\left[-4, -\frac{3}{2}\right]$

<u>12.</u> $\{x \mid -2 < x < 4\}$

<u>13.</u> $\left\{x \mid 5 < x < \frac{25}{3}\right\}$

<u>14.</u> (7, -1), (-1, 7)

<u>15.</u> 9 cm, 4 cm   <u>16.</u> $4x\sqrt{2}$

<u>17.</u> $\frac{1 - y}{3 - 4\sqrt{y} + y}$ <u>18.</u> $3 \pm \sqrt{14}$ <u>19.</u> 6 km/h   <u>20.</u> $\left[\frac{14}{5}, 0\right]$

1.

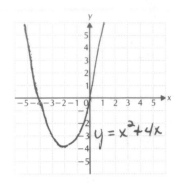

$y = x^2 + 4x$

2.

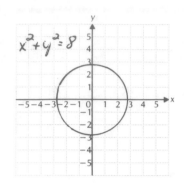

$x^2 + y^2 = 8$

3.

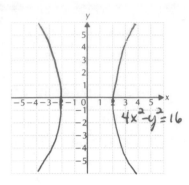

$4x^2 - y^2 = 16$

4.

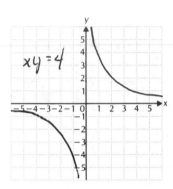

$xy = 4$

5.

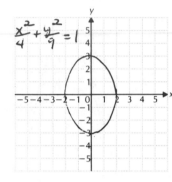

$\dfrac{x^2}{4} + \dfrac{y^2}{9} = 1$

6. (-3, 1); 2

7. $(x - 4)^2 + (y + 6)^2 = 18$

8. $\left[-\dfrac{1}{10},\ 1\right]$

9. $\sqrt{\dfrac{61}{100}} \approx 0.781$

10. (-3, 4)

11. (4, 5), (-4, -5)

12. $\{x \mid -3 \leqslant x \leqslant 0 \text{ or } x \geqslant 3\}$ **13.** $\{x \mid -11 < x < -9\}$ **14.** 3 m × 4 m

15. 60 ft, 48 ft   **16.** 4   **17.** $\dfrac{4 + 5\sqrt{a} + a}{1 - a}$ **18.** $2 \pm \sqrt{5}$ **19.** 45 mph

20. $x^2 + (y - 2)^2 = 13$

Chapter 10, Test Form A

1.

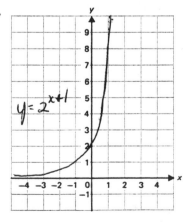

$y = 2^{x+1}$

2.

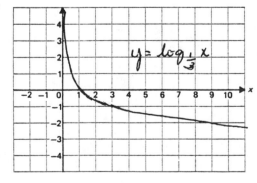

$y = \log_{\frac{1}{3}} x$

3. $9^{\frac{3}{2}} = 27$ 4. $\log_{\frac{1}{2}} 4 = -2$ 5. $2 \log_a x + \frac{1}{3} \log_a y - 5 \log_a z$ 6. $\log \frac{a^{\frac{1}{4}}}{b^2 c}$

7. 2.5302   8. 0.00681   9. -2.2451   10. 7519.6911   11. 2.5249

12. 0.02073   13. $\frac{17}{12}$ 14. 1.2325   15. 6   16. 9   17. 4   18. 2.18 ft/sec

19. $2 + 2i$ 20. $p = \sqrt{\frac{mn}{R}}$ 21. $\sqrt{3}, -\sqrt{3}$ 22. 5, -2   23. -1

Chapter 10, Test Form B

1. $\log_5 \frac{1}{125} = -3$ 2. $2^5 = 32$ 3. $\frac{1}{3} \log x - \log y - 2 \log z$ 4. $\log \sqrt{a^3 c}$

5.

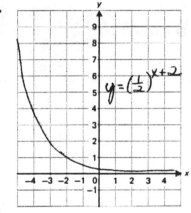

$y = \left(\frac{1}{2}\right)^{x+2}$

6.

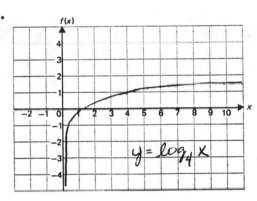

$y = \log_4 x$

7. $0.4548 + (-2)$ or -1.5452 8. 216   9. 6.8941   10. 0.001962   11. -0.6356

12. 15481.035   13. 0.6781   14. $\frac{1}{2}$ 15. 8   16. $\frac{1}{16}$ 17. 1

18. 6.1 billion   19. $8 - 5i$ 20. $Q = \frac{-3 \pm \sqrt{9 + 8A}}{2}$ 21. 1, -2

22. $(3, -1), (1, -3)$ 23. $\log_a (x^3 - 1)$

1.

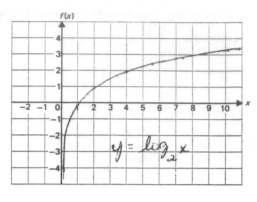

$y = \log_2 x$

2.

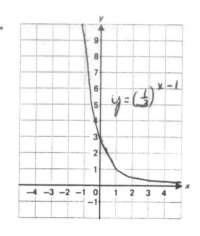

$y = \left(\frac{1}{3}\right)^{x-1}$

3. $\log_8 4 = \frac{2}{3}$ 4. $5^{-2} = \frac{1}{25}$ 5. $\frac{1}{3}(\log_a x + \log_a y - 2\log_a z)$ 6. $\log \frac{ab^2}{c^3}$

7. 1.4698   8. 0.0256   9. -1.7338   10. 326.9641   11. 7.7617

12. 0.0000106   13. 1   14. 1.8956   15. $\frac{1}{2}$ 16. $\frac{1}{8}$ 17. 3   18. $397.49

19. $6 - 8i$ 20. $m = \dfrac{-pq \pm \sqrt{p^2q^2 + 4pn}}{2p}$ 21. $\sqrt{2}, -\sqrt{2}, 2, -2$

22. $(3, -4), (-2, -9)$ 23. $\frac{15}{2}$

Chapter 10, Test Form D

1. $8^{\frac{2}{3}} = 4$ 2. $\log_{32} 8 = \frac{3}{5}$ 3.

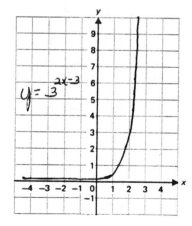

$y = 3^{2x-3}$

4.

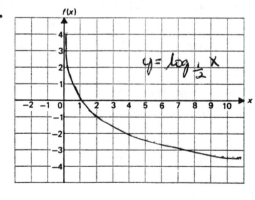

$y = \log_{\frac{1}{2}} x$

5. 3.6160   6. 0.847   7. 5.6895

8. -4.6916   9. 0.004057   10. 40.0288

11. $\frac{1}{5}(\log x + 2\log y - 4\log z)$ 12. $\log \frac{a^2b^{\frac{1}{2}}}{c^3}$ 13. $2\sqrt{2}$ 14. $\frac{1}{9}$ 15. $\frac{4}{3}$

186

Chapter 10, Test Form D   (continued)

16. 1.2684   17. 1   18. 2.23 ft/sec   19. $-\frac{1}{2} - \frac{5}{2}i$ 20. H = $\frac{1}{GK^2}$

21. $-\frac{1}{4}, \frac{1}{3}$ 22. 10 m × 12 m   23. $\frac{1}{3}$, -5

Chapter 10, Test Form E

1.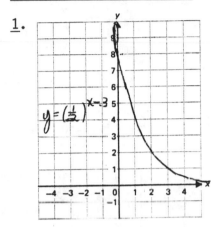

2.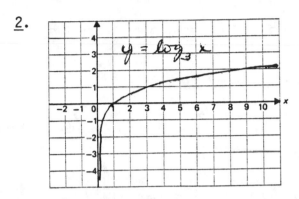

3. $2^3 = 8$ 4. $\log_{\frac{1}{9}} 3 = -\frac{1}{2}$ 5. $3 \log_a x - 2 \log_a z - \log_a y$ 6. $\log \sqrt[4]{\dfrac{a}{b^3c^5}}$

7. 0.9201 + (-1) or -0.0799   8. 63,200   9. 3.3791   10. 0.0000215

11. -4.2787   12. 8.3087   13. $-\frac{3}{2}$ 14. 0.5440   15. 3   16. 3   17. 6

18. 6.8 billion   19. $2\sqrt{5}i$ 20. $t = \sqrt{s^2 - w^2}$ 21. 1, -1, 2, -2

22. (-1, 1), $\left(\frac{13}{15}, \frac{1}{15}\right)$ 23. 7

Chapter 10, Test Form F

1. $\log_{\frac{1}{3}} 3 = -1$ 2. $16^{\frac{1}{2}} = 4$ 3.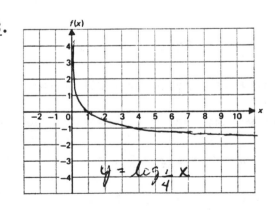

4.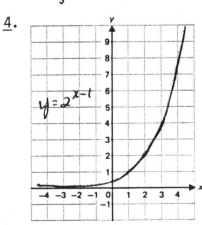

<u>5</u>. 5.8116   <u>6</u>. 0.0400   <u>7</u>. 2.8537   <u>8</u>. -7.0745   <u>9</u>. 0.0003405   <u>10</u>. 66.8466

<u>11</u>. $\frac{1}{4}(3 \log_a x + \log_a y - 2 \log_a z)$ <u>12</u>. $\log \frac{a^2b}{c^{\frac{1}{3}}}$ <u>13</u>. 16   <u>14</u>. 25

<u>15</u>. 1.9586   <u>16</u>. $\frac{7}{2}$ <u>17</u>. 8   <u>18</u>. \$536.56   <u>19</u>. Yes   <u>20</u>. $g = \frac{-k \pm \sqrt{k^2 + 12f}}{6}$

<u>21</u>. 1, -1, $\sqrt{3}$, $-\sqrt{3}$ <u>22</u>. 3 ft, 5 ft   <u>23</u>. 4, -3

Final Examination, Test Form A

<u>1</u>. -2.2   <u>2</u>. $\frac{2}{3}$ <u>3</u>. 7x - 3   <u>4</u>. $\frac{x^{-2}y^4z^{-8}}{9}$ or $\frac{y^4}{9x^2z^8}$ <u>5</u>. 4   <u>6</u>. 4   <u>7</u>. 2

<u>8</u>. 11 ft, 8 ft   <u>9</u>. 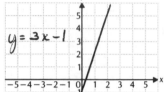   <u>10</u>.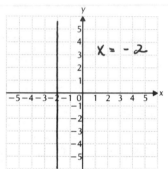

<u>11</u>. y = -4x - 2

<u>12</u>. (6, -3)

<u>13</u>. (-1, 4, -3)

<u>14</u>. 34 dimes,

19 quarters

<u>15</u>. -9   <u>16</u>. {y | y ⩾ 3}   <u>17</u>. {a | a < -1 or a > 2}   <u>18</u>. {4, -5}

<u>19</u>.   <u>20</u>.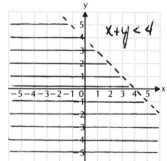

<u>21</u>. Ø   <u>22</u>. $2xy^3 + 2x^2y^2 + x^3y^2$

<u>23</u>. $3a^2 - 7ab + ac + 2b^2 + 3bc - 2c^2$

<u>24</u>. $9x^2 - 6xy + y^2$ <u>25</u>. (2m + n)(2m - n)

<u>26</u>. (3x - 1)(x + 3)   <u>27</u>. $(y + 3)(y^2 - 3y + 9)$

<u>28</u>. a) $x^2 + x - 1$ b) $-x^2 + x - 7$

c) $x^3 - 4x^2 + 3x - 12$ d) $\frac{x - 4}{x^2 + 3}$ e) $x^2 - 8x + 16$ <u>29</u>. 1   <u>30</u>. $\frac{4y^2}{y + 2}$

<u>31</u>. $3y^2 + 4y + 9$, R 14   <u>32</u>. $\frac{x - 4}{x + 3}$ <u>33</u>. $\frac{1}{2}$ <u>34</u>. $\frac{2}{3}$ <u>35</u>. $\frac{24}{7}$ hours

36. 1.1×10^6 **37.** $6|y|$ **38.** $13\sqrt{3}$ **39.** $6a^2b\sqrt{5b}$ **40.** $-\frac{4}{5} - \frac{7}{5}i$

41. $3, 7$ **42.** $\sqrt{45} \approx 6.708$ **43.** $0, 3$ **44.** $\frac{2 \pm \sqrt{6}i}{2}$ **45.** $-\frac{1}{2}, 1$

46. $8, 10, 12; -12, -10, -8$ **47.** 25 **48.** $(3, 0), (-5, 8)$

49. $\{x | x \leqslant -7 \text{ or } x > 5\}$ **50.** $(4, 3), (-4, -3), (3, 4), (-3, -4)$

51. $\sqrt{10} \approx 3.162$ **52.** $(2, -3), 5$ **53.**

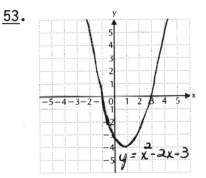

54.

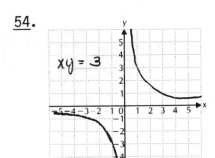

55.

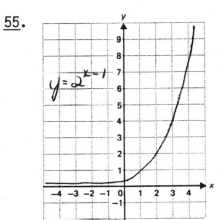

56.

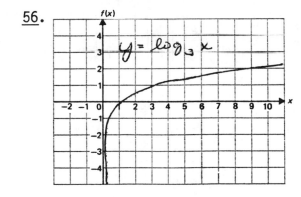

57. $\log_{\frac{1}{3}} 27 = -3$ **58.** $\log \sqrt{\frac{ab^3}{c}}$

59. $\frac{1}{2}$ **60.** 25 **61.** $-\frac{3}{8}$

62. $(x^a + y^{3b})(x^{2a} - x^a y^{3b} + y^{6b})$

Final Examination, Test Form B

1. 1 **2.** $-\frac{1}{12}$ **3.** 5 **4.** $26x - 48$ **5.** $\frac{8x^{-15}y^9}{27}$ or $\frac{8y^9}{27x^{15}}$ **6.** 4

7. $a = \dfrac{2b - cd}{c}$ 8. 20°, 60°, 100°   9.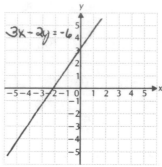

10.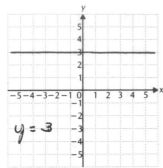

11. $y = -\dfrac{1}{2}x + 1$ 12. (3, 0)   13. (3, 4, -3)   14. (-1, -2)

15. 89, 73, 85   16. $\{x \mid x > 1\}$ 17. $\left\{x \mid -\dfrac{4}{3} < x \leqslant 1\right\}$ 18. $\{x \mid x \leqslant -1 \text{ or } x \geqslant 7\}$

19. 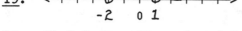   20.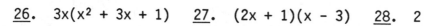

21. $\{1,2,3,4\}$ 22. $x^2 - 4y^2$ 23. $6x^2 + 7x - 3$

24. $(y - 4)^2$ 25. $(a + 0.1)(a^2 - 0.1a + 0.01)$

26. $3x(x^2 + 3x + 1)$ 27. $(2x + 1)(x - 3)$ 28. 2

29. a) $x^2 + x - 3$ b) $x - x^2 - 7$

c) $x^3 - 5x^2 + 2x - 10$ d) $\dfrac{x - 5}{x^2 + 2}$ e) $x^2 - 10x + 25$

30. $\dfrac{1}{y - 2}$ 31. $\dfrac{2}{x - 2}$ 32. $\dfrac{1}{3}$ 33. No solution   34. $138   35. 8 mph

36. -5   37. $|y|$ 38. $\dfrac{\sqrt{15} - \sqrt{6} - \sqrt{10} + 2}{3}$ 39. $\sqrt[6]{(y + 1)^3 y^2}$

40. -1   41. $11 + 10i$ 42. $\sqrt{208} \approx 14.422$ 43. 2   44. $\dfrac{2 \pm \sqrt{2}}{2}$

45. $\sqrt{5}, -\sqrt{5}$ 46. 1, -1, 2, -2   47. 4 m × 7 m   48. $(x + 1)^2 + (y - 4)^2 = 4$

<u>49.</u> $\sqrt{74} \approx 8.602$

<u>50.</u>
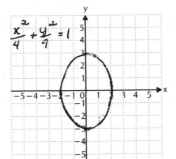

<u>51.</u>
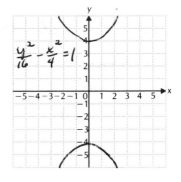

<u>52.</u> $\sqrt{3},\ -\sqrt{3}$

<u>53.</u> $\{x\mid x < -2 \text{ or } x > 3\}$

<u>54.</u> $-7,\ 8$ <u>55.</u> $3^4 = 81$

<u>56.</u> $3 \log_a x + \dfrac{1}{4} \log_a y - \log_a z$

<u>57.</u>
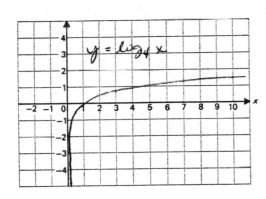

<u>58.</u>
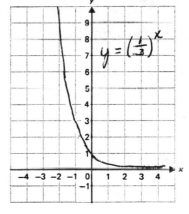

<u>59.</u>   1.431   <u>60.</u>   5   <u>61.</u>   -12   <u>62.</u>   6

Final Examination, Test Form C

<u>1.</u> $-\dfrac{1}{12}$ <u>2.</u>   3   <u>3.</u> $11a - 9$ <u>4.</u> $-6x^{-2}yz^3$ <u>5.</u>   9   <u>6.</u> $y = -2x - 2$

<u>7.</u>
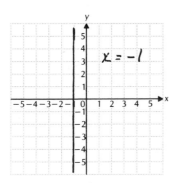

<u>8.</u>
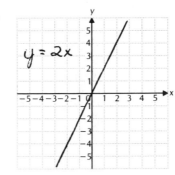

<u>9.</u>   -3   <u>10.</u> $\dfrac{3}{5}$

<u>11.</u>   34, 36   <u>12.</u>   (4, -5)

<u>13.</u>   (3, -2, -1)

<u>14.</u>   Jay: 27 years;

Lisa: 12 years

<u>15.</u>   Inconsistent

16. $\{1, 3, 5\}$ 17. $\{x \mid 1 \leqslant x < 4\}$ 18. $\{y \mid y \geqslant 6\}$ 19. $\{x \mid x < 1 \text{ or } x > 7\}$

20.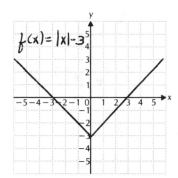

21.

$3x - 4y \leq 12$

22. $3a^3b^4 + 2a^2b^2 - 3ab^3$

23. $2x^2 + 9xy - 5y^2$ 24. $a^2 + 6ab + 9b^2$

25. $(3x + 2)(x - 3)$

26. $(y - 2 + 3z)(y - 2 - 3z)$

27. $(2y - 1)(4y^2 + 2y + 1)$

28. $x^2 - 5x + \dfrac{25}{4}$ 29. $f(x) = |x| - 3$

b) $x - x^2 - 7$

d) $\dfrac{x - 6}{x^2 + 1}$

31. $\dfrac{1}{x - 1}$

33. $3x^2 - 7x + 7, \ R\ -2$

30. a) $x^2 + x - 5$

c) $x^3 - 6x^2 + x - 6$

e) $x^2 - 12x + 36$

32. $\dfrac{x - 1}{2x}$

34. -3

35. Train A: 80 mph;   train B: 100 mph   36. $-\dfrac{1}{4}$

37. $|x - 1|$ 38. 5 39. $12 - 7\sqrt{6}$ 40. $5ab\sqrt{b}$ 41. $12 - 8i$

42. No solution   43. $0, \dfrac{1}{4}$ 44. $-2 \pm 2\sqrt{2}$ 45. $T = \dfrac{3 \pm \sqrt{9 + 8Q}}{2}$

46. $y = \dfrac{xz}{w^2}$ 47. $6\sqrt{6}, \sqrt{6}; \ -6\sqrt{6}, -\sqrt{6}$

48. $x^2 + y^2 = 9$

49. $\dfrac{x^2}{1} + \dfrac{y^2}{4} = 1$

50. $\left(1, -\dfrac{3}{2}\right)$

51. $x^2 + (y + 2)^2 = 25$

52. $\left(\dfrac{1}{3}, \dfrac{1}{3}\right), \ (-1, 3)$

53. $\{x \mid x \leqslant -2 \text{ or } x > 2\}$

54. $3, 12; \ -3, -12$

55.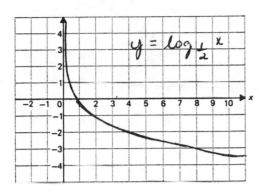

56.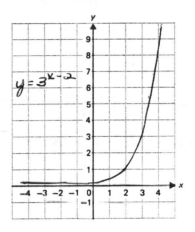

57. $\log \dfrac{a^{\frac{1}{2}}b^3}{c^2}$ 58. $6^0 = 1$ 59. $\dfrac{1}{3}$ 60. 7 61. $\dfrac{7}{2}$, -1 62. $\dfrac{1}{x + 1}$

Final Examination, Test Form D

1. $\{2,3,4,5\}$ 2. 125% 3. 5.0×10^{-5} 4. $-\dfrac{5}{6}$ 5. -14 6. 8

7. $\dfrac{a^6 b^{-2} c^{-8}}{4}$ or $\dfrac{a^6}{4b^2 c^8}$ 8. $4x^2 - 13x - 12$ 9. $4x^2 - 4xy + y^2$ 10. $\dfrac{x}{x^2 - 3x + 9}$

11. $\dfrac{1}{2y}$ 12. $\dfrac{y - 4}{y^2}$ 13. $-\dfrac{1}{2} + \dfrac{1}{2}i$ 14. $\dfrac{|y|}{3}$ 15. a 16. $|a|$

17. $2b\sqrt[3]{2a^2 b}$ 18. $(x + 3)(x + 1)$ 19. $(y^2 + 4)(y + 2)(y - 2)$

20. $(a + 2b)(a^2 - 2ab + 4b^2)$ 21. $(x + 1)(x - 1)(2x - 3)$ 22. -3 23. $1, 5$

24. 2 25. $\dfrac{3}{2}$, $-\dfrac{3}{2}$ 26. $\dfrac{-1 \pm 3i}{2}$ 27. No solution   28. $(-2, 4)$

29. $(1, 0, -1)$ 30. $(2\sqrt{3}, -\sqrt{3})$, $(-2\sqrt{3}, \sqrt{3})$ 31. 4 32. $\dfrac{1}{9}$

33. $\{a \mid a \leqslant 4\}$ 34. $\left\{x \mid x < -\dfrac{1}{3} \text{ or } x > 1\right\}$ 35. $\{x \mid 0 \leqslant x < 4\}$

36. $\{x \mid -3 < x < 1\}$ 37. $(6, -2)$ 38. $k = \dfrac{5}{2}(h - 3)$ 39. $n = \dfrac{m}{Pm - 1}$

40. ![number line with open circles at -4 and -2, shaded to the right]

41.
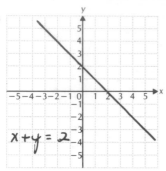
$x + y = 2$

42.
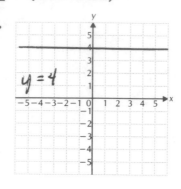
$y = 4$

43.
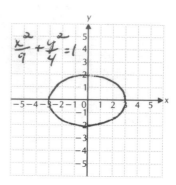
$\frac{x^2}{9} + \frac{y^2}{4} = 1$

44.
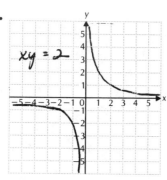
$xy = 2$

45.
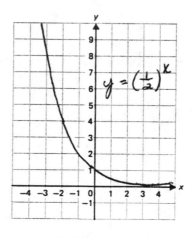
$y = \left(\frac{1}{2}\right)^x$

46.
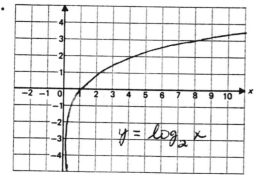
$y = \log_2 x$

47.
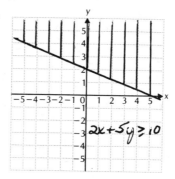
$2x + 5y \geq 10$

48. $y = -2x + 5$ 49. $(-4, 1)$, $\sqrt{13}$ 50. $\sqrt{80} \approx 8.944$ 51. a) $x^2 + x + 3$

b) $x + 3 - x^2$ c) $x^3 + 3x^2$ d) $\frac{x + 3}{x^2}$ e) $x^2 + 6x + 9$ 52. $\log_{16} 2 = \frac{1}{4}$

Final Examination, Test Form D   (continued)

$\underline{53}$. $\frac{1}{3}(2 \log_a x + \log_a y - 2 \log_a z)$ $\underline{54}$. \$650 $\underline{55}$. 70°, 75°, 35°

$\underline{56}$. 24 hours $\underline{57}$. $\sqrt{65} \approx 8.062$ $\underline{58}$. 3025 m² $\underline{59}$. $\frac{3}{2}$ in. $\underline{60}$. 2 cm, 7 cm

$\underline{61}$. $\frac{1}{2} + \frac{13}{10}i$ $\underline{62}$. $\left\{x \middle| x < \frac{1}{2}\right\}$

Final Examination, Test Form E

$\underline{1}$. $\frac{6}{7}$ $\underline{2}$. 1.5 $\underline{3}$. $-\frac{2}{15}$ $\underline{4}$. $\frac{16x^4 y^{-8}}{9}$ or $\frac{16x^4}{9x^8}$ $\underline{5}$. $\frac{y - 5}{4y}$ $\underline{6}$. $\frac{1}{y(y - 1)}$

$\underline{7}$. $a^2 - 9b^2$ $\underline{8}$. $x^2 - 4x - 21$ $\underline{9}$. $5 + 10i$ $\underline{10}$. $7ab^4 + a^2b^3 - 5a^2b$

$\underline{11}$. $-2\sqrt{2}$ $\underline{12}$. 21 $\underline{13}$. $\frac{33}{100}$ $\underline{14}$. $2x + 1$, R -8 $\underline{15}$. $\{1,4\}$ $\underline{16}$. $|x - 8|$

$\underline{17}$. y $\underline{18}$. $3a^2b^2\sqrt{7b}$ $\underline{19}$. $2x(x - 1)^2$ $\underline{20}$. $(y + 2)(y^2 - 2y + 4)$

$\underline{21}$. $(2x - 5)(x + 3)$ $\underline{22}$. $\frac{2}{3}$ $\underline{23}$. $y = \frac{2}{5}x + \frac{19}{5}$ $\underline{24}$. 11 $\underline{25}$. 1

$\underline{26}$. No solution $\underline{27}$. $(5, 3)$ $\underline{28}$. $(7, 4, -8)$ $\underline{29}$. $\frac{1 \pm \sqrt{10}}{3}$ $\underline{30}$. 4, -3

$\underline{31}$. 1, -1, 2, -2 $\underline{32}$. No solution $\underline{33}$. $(-2, 4)$, $(4, -2)$ $\underline{34}$. 125

$\underline{35}$. 2.3 $\underline{36}$. $\left\{x \middle| x < \frac{1}{2} \text{ or } x > 1\right\}$ $\underline{37}$. $\{y | y \leqslant -3\}$

$\underline{38}$. $\left\{x \middle| x \leqslant -3 \text{ or } 1 \leqslant x \leqslant 4\right\}$ $\underline{39}$. $(3, -3)$ $\underline{40}$. $p = \frac{m \pm \sqrt{m^2 + 4nr}}{2n}$

$\underline{41}$.
```
<--+--+--+--⊕--+--+--●--+--+--+-->
        -2    0    2
```

$\underline{42}$.

$y = 4x - 1$

$\underline{43}$.

$y = -3$

$\underline{44}$.

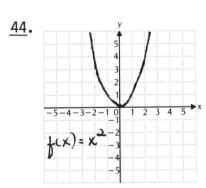

$f(x) = x^2$

45.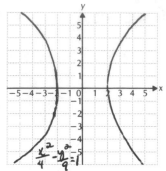

46.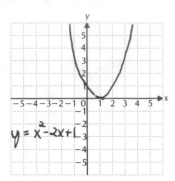

47.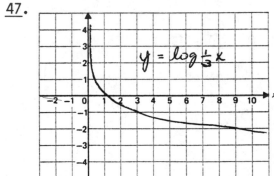

48.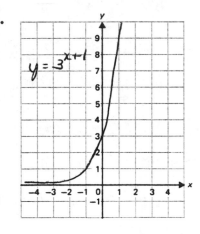

49.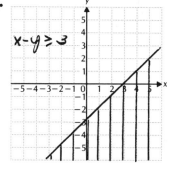

50.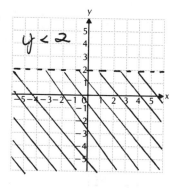

51. $\sqrt[12]{(x + 2)^4 x^3}$

52. $(x - 5)^2 + (y + 1)^2 = 9$

53. $\log \sqrt[5]{\dfrac{a^2}{b}}$

54. $\log_{\frac{1}{4}} 16 = -2$

55. 20 liters of 70% solution, 80 liters of 55% solution   56. $420   57. $\dfrac{3}{16}$ in.   58. First part: 50 km/h; second part: 60 km/h   59. 4 m × 12 m   60. 3 km/h   61. $\left[0, -\dfrac{13}{4}\right]$ 62. -1

196

Final Examination, Test Form F

<u>1.</u> -3   <u>2.</u> 112.5%   <u>3.</u> -48   <u>4.</u> $-\frac{9}{20}$ <u>5.</u> $12x^{-1}y^2z^3$ <u>6.</u> -4x + 2

<u>7.</u> $2xy^3 + 4x^2y - x^3y^4$ <u>8.</u> $6a^2 - 13a + 6$ <u>9.</u> $9y^2 - 12yz^2 + 4z^4$ <u>10.</u> $\frac{x + 3}{2(x - 3)}$

<u>11.</u> $\frac{1}{x + 4}$ <u>12.</u> $(y^2 + yb + b^2)$ <u>13.</u> $8x^2 + 8x + 2$, R 5   <u>14.</u> 32   <u>15.</u> $-\sqrt{5}$

<u>16.</u> 6 + i   <u>17.</u> -6   <u>18.</u> y = -x - 2   <u>19.</u> (-1, 5), 6   <u>20.</u> $9^{-\frac{1}{2}} = \frac{1}{3}$

<u>21.</u> $\log_a x + 3 \log_a y - \frac{1}{2} \log_a z$ <u>22.</u> {5,14}   <u>23.</u> $|x - 3|$ <u>24.</u> $-\frac{1}{3}$

<u>25.</u> $\frac{2 - 3\sqrt{a} + a}{1 - a}$ <u>26.</u> $(4x^2 + 5)(4x^2 - 5)$ <u>27.</u> $(4x + 1)(x - 3)$

<u>28.</u> $(5a - 1)(25a^2 + 5a + 1)$ <u>29.</u> 5   <u>30.</u> $\frac{7}{5}$ <u>31.</u> 4   <u>32.</u> 3 ± i   <u>33.</u> 0, $\frac{5}{4}$

<u>34.</u> 0, -8   <u>35.</u> 9   <u>36.</u> (-5, 4)   <u>37.</u> (-2, -4, 8)   <u>38.</u> $(-\sqrt{6}, \sqrt{6})$,

$(\sqrt{6}, -\sqrt{6})$ <u>39.</u> 6   <u>40.</u> $\frac{5}{9}$ <u>41.</u> {x|x ≥ -2}   <u>42.</u> {x|x < -1 or x > 4}

<u>43.</u> {x|-15 ≤ x < -6}   <u>44.</u> $q - \sqrt{p^2 \quad m^2}$ <u>45.</u>

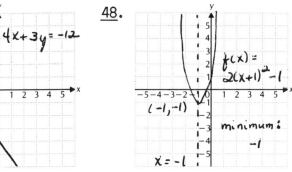

-2   0   3

<u>46.</u>
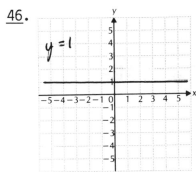

y = 1

<u>47.</u>
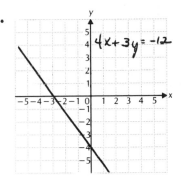

4x + 3y = -12

<u>48.</u>
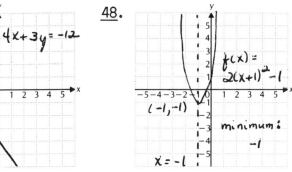

f(x) = 2(x+1)² - 1

(-1, -1)

minimum:
-1

x = -1

<u>49.</u>
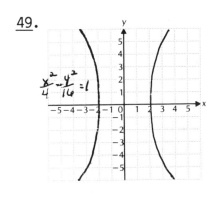

$\frac{x^2}{4} - \frac{y^2}{16} = 1$

<u>50.</u>
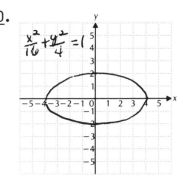

$\frac{x^2}{16} + \frac{y^2}{4} = 1$

51.

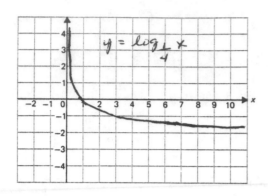

52.

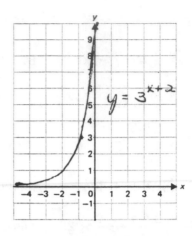

53.

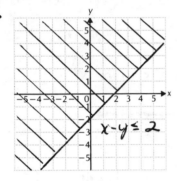

54. $\dfrac{9}{2}$ 55. $\dfrac{15}{2}$ hours   56. 5 m × 10 m

57. $\sqrt{106} \approx 10.296$ 58. $25,000 at 6%; $40,000 at

8%; $15,000 at 10%   59. 20, -10   60. 10 mph

61. $\left\{ a \middle| -\dfrac{3}{2} < a < 4 \right\}$ 62. $\dfrac{\sqrt{6}}{2}, -\dfrac{\sqrt{6}}{2}$

Name _____

Class _____ Score _____ Grade _____

1. Find percent notation: $\frac{13}{20}$

ANSWERS

2. Find decimal notation: 325%

3. Insert > or < to make a true sentence: -8   -7

4. Evaluate $\frac{5a}{b}$ when a = 6 and b = 10.

5. Simplify: $|-3.9|$

Compute.
6. -5 + (-4)   7. 3.2 - 6.4

8. $-\frac{3}{5} \cdot \frac{20}{9}$ 9. $-\frac{4}{15} \div -\frac{8}{5}$

10. Multiply: -2(3x - 2y)

11. Collect like terms: 3w - 5z + w + 8z

Simplify.
12. 9y - [4 - 2(3y + 5)]   13. $(2x^2y^{-3})(-4x^{-1}y^5)$

14. $(-2a^{-4}b^2)^{-3}$ 15. $4^3 - 12 + 3 \cdot 2$

Solve.
16. x - 5 = 4   17. 4y = 18

18. 7a - 4 = 3a + 4   19. 2(4x - 1) = 1 - (x + 3)

ANSWERS

1._____
2._____
3._____
4._____
5._____
6._____
7._____
8._____
9._____
10._____
11._____
12._____
13._____
14._____
15._____
16._____
17._____
18._____
19._____

ANSWERS

20. _____

21. _____

22. _____

23. _____See graph._____

24. _____See graph._____

25. _____See graph._____

26. _____

27. _____

28. _____

29. _____

30. _____

20. Solve: $(2y - 3)(y + 2) = 0$

21. Solve for m: $R = 4p - 3m$

22. Solve: Money is borrowed at 12% simple interest. After one year $1064 pays off the loan. How much was originally borrowed?

Graph.

23. $y = x + 2$

24. $y = 3$

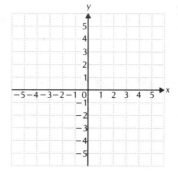

25. $2x + y = 4$

26. Find the slope, if it exists, of a line containing the points $(-4,5)$ and $(2,-1)$.

27. Find an equation of the line with slope 3 and containing the point $(-1,2)$.

28. Find an equation of the line containing the point $(3,-2)$ and parallel to the line $x - 2y = 6$.

Δ————————————————————————————

29. Suppose $x = 2^{5a+2}$ and $y = 2^{3a}$. Find xy^{-3}.

30. Find the slope of the line containing the points $(4a, 2b - c)$ and $(2a, 4b - c)$.

Name _____

Class _____ *Score* _____ *Grade* _____

1. Evaluate $\frac{m + n}{4}$ when m = 11 and n = 9.

ANSWERS

2. Insert > or < to make a true sentence: -2.4   -4.2

1._____

2._____

3. Simplify: $\left|-\frac{13}{4}\right|$

3._____

4._____

4. Find fractional notation: 29%

5._____

5. Find percent notation: 0.147

6._____

7._____

Compute.

6. 3 + (-10)   7. -2.1 - (-5.2)

8._____

9._____

8. $\frac{9}{4} \cdot -\frac{8}{45}$ 9. $-\frac{7}{9} \div -\frac{14}{27}$

10._____

10. Multiply: -5(x - 3y)

11._____

12._____

11. Collect like terms: 2b + 3c - 5b + c

13._____

Simplify.

14._____

12. 7z - [5 - 3(2z + 3)]   13. 3·4 - 2 + 2³

15._____

14. $(-3a^5b^{-3})^{-2}$ 15. $(3x^{-3}y^4)(-2x^{-1}y^2)$

16._____

17._____

Solve.

16. 6y = 15   17. x - 3 = 2

18._____

19._____

18. 8a + 5 = 2a - 1   19. 3(2x + 3) = 5 - (4x - 8)

ANSWERS	
20._____	20. Solve: $(y - 5)(3y + 1) = 0$
	21. Solve for c: $Q = ac + bc$
	22. Solve: Money is borrowed at 12% simple interest. After one year $840 pays off the loan. How much was originally borrowed?

20. Solve: $(y - 5)(3y + 1) = 0$

21. Solve for c: $Q = ac + bc$

22. Solve: Money is borrowed at 12% simple interest. After one year $840 pays off the loan. How much was originally borrowed?

Graph.

23. $y = x - 2$

24. $x + 2y = 4$

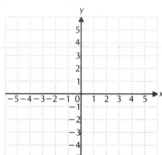 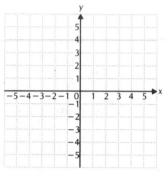

25. $y = -1$

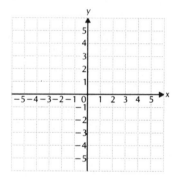

26. Find the slope, if it exists, of the line containing the points $(-5,4)$ and $(-3,2)$.

27. Find an equation of the line with slope 2 and containing the point $(2,-1)$.

28. Find an equation of the line containing the point $(6,-1)$ and parallel to the line $x + 3y = 9$.

Δ ————————————————————————————

29. Simplify: $\left[\left(\dfrac{p^3}{p^{-5}} \right)^{-2} \cdot \left(\dfrac{p^{-4}}{p^2} \right)^3 \right]^{-1}$

30. Find the value of k so that the graphs of the given lines are parallel:

$$ky = 2x - 4$$
$$3x + 2y = 8$$

ANSWERS

20._____

21._____

22._____

23._ See graph._

24._ See graph._

25._ See graph._

26._____

27._____

28._____

29._____

30._____

Name _____

Class _____ Score _____ Grade _____

Compute.

1. -2.9 - (-4.8)

2. $-\frac{1}{4} + \frac{3}{5}$

3. $3 \cdot 8 - 4 \div 2 + 2$

4. $-\frac{25}{24} \div -\frac{35}{6}$

5. Find percent notation: $\frac{29}{25}$

6. Simplify: $\frac{-8a^3b^{-7}}{10ab^{-5}}$

7. Find an equation of the line containing the points (3,5) and (-1,-3).

Graph.

8. x - y = 4

9. y = -3x

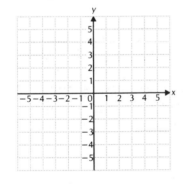

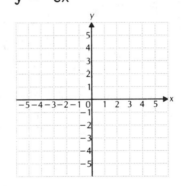

Solve.

10. 4y - 7 = 13

11. 3 - (a + 4) = 2(a + 1)

12. Solve using the substitution method:

$$2x + 3y = 4$$
$$y = x - 2$$

ANSWERS

1._____

2._____

3._____

4._____

5._____

6._____

7._____

8.___See graph.___

9.___See graph.___

10._____

11._____

12._____

ANSWERS	
13._____	13. Solve using the addition method: $$2x + 3y = 1$$ $$3x + 4y = 1$$
14._____	14. Solve: $2x + y + z = 0$ $\quad\quad\quad x - y + 4z = 1$ $\quad\quad\quad 2x + 2y + z = 4$
15._____	15. Evaluate: $\begin{vmatrix} -2 & -3 & 1 \\ 2 & -1 & 0 \\ 4 & 1 & 3 \end{vmatrix}$
16.a)_____	16. Find a) the profit and b) the break-even point: $$C = 250x + 300,000$$ $$R = 400x$$
b)_____	17. Determine whether the system is dependent or independent: $$2x - 3y = 1$$ $$4x - 6y = 3$$
17._____	18. One solution is 40% alcohol and a second is 80% alcohol. How much of each should be mixed together to make 100 liters of a solution that is 58% alcohol?
18._____	19. Simplify: $2(5^{-1} \cdot 5 \cdot 5^{-2} \cdot 5^{0})$
19._____	20. Two solutions of the equation $ax + by = 4$ are $(1,-1)$ and $(2,2)$. Find a and b.
20._____	

Name _____

Class _____ *Score* _____ *Grade* _____

	ANSWERS

1. Find percent notation: $\frac{33}{40}$

1._____

Compute.

2. $3.4 - (-7.9)$ 3. $\frac{3}{10} + \left(- \frac{5}{12}\right)$

2._____

4. $2 \cdot 12 - 6 \div 3 + 3$ 5. $-\frac{5}{16} \div \frac{15}{32}$

3._____

6. Simplify: $\frac{-6a^{-4}b^5}{14a^{-2}b}$

4._____

Graph.

7. $y = -2x$ 8. $x - y = 3$

5._____

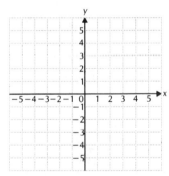   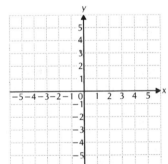

6._____

9. Find an equation of the line containing the points (-2,4) and (-1,6).

7.___See graph.___

8.___See graph.___

Solve.

10. $3y + 9 = 6$ 11. $5(a - 2) = 2 - (a + 7)$

9._____

12. Solve using the substitution method:
$$3x + 2y = 2$$
$$x = y - 6$$

10._____

11._____

12._____

Name _____

ANSWERS	

13._____

13. Solve using the addition method:
$$3x - 2y = 6$$
$$2x + 3y = -9$$

14._____

14. Solve: $2x + y + z = 5$
$$3x + 2y + 3z = 4$$
$$x + 2y + z = 0$$

15.a)_____

15. Find a) the profit and b) the break-even point:
$$C = 200x + 600,000$$
$$R = 600x$$

b)_____

16. Evaluate: $\begin{vmatrix} 1 & 2 & 1 \\ 0 & -2 & 2 \\ 3 & -1 & -3 \end{vmatrix}$

16._____

17. Determine whether the system is dependent or independent:
$$3x - 2y = 4$$
$$-6x + 4y = -6$$

17._____

18. Solve: One solution is 40% alcohol and a second is 80% alcohol. How much of each should be mixed together to make 100 liters of a solution that is 66% alcohol?

18._____

19. Simplify: $(x^{2m-n}x^{m+2n})^5$

19._____

20. Determine a so that the slope of the line through the points $(6a - 2, 4)$ and $(4a + 4, -2)$ is 3.

20._____

Chapters 1 - 4   *Class* _____ *Score* _____ *Grade* _____

Perform the indicated operations and simplify, if possible.

ANSWERS

1. $-\dfrac{2}{9} \div -\dfrac{8}{27}$ 2. $2 \cdot 6 - 4^2 + 8 \div 2$

1._____

2._____

3. $3(y - 3) - 2(y + 1)$ 4. $(2ab^{-3}c^4)^3$

3._____

5. $ab(2c - 3)$

4._____

6. Find an equation of the line with slope −2 and containing the point (−1,5).

5._____

Solve.

6._____

7. $2y + 7 = 1$ 8. $2x + 3y = 5$
                              $3x - 2y = 14$

7._____

9. $3x - 5 \leqslant 5x - 3$ 10. $|2x - 1| \geqslant 9$

8._____

11. The perimeter of a rectangular garden is 36 ft. The width is 2 ft less than the length. Find the dimensions.

9._____

10._____

12. The sum of three numbers is 168. The first is 18 more than twice the second. The third is 15 less than twice the second. Find the numbers.

11._____

12._____

Name _____

ANSWERS	

13. _____

14. _____

15. ___See graph.___

16. ___See graph.___

17. ___See graph.___

18. ___See graph.___

19. _____

20. ___See graph.___

13. Determine whether true or false:

$\{1,4\} \subset \{2,4,6,8\}$

14. Find the intersection: $\{-3,-2,-1,0\} \cap \{-4,0,4\}$

Graph.

15. $x = -2$

16. $y = 2x - 1$

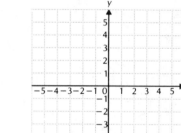

17. $4x + 2y \geqslant 2$

18. Graph on a number line: $-2 < x + 1 \leqslant 1$

19. Solve: $|2x - 5| = x - 3$

20. Graph on a plane: $y \leqslant |x| + 2$

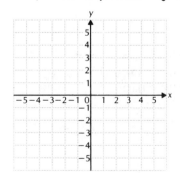

	ANSWERS

1. Find the intersection: $\{-5,-3,-1\} \cap \{-3,0,3\}$

2. Determine whether true or false: $\{1,3\} \subset \{3,5,7,9\}$

Perform the indicated operations and simplify, if possible.

3. $-\dfrac{4}{15} \div -\dfrac{16}{25}$ 4. $3 \cdot 5 - 8^2 \div 4 + 4$

5. $xy(4z - 5)$ 6. $(3a^{-2}bc^{-4})^2$

7. $4(y + 1) - 3(y - 2)$

Solve.

8. $3y - 5 = 1$ 9. $3x + 2y = 4$
                            $5x + 3y = 5$

10. $2x - 7 \leqslant 4x - 5$ 11. $|3x + 2| \geqslant 7$

12. The perimeter of a rectangular garden is 40 ft. The width is 2 ft less than the length. Find the dimensions.

13. The sum of three numbers is 170. The first is 4 less than twice the second. The third is 6 more than three times the second. Find the numbers.

ANSWERS

1._____

2._____

3._____

4._____

5._____

6._____

7._____

8._____

9._____

10._____

11._____

12._____

13._____

ANSWERS	
14._____	14. Find an equation of the line with slope 5 and containing the point (2,-3).

15. Graph on a number line: $-3 < x + 2 \leqslant 2$

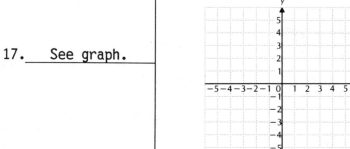

Graph.

16. $x = 3$

17. $y = 3x + 1$

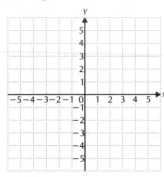

18. $4x + 2y > -8$

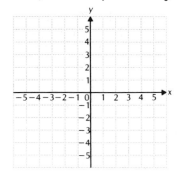

19. Graph on a plane: $y \geqslant |x| - 2$

20. Solve: $|4x - 1| = x - 2$

15. See graph.	
16. See graph.	
17. See graph.	
18. See graph.	
19. See graph.	
20._____	

CUMULATIVE TEST, FORM A

Name _____

Chapters 1 - 5

Class _____ *Score* _____ *Grade* _____

Compute.

1. $-\frac{5}{2} - \left(-\frac{5}{6}\right)$

2. $3 \cdot 6 - 2^3 + 2$

3. Subtract: $(8x^3y - 5x^2y^4 - 3xy) - (5x^3y - 4xy + 2x^2y^4)$

Multiply.

4. $(2x - 3)(3x + 1)$

5. $(4x + y)(4x - y)$

Factor.

6. $4x^2 - 4x + 1$

7. $2x^2 + 3x - 2$

Solve.

8. $8x - 1 = 5x + 11$

9. $x^2 + 5x = 6$

10. $2x + 3y = -3$
    $3x + 2y = 3$

11. $2x - y - z = 3$
    $x + y - 2z = 3$
    $3x - 2y + z = -2$

ANSWERS

1._____

2._____

3._____

4._____

5._____

6._____

7._____

8._____

9._____

10._____

11._____

ANSWERS	

Solve.

12. _____

13. _____

14. _____

15. _____

16. _____

17. ___See graph.___

18.a) _____

  b) _____

  c) _____

  d) _____

  e) _____

19. _____

20. _____

Solve.

12. $9x + 7 < 5x - 1$ 13. $-4 \leqslant 4x + 1 < 3$

14. $|2x - 3| \geqslant 5$

15. A person receives an 8% raise in salary, bringing the salary to $23,220. What was the original salary?

16. A collection of dimes and quarters is worth $24.50. The total number of coins is 125. How many of each type of coin are there?

17. Graph: $5x - 2y = 10$

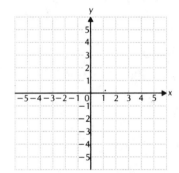

18. Given the functions $f(x) = x - 4$ and $g(x) = x^2 + 2$, find a) $(f + g)(x)$ b) $(f - g)(x)$ c) $(fg)(x)$ d) $(f/g)(x)$ e) $(ff)(x)$.

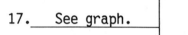

19. Factor: $a^2 - 8ab + 16b^2 - 9x^2 + 6xy - y^2$

20. Solve: $|x - 2| > |x + 3|$

212

Name _____

Class _____ *Score* _____ *Grade* _____

Compute.

ANSWERS

1. $-\dfrac{1}{6} - \left(-\dfrac{3}{2}\right)$

2. $2 \cdot 5 - 3^3 + 3$

1._____

2._____

3. Graph: $2x + 5y = 10$

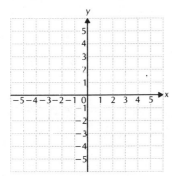

3.___See graph.___

4._____

5._____

6._____

4. Subtract: $(7xy^3 - 4x^4y^2 - 2x^2y) - (5xy^3 - 3x^2y + 2x^4y^2)$

Multiply.

5. $(x - 3y)(x + 3y)$

6. $(4x - 1)(3x + 2)$

7.a)_____

b)_____

c)_____

7. Given the functions $f(x) = x + 2$ and $g(x) = x^2 + 4$,
find a) $(f + g)(x)$ b) $(f - g)(x)$ c) $(fg)(x)$
d) $(f/g)(x)$ e) $(ff)(x)$.

d)_____

e)_____

Factor.

8. $3x^2 + 7x + 2$

9. $9x^2 - 6x + 1$

8._____

9._____

Solve.

10. $6x - 5 = 2x + 15$

11. $x^2 - 4x = 5$

10._____

11._____

ANSWERS	

Solve.

12. $3x + 4y = 2$
    $2x + 5y = 6$

13. $x - y - 2z = 3$
    $2x + y - 5z = -1$
    $x - 3y + z = 3$

12._____

13._____

14. $-3 \leqslant 3x + 2 < 5$

15. $7x + 9 \leqslant 4x - 3$

14._____

16. $|3x - 1| \geqslant 5$

15._____

17. A person receives a 6% raise in salary, bringing the salary to $24,380. What was the original salary?

16._____

18. A collection of dimes and quarters is worth $20.50. The total number of coins is 115. How many of each type of coin are there?

17._____

18._____

19. Factor: $x^{12a} - y^{9b}$

19._____

20. Solve: $4y - 5 < 2y + 3 < 3y + 4$

20._____

Name _____

Class _____ *Score* _____ *Grade* _____

Perform the indicated operations and simplify, if possible.

1. $8 - [5 - 3(2a - 1)]$

2. $(4x^{-5}y^3)^3$

3. $\dfrac{x^2 - 2x + 1}{x^2 - 4x + 3} \div \dfrac{2x^2 - 2x}{x^3 - 27}$

4. $\dfrac{3x}{x + 2} - \dfrac{2x}{x - 3} + \dfrac{30}{x^2 - x - 6}$

5. $(5x - 1)(2x + 3)$

6. Factor: $y^4 - 16$

7. Find an equation of the line containing the points $(4,-3)$ and $(2,0)$.

Graph.

8. $x - y = 3$

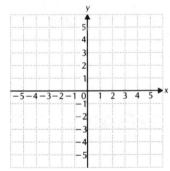

9. $f(x) = x^2 + 1$

10. $2x + 3y \geqslant -6$

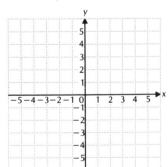

ANSWERS

1._____

2._____

3._____

4._____

5._____

6._____

7._____

8.___See graph.___

9.___See graph.___

10.___See graph.___

215

ANSWERS	

Solve.

11. _____

11. $10x - 3 = 5$

12. $3x - 2y = 3$

     $2x + 3y = -11$

12. _____

13. $\dfrac{1}{x + 5} = \dfrac{-2}{x - 4}$

14. $5x - 3 \leqslant 2x + 6$

13. _____

15. $-3 < x + 2 \leqslant 4$

16. Find two consecutive integers such that three times the first plus two times the second is 77.

14. _____

17. In triangle ABC, the measure of angle B is 5° more than twice the measure of angle A. The measure of angle C is 5° less than six times the measure of angle A. Find the angle measures.

15. _____

16. _____

18. Train A travels 40 km/h faster than train B. Train A travels 510 km in the same time it takes train B to travel 340 km. Find the speed of each train.

17. _____

Δ _____

19. Simplify: $\dfrac{a^2 - 2ab + b^2}{a^2 + b^2 + a - b - 2ab}$

18. _____

20. Find k so that when $2x^3 + kx^2 - 5x + 2k$ is divided by $x + 2$ the remainder is 0.

19. _____

20. _____

Perform the indicated operations and simplify, if possible.

ANSWERS

1. $(5x^3y^{-6})^2$

2. $7 - [6 - 2(4a + 3)]$

1._____

3. $(6x + 5)(x - 4)$

4. $\dfrac{2x}{x - 5} - \dfrac{x}{x + 1} + \dfrac{6}{x^2 - 4x - 5}$

2._____

3._____

5. $\dfrac{x^3 - 1}{4x + 8} \div \dfrac{x^2 - 1}{x^2 + 3x + 2}$

4._____

6. Factor: $y^4 - 81$

5._____

Solve.

6._____

7. $12x - 5 = 3$

8. $3x + 2y = 2$
   $2x + 3y = 8$

7._____

9. $\dfrac{2}{x + 1} = \dfrac{1}{x + 2}$

10. $4x + 1 \geqslant x + 5$

8._____

9._____

11. $-5 < x - 3 < 1$

10._____

12. Find two consecutive integers such that three times the first plus two times the second is 57.

11._____

12._____

ANSWERS
13._____
14._____
15._____
16.___See graph.___
17.___See graph.___
18.___See graph.___
19._____
20._____

13. In triangle ABC, the measure of angle A is 5° less than twice the measure of angle B. The measure of angle C is 5° more than six times the measure of angle B. Find the angle measures.

14. Train A travels 40 km/h faster than train B. Train A travels 320 km in the same time it takes train B to travel 192 km. Find the speed of each train.

15. Find an equation of the line containing the points (-5,1) and (0,4).

Graph.

16. $x + y = 3$

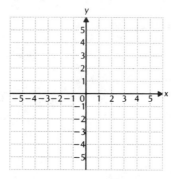

17. $f(x) = x^2 - 2$

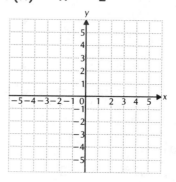

18. $2x - 3y \leqslant 6$

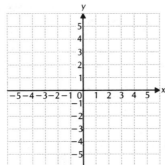

19. Simplify: $\dfrac{x^2 + y^2 - 9z^2 - 2xy}{x^2 - xy + 3xz}$

20. Find k so that when $3x^2 + 2kx - 6x + k$ is divided by $x + 1$ the remainder is 0.

Assume that ALL expressions under radical signs represent positive numbers.

ANSWERS

1. Find percent notation: $\frac{7}{8}$

1.

Perform the indicated operations and simplify, if possible.

2.

2. $\frac{1}{x} - \frac{1}{x + 2} + \frac{2}{2x + 4}$ 3. $3\sqrt{20} + \sqrt{80} - 4\sqrt{45}$

3._____

4. $(3 - 2i)(1 + 3i)$

5. Given the function described by $f(x) = x^2 - 4x - 5$, find $f(-2)$.

4._____

6. Graph: $y = 2$

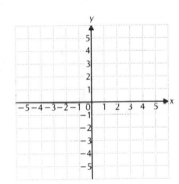

5._____

6.   See graph.

7._____

Solve.

7. $4x + 3 = -1$ 8. $4x^2 = 8x$

8._____

9. $2x + y + z = 2$ 10. $\frac{2}{3x + 1} = \frac{2}{6x - 1}$

   $x - 3y - z = 4$

   $3x + 2y + 2z = 2$

9._____

10._____

ANSWERS	Solve.

11. _____

11. $\sqrt{x + 9} + 1 = \sqrt{x + 14}$ 12. $3x - 7 < 8x + 3$

13. $|x - 4| \geqslant 1$

12. _____

14. Jack is five years older than Annie. In one year Jack will be twice as old as Annie. Find their ages now.

13. _____

15. Pat can clean the garage in 5 hours. Working together, it takes Pat and Lynn 2 hours to do the same job. How long would it take Lynn to clean the garage working alone?

14. _____

16. Solve for q: $m = \frac{4}{5}q + n$

15. _____

17. Rationalize the denominator: $\dfrac{1 - \sqrt{x}}{3 + \sqrt{x}}$

16. _____

18. Use fractional exponents to write a single radical expression:

$$\sqrt[3]{x} \quad \sqrt[4]{x - 1}$$

17. _____

Δ———————————————————————————

18. _____

19. Multiply and simplify.

$$(\sqrt{3} + \sqrt[3]{2} + \sqrt{5})(\sqrt{2} + \sqrt{3} - \sqrt{5})$$

19. _____

20. Subtract and multiply: $\dfrac{2}{1 + i} - \dfrac{1}{2 + 3i}$

20. _____

1. Find percent notation: $\frac{5}{8}$

Perform the indicated operations and simplify, if possible.

2. $(2 + 5i)(1 - i)$ 3. $\sqrt{27} + 3\sqrt{12} - 4\sqrt{75}$

4. $\dfrac{2x}{x + 1} - \dfrac{2}{x} + \dfrac{6}{3x + 3}$

Solve.

5. $3x + 4 = -2$ 6. $3x^2 = 9x$

7. $\dfrac{1}{4x + 1} = \dfrac{2}{4x + 3}$ 8. $2x - y + 3z = 2$
$\qquad\qquad\qquad\qquad\qquad\quad x - 2y + z = -5$
$\qquad\qquad\qquad\qquad\quad 3x - 2y - z = 1$

9. $\sqrt{x + 12} = 1 + \sqrt{x + 7}$ 10. $4x - 5 < 6x + 3$

11. $|x + 3| \geqslant 2$

ANSWERS

1._____

2._____

3._____

4._____

5._____

6._____

7._____

8._____

9._____

10._____

11._____

ANSWERS	

12. _____

13. _____

14. _____

15.   See graph.

16. _____

17. _____

18. _____

19. _____

20. _____

12. Solve for c: $E = 2b - 5c$

Solve.

13. Jim is 20 years older than Teri. In five years Jim will be three times as old as Teri. Find their ages now.

14. Jeff can paint a shed in 6 hours. Working together, it takes Jeff and Mary 4 hours to do the same job. How long would it take Mary to paint the shed working alone?

15. Graph: $x = 2$

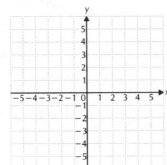

16. Given the function described by $f(x) = x^2 - 3x - 6$, find $f(-2)$.

17. Use fractional exponents to write a single radical expression:

$$\sqrt{x + 2} \ \ \sqrt[5]{x}$$

18. Rationalize the denominator: $\dfrac{3 + \sqrt{x}}{2 - \sqrt{x}}$

19. Multiply and simplify.

$$(\sqrt{3} + \sqrt{5} - \sqrt{8})(\sqrt{5} + \sqrt{3} + \sqrt{8})$$

20. Divide: $\dfrac{2\sqrt{3} + \sqrt{2}i}{3\sqrt{3} - 2\sqrt{2}i}$

Name _____

Class _____ *Score* _____ *Grade* _____

Simplify.

1. $(5a^2b^{-3}c^4)(-2ab^{-1}c^{-7})$

2. $\dfrac{x - \dfrac{4}{x}}{1 - \dfrac{2}{x}}$

Factor.

3. $2y^3 - 128$

4. $x^2 - 10x + 24$

5. Find an equation of the line with slope -5 and containing the point (-3,1).

Graph.

6. $3x - y = 3$

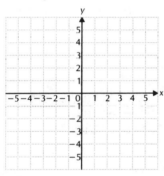

7. $4x + 3y \leqslant -12$

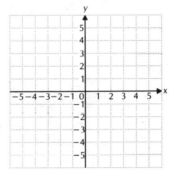

8. a) Graph $f(x) = 2(x - 2)^2 - 1$

   b) Label the vertex.

   c) Draw the line of symmetry.

   d) Find the maximum or minimum value of the function.

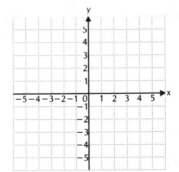

9. Simplify. Assume that letters can represent ANY real number.

$$\sqrt{x^2 - 4x + 4}$$

	ANSWERS
1.	_____
2.	_____
3.	_____
4.	_____
5.	_____
6.	See graph.
7.	See graph.
8.	See graph.
9.	_____

ANSWERS	Solve. Assume that ALL expressions under radical signs represent positive numbers.

10. $4x - 9 = 5$ 11. $2x^2 = 2x + 1$

10. _____

12. $5x + 2y = -1$ 13. $\dfrac{x + 3}{2x + 1} = \dfrac{4}{x - 1}$
    $2x + 3y = 15$

11. _____

14. $\sqrt{2x + 5} - 1 = \sqrt{2x}$ 15. $8x - 1 > 2x - 7$

12. _____

16. Solve for g: $H = \dfrac{gk}{g + k}$

13. _____

Solve.

14. _____

17. Find the length of a diagonal of a rectangle with sides of length 5 cm and 7 cm. Give an exact answer and an approximation to three decimal places.

15. _____

18. The length of a rectangle is 3 ft more than the width. The area is 180 ft². Find the dimensions.

16. _____

17. _____

Δ

Solve.

19. $\left(\dfrac{x + 1}{x - 1}\right)^2 + 4 = 4\left(\dfrac{x + 1}{x - 1}\right)$

18. _____

19. _____

20. $(20x^4 - 13x^3 - 21x^2)(8x - 12) = 0$

20. _____

Name _____

Class _____ Score _____ *Grade* _____

Factor.

1. $2y^3 + 54$

2. $x^2 - 11x + 30$

Simplify.

3. $(-4a^{-1}b^2c^5)(2a^2b^{-5}c)$

4. $\dfrac{x - \frac{x}{y}}{x + \frac{x}{y}}$

5. Simplify. Assume that letters can represent ANY real number.

$$\sqrt{x^2 - 6x + 9}$$

Solve. Assume that ALL expressions under radical signs represent positive numbers.

6. $6x - 7 = 3$

7. $2x + 3y = -2$
    $3x + 2y = 12$

8. $3x^2 - 3 = 2x$

9. $\dfrac{x + 4}{3x + 4} = \dfrac{3}{x - 1}$

10. $\sqrt{2x + 2} - 1 = \sqrt{2x - 1}$

11. $7x - 3 > x - 9$

12. Solve for m: $P = \dfrac{Q}{m(n - t)}$

ANSWERS
1._____
2._____
3._____
4._____
5._____
6._____
7._____
8._____
9._____
10._____
11._____
12._____

ANSWERS	

Solve.

13. _____

13. The length of a rectangle is 5 ft more than the width. The area is 104 ft². Find the dimensions.

14. Find the length of a diagonal of a rectangle with sides of length 3 cm and 6 cm. Give an exact answer and an approximation to three decimal places.

14. _____

15. Find an equation of the line with slope –4 and containing the point (4,-1).

Graph.

15. _____

16. $x - 3y = 3$

17. $3x - 4y \leqslant 12$

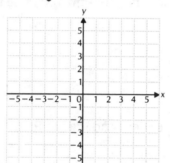

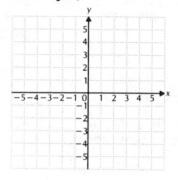

16. ___See graph.___

17. ___See graph.___

18. a) Graph $f(x) = 2(x - 1)^2 + 1$

b) Label the vertex.

c) Draw the line of symmetry.

d) Find the maximum or minimum value of the function.

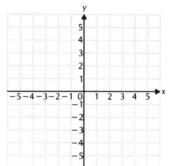

18. ___See graph.___

19. _____

Solve.

19. $2y^3 + 3y^{3/2} - 9 = 0$ 20. $x^2 - 3\sqrt{2}x + 0.5 = 0$

20. _____

Name _____

Class _____ *Score* _____ *Grade* _____

Assume that ALL expressions under radical signs represent positive numbers.

Perform the indicated operations and simplify, if possible.

1. $\dfrac{8}{x^2 - 4} - \dfrac{x}{x + 2} + \dfrac{2x}{x - 2}$

2. $\dfrac{3 - i}{2 + 3i}$

3. Given the functions $f(x) = x + 1$ and $g(x) = x^2 - 3$, find a) $(f + g)(x)$ b) $(f - g)(x)$ c) $(fg)(x)$ d) $(f/g)(x)$ e) $(ff)(x)$.

Graph.

4. $x - 5y = 5$

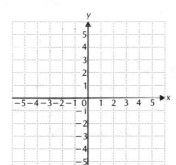

5. $xy = 4$

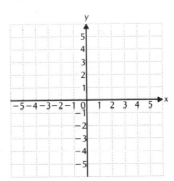

6. $\dfrac{x^2}{9} + \dfrac{y^2}{4} = 1$

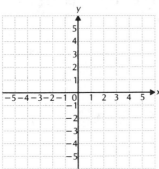

Solve.

7. $3x - 4 = x + 7$

8. $\dfrac{2}{x + 1} = \dfrac{3}{x - 1}$

ANSWERS ——

1._____

2._____

3.a)_____

b)_____

c)_____

d)_____

e)_____

4.___See graph.___

5.___See graph.___

6.___See graph.___

7._____

8._____

ANSWERS	Solve.

9._____

9. $x^2 + 4x = 2$

10._____

10. $x^{-2} + 8x^{-1} + 15 = 0$

11. $x + y + z = 0$
$2x + y - z = 14$
$3x + 2y - z = 20$

12. $x^2 - 5y^2 = 5$
$x + y = 3$

11._____

12._____

13. $\sqrt{x + 2} + 1 = \sqrt{x + 9}$

14. $x + 5 \geqslant 5x - 3$

13._____

15. $|4x + 5| > 7$

16. $x^2 - 3x \geqslant 4$

14._____

17. Money is borrowed at 12% simple interest. After one year $1400 pays off the loan. How much was originally borrowed?

15._____

18. The sum of the squares of two consecutive positive integers is 265. Find the integers.

16._____

17._____

19. Find an equation of the circle with center (2,0) passing through $(1, -2\sqrt{2})$.

18._____

20. Find the point on the line $y = 1$ that is equidistant from (3,4) and (-2,-3).

19._____

20._____

228

Assume that ALL expressions under radical signs represent positive numbers.

1. Given the functions $f(x) = x - 3$ and $g(x) = x^2 + 1$, find a) $(f + g)(x)$ b) $(f - g)(x)$ c) $(fg)(x)$ d) $(f/g)(x)$ e) $(ff)(x)$.

Perform the indicated operations and simplify, if possible.

2. $\dfrac{2}{x^2 - 1} - \dfrac{x}{x + 1} + \dfrac{2x}{x - 1}$ 3. $\dfrac{4 + 2i}{3 - i}$

Solve.

4. $5x + 3 = 2x + 1$ 5. $x^2 + 2x = 4$

6. $\dfrac{3}{x + 2} = \dfrac{2}{x - 2}$ 7. $x^{-2} + 7x^{-1} + 12 = 0$

8. $2x^2 - y^2 = 2$ 9. $x + y + z = -1$
   $x + y = 1$ $3x + y - z = 11$
                               $2x + 3y + 2z = 1$

10. $\sqrt{x + 3} + 1 = \sqrt{x + 10}$ 11. $x - 4 \leqslant 4x + 2$

12. $|5x + 3| > 7$ 13. $x^2 + x \geqslant 6$

ANSWERS
1.a)_____
b)_____
c)_____
d)_____
e)_____
2._____
3._____
4._____
5._____
6._____
7._____
8._____
9._____
10._____
11._____
12._____
13._____

ANSWERS	

Solve.

14. _____

14. Money is borrowed at 11% simple interest. After 1 year $1221 pays off the loan. How much was originally borrowed?

15. The sum of the squares of two consecutive positive integers is 481. Find the integers.

15. _____

Graph.

16. $5x + y = 5$　　　　　17. $\dfrac{x^2}{4} + \dfrac{y^2}{16} = 1$

16. ___See graph.___

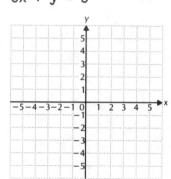

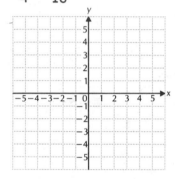

17. ___See graph.___

18. $xy = 6$

18. ___See graph.___

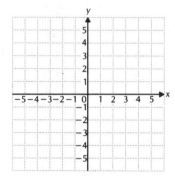

19. _____

19. Find an equation of the circle that passes through $(1,-7)$ and $(-3,5)$ and whose center is on the line $4x - y = 1$.

20. Find the point on the line $x = 2$ that is equidistant from $(4,5)$ and $(-1,-2)$.

20. _____

ANSWER KEYS FOR CUMULATIVE TESTS, FORMS A AND B

Cumulative Test, Form A, Chapters 1 and 2

__1__. 65%   __2__. 3.25   __3__. <   __4__. 3   __5__. 3.9   __6__. -9   __7__. -3.2   __8__. $-\frac{4}{3}$

__9__. $\frac{1}{6}$ __10__. -6x + 4y   __11__. 4w + 3z   __12__. 15y + 6   __13__. -8xy²

__14__. $-\frac{a^{12}b^{-6}}{8}$ or $-\frac{a^{12}}{8b^6}$ __15__. 58   __16__. 9   __17__. $\frac{9}{2}$ __18__. 2   __19__. 0   __20__. $\frac{3}{2}$, -2

__21__. $m = \frac{4p - R}{3}$ __22__. $950   __23__.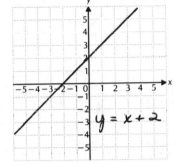

__24__. 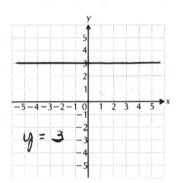   __25__.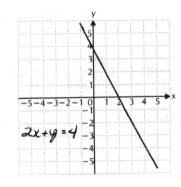

__26__. -1   __27__. y = 3x + 5

__28__. $y = \frac{1}{2}x - \frac{7}{2}$ __29__. 2^{-4a+2} __30__. $-\frac{b}{a}$

Cumulative Test, Form B, Chapters 1 and 2

__1__. 5   __2__. >   __3__. $\frac{13}{4}$ __4__. $\frac{29}{100}$ __5__. 14.7%   __6__. -7   __7__. 3.1   __8__. $-\frac{2}{5}$

__9__. $\frac{3}{2}$ __10__. -5x + 15y   __11__. -3b + 4c   __12__. 13z + 4   __13__. 18

__14__. $\frac{a^{-10}b^6}{9}$ or $\frac{b^6}{9a^{10}}$ __15__. -6x⁻⁴y⁶   __16__. $\frac{5}{2}$ __17__. 5   __18__. -1   __19__. $\frac{2}{5}$

Cumulative Test, Form B, Chapters 1 and 2   (continued)

<u>20</u>. 5, $-\frac{1}{3}$ <u>21</u>. $c = \dfrac{Q}{a + b}$ <u>22</u>. \$750   <u>23</u>.

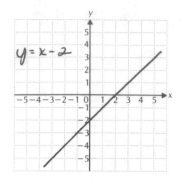

<u>24</u>.

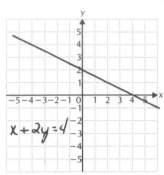

<u>25</u>.

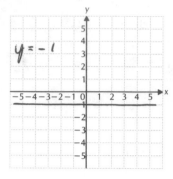

<u>26</u>. -1   <u>27</u>. y = 2x - 5

<u>28</u>. $y = -\frac{1}{3}x + 1$ <u>29</u>. p^{34} <u>30</u>. $-\frac{4}{3}$

Cumulative Test, Form A, Chapters 1 - 3

<u>1</u>. 1.9   <u>2</u>. $\frac{7}{20}$ <u>3</u>. 24   <u>4</u>. $\frac{5}{28}$ <u>5</u>. 116%   <u>6</u>. $-\dfrac{4a^2 b^{-2}}{5}$ or $-\dfrac{4a^2}{5b^2}$

<u>7</u>. y = 2x - 1   <u>8</u>.   <u>9</u>.

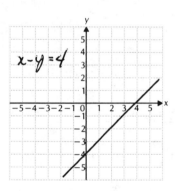

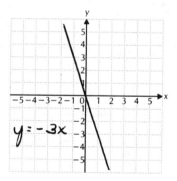

<u>10</u>. 5   <u>11</u>. -1   <u>12</u>. (2, 0)   <u>13</u>. (-1, 1)   <u>14</u>. (-3, 4, 2)   <u>15</u>. 30

<u>16</u>. a) P = 150x - 300,000 b) 2000 units   <u>17</u>. Independent

<u>18</u>. 55 liters of 40% solution, 45 liters of 80% solution   <u>19</u>. $\frac{2}{25}$

<u>20</u>. a = 3, b = -1

Cumulative Test, Form B, Chapters 1 - 3

<u>1</u>. 82.5%   <u>2</u>. 11.3   <u>3</u>. $\frac{-7}{60}$ <u>4</u>. 25   <u>5</u>. $-\frac{2}{3}$ <u>6</u>. $-\dfrac{3a^{-2}b^4}{7}$ or $-\dfrac{3b^4}{7a^2}$

232

Cumulative Test, Form B, Chapters 1 - 3 (continued)

7. 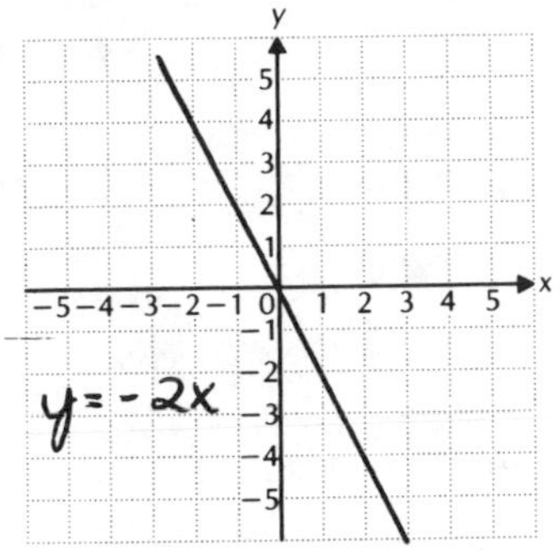

8. 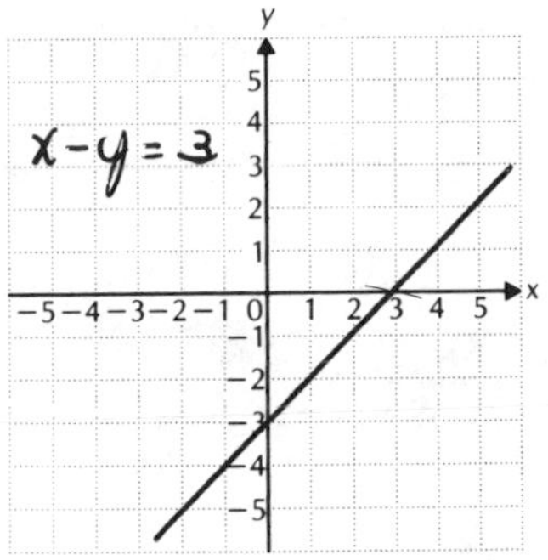

9. $y = 2x + 8$

10. -1 11. $\frac{5}{6}$

12. $(-2, 4)$

13. $(0, -3)$

14. $(4, -1, -2)$

15. a) $P = 400x - 600{,}000$ b) 1500 units 16. 26 17. Independent

18. 35 liters of 40% solution, 65 liters of 80% solution 19. x^{15m+5n}

20. 4

Cumulative Test, Form A, Chapters 1 - 4

1. $\frac{3}{4}$ 2. 0 3. $y - 11$ 4. $8a^3b^{-9}c^{12}$ or $\frac{8a^3c^{12}}{b^9}$ 5. $2abc - 3ab$

6. $y = -2x + 3$ 7. -3 8. $(4, -1)$ 9. $\{x \mid x \geq -1\}$ 10. $\{x \mid x \leq -4 \text{ or } x \geq 5\}$

11. 8 ft × 10 ft 12. 84, 33, 51 13. False 14. $\{0\}$

15. 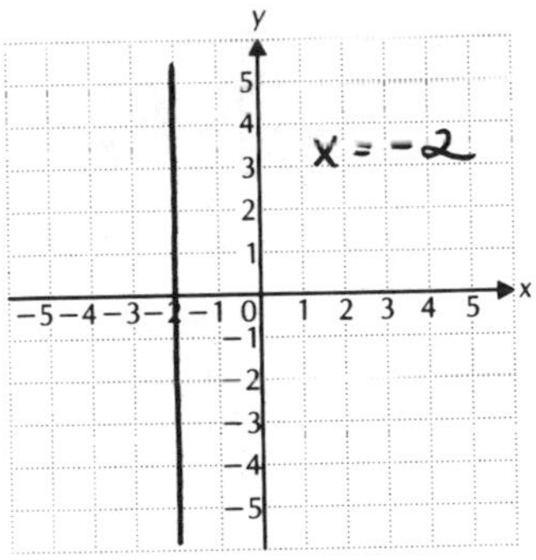

16. 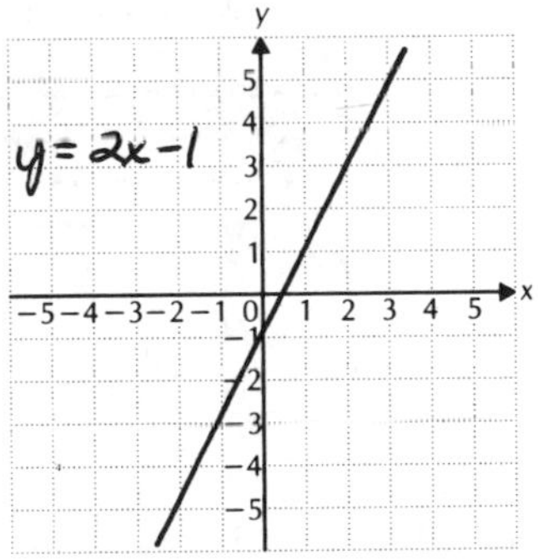

17. 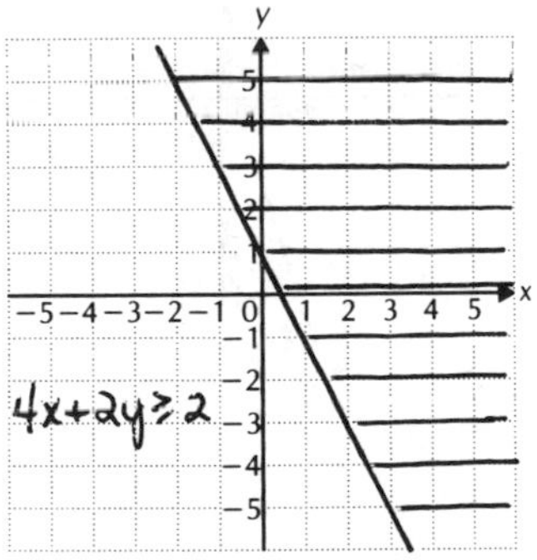

18. 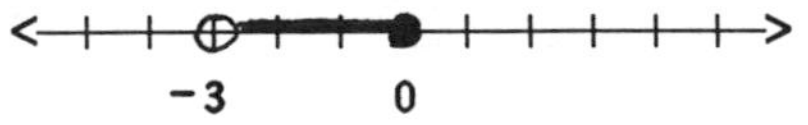

19. No solution

<u>20</u>. $y \leqslant |x| + 2$

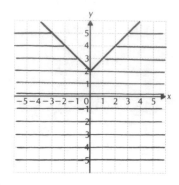

Cumulative Test, Form B, Chapters 1 – 4

<u>1</u>. {-3}   <u>2</u>. False   <u>3</u>. $\frac{5}{12}$ <u>4</u>. 3   <u>5</u>. $4xyz - 5xy$ <u>6</u>. $9a^{-4}b^2c^{-8}$ or $\frac{9b^2}{a^4c^8}$

<u>7</u>. $y + 10$ <u>8</u>. 2   <u>9</u>. (-2, 5)   <u>10</u>. $\{x \mid x \geqslant -1\}$ <u>11</u>. $\left\{x \mid x \leqslant -3 \text{ or } x \geqslant \frac{5}{3}\right\}$

<u>12</u>. 9 ft × 11 ft   <u>13</u>. 52, 28, 90   <u>14</u>. $y = 5x - 13$

<u>15</u>.

<u>16</u>.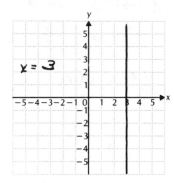

<u>17</u>.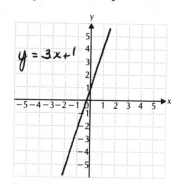

$y = 3x + 1$

<u>18</u>.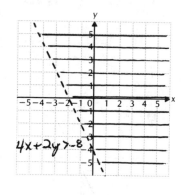

$4x + 2y > -8$

<u>19</u>.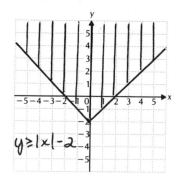

$y \geqslant |x| - 2$

<u>20</u>. No solution

234

Cumulative Test, Form A, Chapters 1 - 5

<u>1.</u> $-\dfrac{5}{3}$ <u>2.</u> 12   <u>3.</u> $3x^3y - 7x^2y^4 + xy$ <u>4.</u> $6x^2 - 7x - 3$ <u>5.</u> $16x^2 - y^2$

<u>6.</u> $(2x - 1)^2$ <u>7.</u> $(2x - 1)(x + 2)$ <u>8.</u> 4   <u>9.</u> 1, -6   <u>10.</u> (3, -3)

<u>11.</u> (-1, -2, -3)   <u>12.</u> $\{x \mid x < -2\}$ <u>13.</u> $\left\{x \mid -\dfrac{5}{4} \leqslant x < \dfrac{1}{2}\right\}$

<u>14.</u> $\{x \mid x \leqslant -1 \text{ or } x \geqslant 4\}$ <u>15.</u> $21,500   <u>16.</u> 45 dimes, 80 quarters

<u>17.</u>
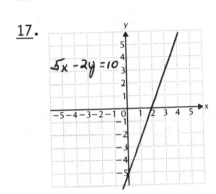

<u>18.</u> a) $x^2 + x - 2$ b) $x - x^2 - 6$

c) $x^3 - 4x^2 + 2x - 8$ d) $\dfrac{x - 4}{x^2 + 2}$ e) $x^2 - 8x + 16$

<u>19.</u> $(a - 4b + 3x - y)(a - 4b - 3x + y)$

<u>20.</u> $\left\{x \mid x < -\dfrac{1}{2}\right\}$

Cumulative Test, Form B, Chapters 1 - 5

<u>1.</u> $\dfrac{4}{3}$ <u>2.</u> -14   <u>3.</u>
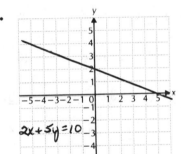

<u>4.</u> $2xy^3 - 6x^4y^2 + x^2y$

<u>5.</u> $x^2 - 9y^2$

<u>6.</u> $12x^2 + 5x - 2$

<u>7.</u> a) $x^2 + x + 6$

b) $x - x^2 - 2$

c) $x^3 + 2x^2 + 4x + 8$

d) $\dfrac{x + 2}{x^2 + 4}$

e) $x^2 + 4x + 4$

<u>8.</u> $(3x + 1)(x + 2)$

<u>9.</u> $(3x - 1)^2$

<u>10.</u> 5   <u>11.</u> 5, -1

<u>12.</u> (-2, 2)   <u>13.</u> (-4, -3, -2)   <u>14.</u> $\left\{x \mid -\dfrac{5}{3} \leqslant x < 1\right\}$ <u>15.</u> $\{x \mid x \leqslant -4\}$

<u>16.</u> $\left\{x \mid x \leqslant -\dfrac{4}{3} \text{ or } x \geqslant 2\right\}$ <u>17.</u> $23,000   <u>18.</u> 55 dimes, 60 quarters

<u>19.</u> $(x^{4a} - y^{3b})(x^{8a} + x^{4a}y^{3b} + y^{6b})$ <u>20.</u> $\{y \mid -1 < y < 4\}$

Cumulative Test, Form A, Chapters 1 - 6

1. 6a   **2.** $64x^{-15}y^9$ or $\dfrac{64y^9}{x^{15}}$ **3.** $\dfrac{x^2 + 3x + 9}{2x}$ **4.** $\dfrac{x - 10}{x + 2}$ **5.** $10x^2 + 13x - 3$

6. $(y^2 + 4)(y + 2)(y - 2)$ **7.** $y = -\dfrac{3}{2}x + 3$ **8.**

9.

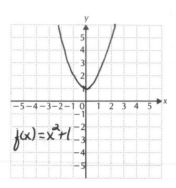

$f(x) = x^2 + 1$

10.

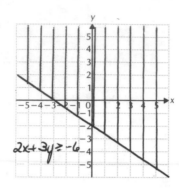

$2x + 3y \geq -6$

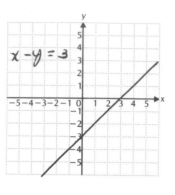

$x - y = 3$

11. $\dfrac{4}{5}$ **12.** $(-1, -3)$ **13.** -2 **14.** $\{x \mid x \leqslant 3\}$ **15.** $\{x \mid -5 < x \leqslant 2\}$

16. 15, 16   **17.** $20°, 45°, 115°$ **18.** Train A: 120 km/h; train B: 80 km/h

19. $\dfrac{a - b}{a - b + 1}$ **20.** 1

Cumulative Test, Form B, Chapters 1 - 6

1. $25x^6y^{-12}$ or $\dfrac{25x^6}{y^{12}}$ **2.** $7 + 8a$ **3.** $6x^2 - 19x - 20$ **4.** $\dfrac{x + 6}{x - 5}$

5. $\dfrac{x^2 + x + 1}{4}$ **6.** $(y^2 + 9)(y + 3)(y - 3)$ **7.** $\dfrac{2}{3}$ **8.** $(-2, 4)$ **9.** -3

10. $\left\{x \mid x \geqslant \dfrac{4}{3}\right\}$ **11.** $\{x \mid -2 < x < 4\}$ **12.** 11, 12   **13.** $20°, 35°, 125°$

14. Train A: 100 km/h; train B: 60 km/h   **15.** $y = \dfrac{3}{5}x + 4$

16.

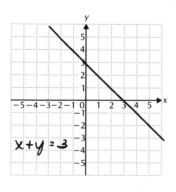

$x + y = 3$

17.

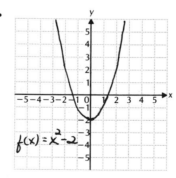

$f(x) = x^2 - 2$

18.

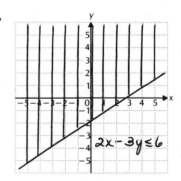

$2x - 3y \leq 6$

19. $\dfrac{x - y - 3z}{x}$ 20. -1

Cumulative Test, Form A, Chapters 1 - 7

1. 87.5%   2. $\dfrac{1}{x}$ 3. $-2\sqrt{5}$ 4. $9 + 7i$ 5. 7   6.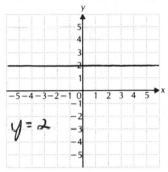

7. -1   8. 0, 2   9. (2, 0, -2)   10. $\dfrac{2}{3}$ 11. -5

12. $\{x \mid x > -2\}$ 13. $\{x \mid x \leqslant 3 \text{ or } x \geqslant 5\}$

14. Jack: 9 years; Annie: 4 years   15. $\dfrac{10}{3}$ hours

16. $q = \dfrac{5}{4}(m - n)$ 17. $\dfrac{3 - 4\sqrt{x} + x}{9 - x}$

18. $\sqrt[12]{x^4(x - 1)^3}$ 19. $2\sqrt{6}$ 20. $\dfrac{11}{13} - \dfrac{10}{13}i$

Cumulative Test, Form B, Chapters 1 - 7

1. 62.5%   2. $7 + 3i$ 3. $-11\sqrt{3}$ 4. $\dfrac{2(x - 1)}{x}$ 5. -2   6. 0, 3   7. $\dfrac{1}{4}$

8. (3, 4, 0)   9. -3   10. $\{x \mid x > -4\}$ 11. $\{x \mid x \leqslant -5 \text{ or } x \geqslant -1\}$

12. $c = \dfrac{2b - E}{5}$ 13. Jim: 25 years; Teri: 5 years   14. 12 hours

15. 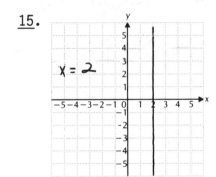   16. 4   17. $\sqrt[10]{(x + 2)^5 x^2}$ 18. $\dfrac{6 + 5\sqrt{x} + x}{4 - x}$

19. $2\sqrt{15}$ 20. $\dfrac{2}{5} + \dfrac{\sqrt{6}}{5}i$

Cumulative Test, Form A, Chapters 1 - 8

1. $-10a^3 b^{-4} c^{-3}$ or $-\dfrac{10a^3}{b^4 c^3}$ 2. $x + 2$ 3. $2(y - 4)(y^2 + 4y + 16)$ 4. 4, 6

5. $y = -5x - 14$

6.
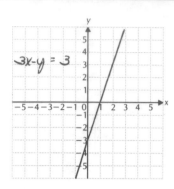
$3x - y = 3$

7.
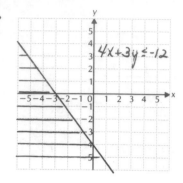
$4x + 3y \leq -12$

8.
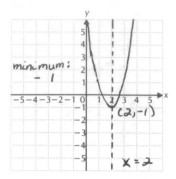
minimum: -1
$(2, -1)$
$x = 2$

9. $|x - 2|$ **10.** $\dfrac{7}{2}$ **11.** $\dfrac{1 \pm \sqrt{3}}{2}$ **12.** $(-3, 7)$ **13.** $7, -1$ **14.** 2

15. $\{x \mid x > -1\}$ **16.** $g = \dfrac{Hk}{k - H}$ **17.** $\sqrt{74} \approx 8.602$ cm   **18.** 12 ft × 15 ft

19. 3 **20.** $0, \dfrac{7}{5}, -\dfrac{3}{4}, \dfrac{3}{2}$

Cumulative Test, Form B, Chapters 1 - 8

1. $2(y + 3)(y^2 - 3y + 9)$ **2.** $(x - 5)(x - 6)$ **3.** $-8ab^{-3}c^6$ or $-\dfrac{8ac^6}{b^3}$

4. $\dfrac{y - 1}{y + 1}$ **5.** $|x - 3|$ **6.** $\dfrac{5}{3}$ **7.** $(8, -6)$ **8.** $\dfrac{1 \pm \sqrt{10}}{3}$ **9.** $8, -2$ **10.** 1

11. $\{x \mid x > -1\}$ **12.** $m = \dfrac{Q}{P(n - t)}$ **13.** 8 ft × 13 ft   **14.** $\sqrt{45} \approx 6.708$ cm

15. $y = -4x + 15$

16.
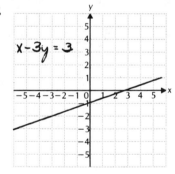
$x - 3y = 3$

17.
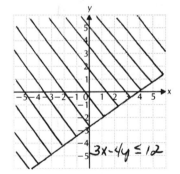
$3x - 4y \leq 12$

18.
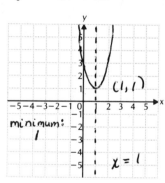
$(1, 1)$
minimum: 1
$x = 1$

19. $\sqrt[3]{\dfrac{9}{4}}$ **20.** $\dfrac{3\sqrt{2} \pm 4}{2}$

Cumulative Test, Form A, Chapters 1 - 9

1. $\dfrac{x + 4}{x - 2}$ 2. $\dfrac{3}{13} - \dfrac{11}{13}i$ 3. a) $x^2 + x - 2$ b) $x - x^2 + 4$ c) $x^3 + x^2 - 3x - 3$

d) $\dfrac{x + 1}{x^2 - 3}$ e) $x^2 + 2x + 1$ 4.

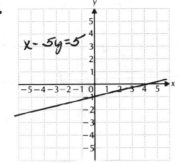

5.

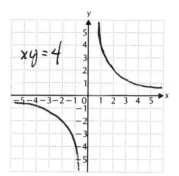

6.

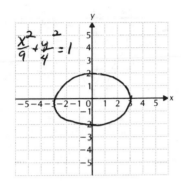

7. $\dfrac{11}{2}$ 8. -5 9. $-2 \pm \sqrt{6}$ 10. $-\dfrac{1}{5}, -\dfrac{1}{3}$ 11. $(2, 4, -6)$

12. $\left(\dfrac{5}{2}, \dfrac{1}{2}\right)$, $(5, -2)$ 13. 7 14. $\{x \mid x \leqslant 2\}$ 15. $\left\{x \mid x < -3 \text{ or } x > \dfrac{1}{2}\right\}$

16. $\{x \mid x \leqslant -1 \text{ or } x \geqslant 4\}$ 17. $\$1250$ 18. $11, 12$ 19. $(x - 2)^2 + y^2 = 9$

20. $\left[-\dfrac{1}{5}, 1\right]$

Cumulative Test, Form B, Chapters 1 - 9

1. a) $x^2 + x - 2$ b) $x - x^2 - 4$ c) $x^3 - 3x^2 + x - 3$ d) $\dfrac{x - 3}{x^2 + 1}$ e) $x^2 - 6x + 9$

2. $\dfrac{x + 2}{x - 1}$ 3. $1 + i$ 4. $-\dfrac{2}{3}$ 5. $-1 \pm \sqrt{5}$ 6. 10 7. $-\dfrac{1}{4}, -\dfrac{1}{3}$

8. $(-3, 4),(1, 0)$ 9. $(1, 3, -5)$ 10. 6 11. $\{x \mid x \geqslant -2\}$

12. $\left\{x \mid x < -2 \text{ or } x > \dfrac{4}{5}\right\}$ 13. $\{x \mid x \leqslant -3 \text{ or } x \geqslant 2\}$ 14. $\$1100$ 15. $15, 16$

16.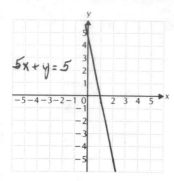

17.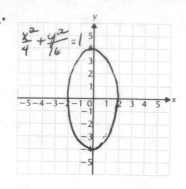

18.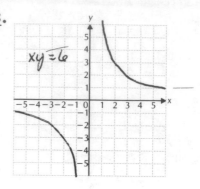

19. $\left(x - \dfrac{5}{13}\right)^2 + \left(y + \dfrac{7}{13}\right)^2 = \dfrac{7120}{169}$ 20. $\left(2, \dfrac{8}{7}\right)$

Example: Three plus six times a number is 7 more than four times the number.
          What is the number?

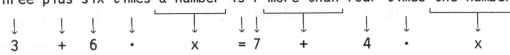

          Three plus six times a number is 7 more than four times the number.

          $$3 + 6 \cdot x = 7 + 4 \cdot x$$

          Solve: $3 + 6x = 7 + 4x$

                  $3 + 2x = 7$

                  $2x = 4$

                  $x = 2$

          The value 2 checks in the original problem. The number is 2.

Solve.

1. Three plus twice a number is seven less than four times the number. What is
   the number? _____

2. The perimeter of a rectangle is 18 inches. The length is three inches more
   than the width. What is the length? _____

3. The cost of renting a car is $18 per day plus 16¢ per mile. Find the cost of
   renting a car for a three-day trip of 1000 miles. _____

4. Two minus five times a number is sixteen more than twice the number. What is
   the number? _____

5. The second angle of a triangle is twice the first. The third angle is six
   times the first. Find the measure of the third angle. _____

6. Six plus four times a number is 12 more than twice the number. What is the
   number? _____

7. Find two consecutive odd integers such that four times the first plus three
   times the second is 27. _____

8. Seven minus four times a number is three minus twice the number. What is the
   number? _____

9. After a person gets a 30% raise in salary, the new salary is $20,800. What was the old salary? _____

10. The sum of four consecutive integers is 90. Find the integers. _____

11. The perimeter of a flower bed is 42 ft. The length is 3 ft less than twice the width. What are the dimensions? _____

12. Thirteen less than twice a number is seventeen more than half the number. What is the number? _____

13. Money is invested in a savings account at 6% simple interest. After one year there is $2756 in the account. How much was originally invested? _____

14. A piece of ribbon 98 in. long is cut into two pieces so that one piece is two-fifths as long as the other. Find the length of each piece. _____

15. Three more than twice a number is twelve less than five times the number. Find the number. _____

16. Money is borrowed at 10% simple interest. After one year $1045 pays off the loan. How much was originally borrowed? _____

17. A sporting goods store drops the price of a tennis racket 35% to a sale price of $136.50. What was the former price? _____

18. Find three consecutive odd integers such that the sum of the first, three times the second, and twice the third is 68. _____

19. After a 12% increase in the price, the new car price is $9184. What was the former price? _____

20. The second angle of a triangle is 5° more than the first, and the third is 5° less than twice the first. Find the measures of the angles. _____

Examples: Graph.

a) $y = -\frac{2}{3}x + 1$

x	y
-3	3
0	1
3	-1

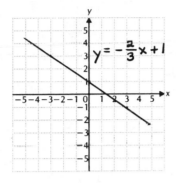

b) $3y - 2x = 6$

x	y
0	2
-3	0
3	4

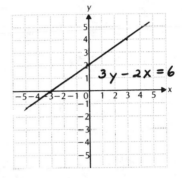

c) $x = 3$

x	y
3	-5
3	0
3	2

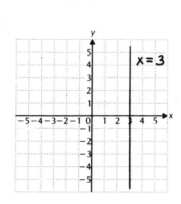

d) $y = -4$

x	y
-1	-4
0	-4
3	-4

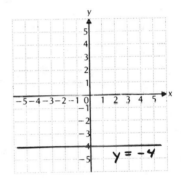

Graph.

1. $y = 4x - 3$

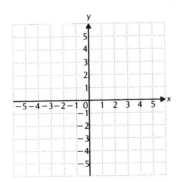

2. $y = 6x$

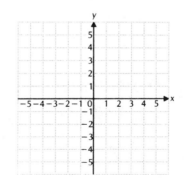

3. $x = 2$

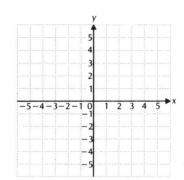

4. $y = -0.5x$

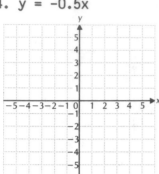

5. $3x + 6y = 18$

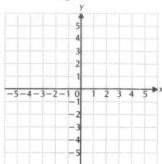

6. $y = -3x + 4$

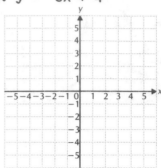

7. $y = -1$

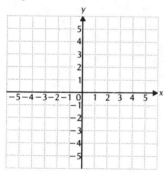

8. $-3x - 2y = 12$

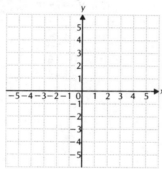

9. $y = \frac{3}{2}x$

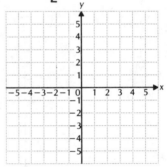

10. $y = \frac{1}{2}x - 3$

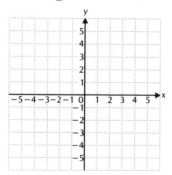

11. $4y + x = 0$

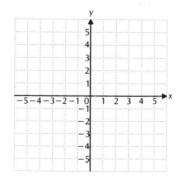

12. $x = -\frac{3}{2}$

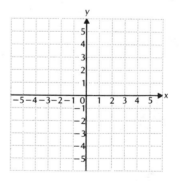

13. $y = \frac{2}{3}x$

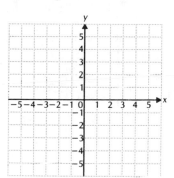

14. $y = 5$

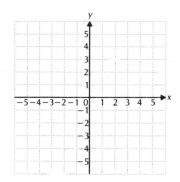

15. $2y - 10 = 5x$

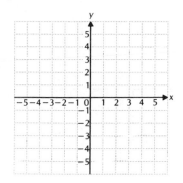

16. $4x + y = 4$

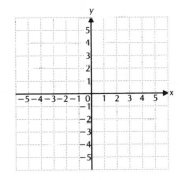

17. $y = -\frac{3}{5}x$

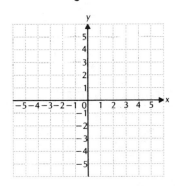

18. $y = x + 4$

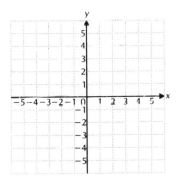

19. $x = -4$

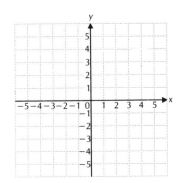

20. $3x + 15 = -5y$

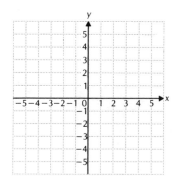

21. $y = -\frac{3}{4}x + 2$

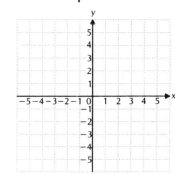

22. $y = 5x - 6$

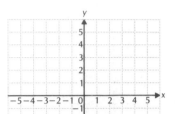

23. $4x - 4y = 16$

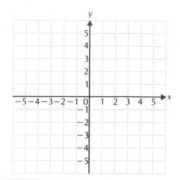

24. $y = -x$

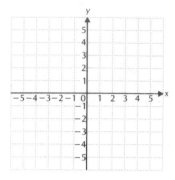

25. $y = -2x - 1$

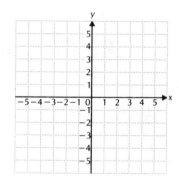

26. $y = \dfrac{9}{2}$

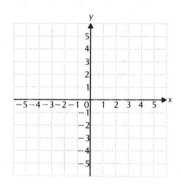

27. $x - 5y = 5$

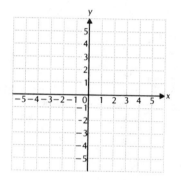

28. $y = -\dfrac{1}{5}x$

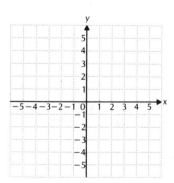

29. $y = 3x - 5$

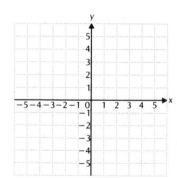

30. $y = 0.5x - 1$

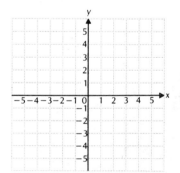

Example: The campus bookstore sells two kinds of hooded raincoats. The plastic
ones sell for $4.50, and the nylon ones sell for $8.50. During the
first semester a total of 110 raincoats were sold at a total value of
$595. How many of each kind were sold?

We let x represent the number of plastic raincoats sold and y represent
the number of nylon raincoats sold.

The total sold was 110, so we have x + y = 110.
The total amount taken in was $595, thus we have 4.50x + 8.50y = 595.

We solve the following system.

$$x + y = 110 \qquad \text{or} \qquad x + y = 110$$
$$4.5x + 8.5y = 595 \qquad\qquad 45x + 85y = 5950 \text{ (Multiplying by 10)}$$

The solution of the system is x = 85 and y = 25. These values check.
Thus 85 plastic and 25 nylon raincoats were sold.

Solve.

1. The sum of two numbers is -18. The first number minus twice the second is 66.
Find the numbers. _____

2. A collection of pennies and dimes is worth $5.53. There are 130 coins in all.
How many of each kind of coin are there? _____

3. Two investments are made totaling $14,000. For a certain year these
investments yield $1064 in simple interest. Part of the $14,000 is invested
at 6% and the rest at 8%. How much is invested at 8%? _____

4. The difference between two numbers is 12. Twice the smaller is sixteen less
than the larger. What are the numbers? _____

5. The perimeter of a lot is 72 feet. The length exceeds the width by 8 feet.
Find the length and the width. _____

6. Sarah is 5 years younger than her cousin Fred. In two years, Sarah will be $\frac{3}{4}$ as old as Fred. How old is Fred now? _____

7. The sum of two numbers is -55. The first number minus the second number is 105. Find the numbers. _____

8. One week a business sold 120 pairs of sweatpants. Polyester ones cost $9.95 and cotton ones cost $11.95. In all, $1334 worth of sweatpants were sold. How many of each kind were sold? _____

9. The perimeter of a rectangular field is 184 feet. The length is 8 feet more than twice the width. Find the dimensions. _____

10. A chemist has one solution of acid and water that is 20% acid and a second that is 65% acid. How many gallons of each should be mixed together to get 120 gallons of a solution that is 50% acid? _____

11. The sum of a certain number and a second number is 22. The second number minus the first number is -86. Find the numbers. _____

12. Two investments are made totaling $12,000. For a certain year these investments yield $885 in simple interest. Part of the $12,000 is invested at 6% and the rest at 9%. How much is invested at each rate? _____

Examples: Solve.

a) $3 - 6x < -12$

   $-3 + 3 - 6x < -3 + (-12)$

          $-6x < -15$

   $-\frac{1}{6} \cdot (-6x) > -\frac{1}{6} \cdot (-15)$

          $x > \frac{15}{6}$

          $x > \frac{5}{2}$

   The solution set is $\left\{x \mid x > \frac{5}{2}\right\}$.

b) $5y - 4 \geqslant 3y - 23$

   $5y - 4 + 4 \geqslant 3y - 23 + 4$

          $5y \geqslant 3y - 19$

   $-3y + 5y \geqslant -3y + 3y - 19$

          $2y \geqslant -19$

   $\frac{1}{2} \cdot 2y \geqslant \frac{1}{2} \cdot (-19)$

          $y \geqslant -\frac{19}{2}$

   The solution set is $\left\{y \mid y \geqslant -\frac{19}{2}\right\}$.

Solve.

1. $3x + 7 \leqslant 25$ _____

2. $3y - 8 \geqslant 10y - 2$ _____

3. $14y - 1 < 5y - 13$ _____

4. $0.4x < 2.6 - 0.6x$ _____

5. $5x + 4 - 8x \geqslant 10 - x$ _____

6. $-6y + 7 < -5$ _____

7. $12 - 3x > 8x + 7$ _____

8. $5y - 9 \leqslant 10y - 4$ _____

9. $\frac{1}{2}y - 13 < 13$ _____

10. $1 - y > y + 1$ _____

EXTRA PRACTICE 6
Solving Inequalities With Both Principles
Use after Section 4.2

11. $9x - 6 \leqslant 8x + 6$ _____

12. $48 \geqslant 7y - 1$ _____

13. $-4x + 5 > -23$ _____

14. $y - 20 + \frac{1}{2}y \leqslant -50$ _____

15. $0.7y > 0.5y - 12$ _____

16. $2x - \frac{4}{5} < \frac{1}{5} - 2x$ _____

17. $6x + 0.6 \leqslant -0.4$ _____

18. $0.5y - 1 \geqslant 1$ _____

19. $8y - 5 > 17$ _____

20. $10 - 7x \leqslant x + 3$ _____

21. $5 - 0.4y \leqslant 0.4y - 3$ _____

22. $11x - 4 - 14x > 5$ _____

23. $1 \geqslant 5 - 2x$ _____

24. $\frac{7}{4} - 2x < \frac{3}{4} - 3x$ _____

25. $23 - 4x < 8x - 2$ _____

26. $\frac{1}{3} \geqslant 1 - \frac{4}{3}y$ _____

27. $47 \geqslant 11x - 8$ _____

28. $4 - y \leqslant y - 4$ _____

29. $-3.2y - 13 < 51$ _____

30. $\frac{2}{3}x - 3 \geqslant \frac{1}{3}x + 12$ _____

254

Examples. Factor completely.

a) $81x^2 - 64 = (9x)^2 - 8^2 = (9x + 8)(9x - 8)$

b) $18x^2 - 84x + 98 = 2(9x^2 - 42x + 49) = 2(3x - 7)^2$

c) $y^3 + 1000 = y^3 + 10^3 = (y + 10)(y^2 - 10y + 100)$

d) $2x^2 + 13x - 7 = (2x - 1)(x + 7)$

e) $27x^3 - 8 = (3x)^3 - 2^3 = (3x - 2)(9x^2 + 6x + 4)$

f) $x^3 - 9x^2 - 36x = x(x - 12)(x + 3)$

Factor completely.

1. $125x^3 - 1 = $ _____

2. $w^2 - 49 = $ _____

3. $y^2 - 10y + 25 = $ _____

4. $x^2 - 5x - 66 = $ _____

5. $a^3 - 3a^2 + 2a = $ _____

6. $49b^2 + 100d^2 = $ _____

7. $(x - 4)(x + 8) + (x - 4)(x - 1) = $

_____

8. $5x^2 - 20x + 20 = $ _____

9. $b^2 - 15b + 56 = $ _____

10. $21 + 4q - q^2 = $ _____

11. $2x^5 - 4x^2 = $ _____

12. $128x^3 + 2 = $ _____

13. $5x^4y - 5yz^4 = $ _____

14. $3y^4 + 5y^3 - 50y^2 = $ _____

15. $27x^2 + 39x - 10 = $ _____

16. $w^2 + 16w - 36 = $ _____

17. $0.09a^2 + 0.24a + 0.16 = $ _____

18. $5x^3 + 60x^2 + 135x = $ _____

19. $8y^3 + 125 = $ _____

20. $\frac{1}{36} - x^2 = $ _____

21. $3x^2 - x + 4 =$ _____

22. $x^3 - 216 =$ _____

23. $42y^2 - 10y - 8 =$ _____

24. $15ad - 10ac + ab =$ _____

25. $1000c^6 - 27d^6 =$ _____

26. $16 - 8w + w^2 =$ _____

27. $x^4 + 2x^3 + x^2 =$ _____

28. $yx - yz - wx + wz =$ _____

29. $y^2 + 18y - 40 =$ _____

30. $x^2 - 14x - 15 =$ _____

31. $8a^2 - 8b^2 =$ _____

32. $27 - a^3 =$ _____

33. $64 + 16x + x^2 =$ _____

34. $a^2 + 4a - 60 =$ _____

35. $q^4 - 16q^3 + 15q^2 =$ _____

36. $16x^4 - 9x^2y^2 =$ _____

37. $65 - 8x - x^2 =$ _____

38. $x^2 - 6x + 4 =$ _____

39. $5y^3 + 135 =$ _____

40. $a^3 - 20a^2 + 100a =$ _____

41. $4y^2 - 41y - 33 =$ _____

42. $b^2 + 6b + 9 =$ _____

43. $x^2 - 169 =$ _____

44. $48 + 2a - a^2 =$ _____

45. $4y^3 + 20y^2 + 25y =$ _____

46. $x^3 + \dfrac{1}{125} =$ _____

47. $12w^2 - 7w - 10 =$ _____

48. $12x^2 + 52x - 9 =$ _____

49. $14x^2 + 53x - 45 =$ _____

50. $x^6 - 1 =$ _____

51. $x^2 - 0.2x + 0.01 =$ _____

52. $5x^2 - 31x - 72 =$ _____

53. $27x^6 - 100 =$ _____

54. $36x^3 - 12x^2 + x =$ _____

55. $20r^2 + 7r - 3 =$ _____

56. $11w^2 + 11w - 66 =$ _____

57. $0.01a^2 - 0.25b^2 =$ _____

58. $x^4y + 5x^3y - 24x^2y =$ _____

59. $3x^6 - 24y^6 =$ _____

60. $\dfrac{1}{4}x^2 - 3x + 9 =$ _____

Addition And Subtraction Of Fractional Expressions
Use after Section 6.3   Name _____

Example: Do this calculation.

$$\frac{5}{3x + 6} + \frac{2}{x + 2} - \frac{3}{x - 2}$$

$$= \frac{5}{3(x + 2)} + \frac{2}{x + 2} - \frac{3}{x - 2}, \; LCM = 3(x + 2)(x - 2)$$

$$= \frac{5}{3(x + 2)} \cdot \frac{x - 2}{x - 2} + \frac{2}{x + 2} \cdot \frac{3(x - 2)}{3(x - 2)} - \frac{3}{x - 2} \cdot \frac{3(x + 2)}{3(x + 2)}$$

$$= \frac{5(x - 2) + 6(x - 2) - 9(x + 2)}{3(x + 2)(x - 2)}$$

$$= \frac{5x - 10 + 6x - 12 - 9x - 18}{3(x + 2)(x - 2)}$$

$$= \frac{2x - 40}{3(x + 2)(x - 2)}$$

Do these calculations. Simplify by removing a factor of 1 when possible.

1. $\dfrac{5}{x - 1} + \dfrac{x}{x^2 - 1} =$ _____

2. $\dfrac{x}{3y} + \dfrac{2x}{-3y} =$ _____

3. $\dfrac{3x}{x - y} + \dfrac{2}{y - x} =$ _____

4. $\dfrac{rs}{r + s} - \dfrac{r}{2} =$ _____

5. $\dfrac{1}{2x^2 - x - 1} - \dfrac{1}{3x^2 - x - 2} =$

_____

6. $\dfrac{2a^2}{a + b} + \dfrac{2b^2}{-b - a} =$ _____

7. $\dfrac{a + b}{a - 2} + \dfrac{4}{b} =$ _____

8. $\dfrac{x}{x + y} + \dfrac{2}{x} =$ _____

9. $\dfrac{x - 2}{x} + \dfrac{1}{y} =$ _____

10. $\dfrac{a + b}{2a - 3} - \dfrac{a - b}{3 - 2a} =$ _____

11. $\dfrac{7}{2x^2 + 3x - 2} - \dfrac{7}{x^2 - x - 6} =$ _____

12. $\dfrac{3x + 1}{x^2 - 9} + \dfrac{x}{3x^2 + 8x - 3} =$ _____

13. $\dfrac{4(2x - 1)}{x^2 - 4} + \dfrac{x}{x + 2} - \dfrac{3}{x - 2} =$ _____

14. $\dfrac{x}{x^2 + 3x + 2} + \dfrac{2x}{2x^2 - x - 3} =$ _____

15. $\dfrac{a - b}{ab} + \dfrac{b - c}{bc} - \dfrac{a - c}{ac} =$ _____

16. $\dfrac{y}{y + 2} + \dfrac{y}{y - 2} - 1 =$ _____

17. $\dfrac{x}{3x - 9} - \dfrac{3}{3x - x^2} - \dfrac{2}{x - 3} =$ _____

18. $\dfrac{2m}{m^2 - 36} - \dfrac{1}{m - 6} + \dfrac{1}{m + 6} =$ _____

19. $\dfrac{1}{y^2 - 9} - \dfrac{1}{y - 3} + y =$ _____

20. $\dfrac{1}{x^2 - 1} - \dfrac{1}{x^2 + x - 2} + \dfrac{1}{x^2 + 3x + 2} =$ _____

Solving Fractional Equations Including Problem Solving
Use after Sections 6.4 and 6.5   Name _____

Example: Solve.

$$\frac{y-2}{10y} - \frac{y+1}{15y} = \frac{1}{6}$$

The LCM is 30y.

$$30y\left(\frac{y-2}{10y} - \frac{y+1}{15y}\right) = 30y \cdot \frac{1}{6}$$

$$3(y-2) - 2(y+1) = 5y$$

$$3y - 6 - 2y - 2 = 5y$$

$$y - 8 = 5y$$

$$-8 = 4y$$

$$-2 = y$$

Check:

$$\frac{y-2}{10y} - \frac{y+1}{15y} = \frac{1}{6}$$

$$\begin{array}{c|c} \dfrac{-2-2}{10(-2)} - \dfrac{-2+1}{15(-2)} & \dfrac{1}{6} \\[2mm] \dfrac{-4}{-20} - \dfrac{-1}{-30} & \\[2mm] \dfrac{1}{5} - \dfrac{1}{30} & \\[2mm] \dfrac{6}{30} - \dfrac{1}{30} & \\[2mm] \dfrac{5}{30} & \\[2mm] \dfrac{1}{6} & \end{array}$$

The solution is -2.

Solve.

1. $3x - \dfrac{2}{x} = -1$ _____

2. $\dfrac{y-8}{y+3} = \dfrac{2}{9}$ _____

3. $\dfrac{8}{5x-1} = \dfrac{2}{3x}$ _____

4. $2x + \dfrac{6}{x} = -7$ _____

5. $\dfrac{10}{x} - \dfrac{1}{x} = 3 - \dfrac{7}{x}$ _____

6. $\dfrac{16}{y} - \dfrac{16}{y+5} = \dfrac{8}{y}$ _____

7. $\dfrac{2}{y} + \dfrac{1}{y+2} = \dfrac{4}{y^2+2y}$ _____

8. $\dfrac{2}{x-2} + \dfrac{2x}{x^2-4} = \dfrac{3}{x+2}$ _____

9. $\dfrac{3}{x+2} - \dfrac{2}{x+3} = \dfrac{12}{x^2+5x+6}$ _____

10. $\dfrac{5}{t^2+5t} - \dfrac{1}{t^2-5t} = \dfrac{1}{t^2-25}$ _____

EXTRA PRACTICE 10
Solving Fractional Equations Including Problem Solving
Use after Sections 6.4 and 6.5

See Section 6.5 for examples of problem solving involving work and motion problems.

Solve.

11. One machine takes 20 minutes to do a certain job. Another machine takes 25 minutes to do the same job. Find the time it would take both machines, working together, to do the same job. _____

12. An airplane flies 1275 miles in the same time that a boat travels 25 miles. If the airplane travels 450 miles per hour faster than the boat, how fast is the plane flying? _____

13. One water pipe of a certain size can fill a tank in 4 hours. Another pipe can fill the same tank in 2 hours. How long will it take to fill the tank if both pipes are used together? _____

14. On a river a boat travels 210 miles downstream in the same amount of time that it takes to travel 150 miles upstream. The speed of the boat in still water is 22 mph. Find the speed of the river. _____

15. An operator using a keypunch machine takes 6 hours to input a certain amount of data to the computer. Another operator using a CRT spends only 2 hours to input the same amount of data. How long will it take to input the data if both operators are working together? _____

16. A train leaves Pine Valley traveling north at 40 mph. Two hours later a second train leaves on a parallel track also traveling north but at 60 mph. How far from Pine Valley will the trains be when the second train catches the first? _____

17. A student working at a pizza parlor takes 2 times longer to make pizza than her manager does. Working together they can make 36 pizzas each hour. How long would it take the student to make 36 pizzas working by herself?

_____

18. The wind is blowing 30 mph. An airplane can fly 40 miles upwind in the same amount of time it takes to fly 50 miles downwind. What is the speed of the airplane when there is no wind at all? _____

19. A new machine takes one-third the time to complete a certain job that an old machine does. Working together they can complete the job in 7 minutes. How long would it take the old machine to complete the job if it were working alone? _____

20. An airliner leaves Medford traveling south at 540 mph. Two hours later a second airliner leaves on the same course but at 630 mph. How far south will the planes be when the second catches the first? _____

262

Example: Simplify.

$$\frac{\frac{3}{x} - \frac{3}{y}}{\frac{x^2 - y^2}{3xy}} = \frac{\frac{3}{x} \cdot \frac{y}{y} - \frac{3}{y} \cdot \frac{x}{x}}{\frac{x^2 - y^2}{3xy}} = \frac{\frac{3y - 3x}{xy}}{\frac{x^2 - y^2}{3xy}}$$

$$= \frac{3(y - x)}{xy} \cdot \frac{3xy}{(x + y)(x - y)} = \frac{-3(x - y)}{xy} \cdot \frac{3xy}{(x + y)(x - y)}$$

$$= \frac{xy(x - y)}{xy(x - y)} \cdot \frac{-3 \cdot 3}{x + y} = - \frac{9}{x + y}$$

Simplify.

1. $\dfrac{x - \dfrac{1}{x}}{1 + \dfrac{1}{x}} =$ _____

2. $\dfrac{\dfrac{a}{b} - \dfrac{b}{a}}{\dfrac{1}{b} - \dfrac{1}{a}} =$ _____

3. $\dfrac{\dfrac{1}{z} - \dfrac{2}{w}}{\dfrac{8}{w} - \dfrac{9}{z}} =$ _____

4. $\dfrac{3}{\dfrac{1}{a} + \dfrac{1}{b}} =$ _____

5. $\dfrac{\dfrac{1}{y} + 1}{\dfrac{1}{y} - 2} =$ _____

6. $\dfrac{r - \dfrac{2r}{s}}{\dfrac{s}{r} - s} =$ _____

7. $\dfrac{\frac{1}{a} + \frac{1}{b}}{a^2 - b^2} =$ _____

8. $\dfrac{\frac{x}{2} - 3x}{x + \frac{1}{x}} =$ _____

9. $\dfrac{\frac{2}{a} + \frac{2}{d}}{\frac{a^2 - d^2}{4ad}} =$ _____

10. $\dfrac{\frac{1}{x} + 1}{\frac{1}{x^2} - 1} =$ _____

11. $\dfrac{x^2 - y^2}{\frac{1}{y} - \frac{1}{x}} =$ _____

12. $\dfrac{\frac{c^2 - d^2}{cd}}{\frac{c + d}{c}} =$ _____

13. $\dfrac{\frac{x^2 - 25}{x^2 - 1}}{\frac{2x^2 - 5x - 25}{x^2 + 2x - 3}} =$ _____

14. $\dfrac{\frac{1}{a^2} - 2}{\frac{1}{a^2} + 4} =$ _____

15. $\dfrac{x - \frac{1}{2}}{x - \frac{1}{8}} =$ _____

16. $\dfrac{\frac{x^2 + 7x + 10}{x^3 + 1}}{\frac{x^2 - 4}{x^2 - x + 1}} =$ _____

Name _____

Examples: Divide.

a) $(18x^7 + 12x^5 - 36x^4) \div 3x^3$

$$\frac{18x^7 + 12x^5 - 36x^4}{3x^3}$$

$$= \frac{18x^7}{3x^3} + \frac{12x^5}{3x^3} - \frac{36x^4}{3x^3}$$

$$= 6x^4 + 4x^2 - 12x$$

Answer: $6x^4 + 4x^2 - 12x$

b) $(x^4 - 5x^2 + x - 10) \div (x - 3)$

$$
\begin{array}{r}
x^3 + 3x^2 + 4x + 13 \\
x - 3 \overline{\smash{)}\, x^4 + 0x^3 - 5x^2 + x - 10} \\
\underline{x^4 - 3x^3} \\
3x^3 - 5x^2 \\
\underline{3x^3 - 9x^2} \\
4x^2 + x \\
\underline{4x^2 - 12x} \\
13x - 10 \\
\underline{13x - 39} \\
29
\end{array}
$$

Answer: $x^3 + 3x^2 + 4x + 13$, R 29

Divide.

1. $(12x^4 + 8x^3 - 16x^2) \div 4x^2 =$

_____

2. $(10x^2 - 23x + 12) \div (2x - 3) =$

_____

3. $(3x^2 + x - 10) \div (3x - 5) =$

_____

4. $(6x^3 + 8x^2 - 5x + 2) \div (x + 2) =$

_____

5. $(8y^3 - 12y^2 + 4y - 2) \div (4y - 2) =$

_____

6. $(25x^2 + 10x^4 - 15x^3) \div 5x^2 =$

_____

7. $(y^4 - 1) \div (y + 1) =$

_____

8. $(a^4 - a^2 - 12) \div (a - 4) =$

_____

9. $(r^5 - r^3 + 2r - 4) \div (r + 2) =$

10. $(x^3 - 1000) \div (x - 10) =$

11. $(2x^3 + 3x^6 - 5x^2) \div x =$

12. $(x^8 - 1) \div (x^2 - 1) =$

13. $(2s^2 - 5s + 2) \div (s - 2) =$

14. $(12t^2 + 5t - 2) \div (3t + 2) =$

15. $(6a^2 - 17a + 5) \div (3a - 1) =$

16. $(3x^2 - 7x + 8) \div (x - 4) =$

17. $(18y^3 + 6y^2 - 42y - 16) \div (6y + 2) =$

18. $(3x^3 - 10x^2 + 8x) \div (x - 2) =$

19. $(b^3 - b^2 + b - 10) \div (b + 3) =$

20. $(8x^3 + 26x^2 - 12x) \div 2x =$

21. $(21x^3 + 14x + 7) \div (x + 2) =$

22. $(x^8 - x^6 + 4x^4 - 24) \div (x^2 - 2) =$

23. $(x^6 - 6x^2 + 16) \div (x - 4) =$

24. $(x^{10} - x^5 + 5) \div (x^5 - 5) =$

Example. Graph: $f(x) = -x^2 + 6x - 7$

$f(x) = -(x^2 - 6x) - 7$

$\quad = -[x^2 - 6x + (9 - 9)] - 7$

$\quad = -(x^2 - 6x + 9) + 9 - 7$

$\quad = -(x - 3)^2 + 2$

Line of symmetry: $x = 3$

Vertex: (3, 2)

x	f(x)
3	2
4	1
2	1
5	-2
1	-2

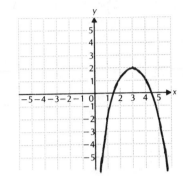

Graph.

1. $f(x) = 2x^2$

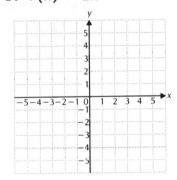

2. $f(x) = (x - 2)^2$

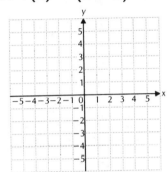

3. $f(x) = (x - 1)^2 + 4$

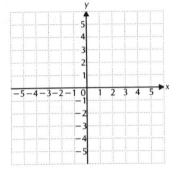

4. $f(x) = 2(x - 1)^2 + 3$

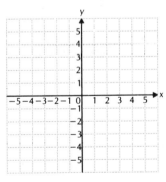

5. $f(x) = x^2 - 4x + 7$

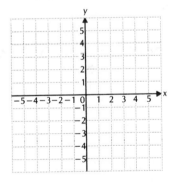

6. $f(x) = -3x^2$

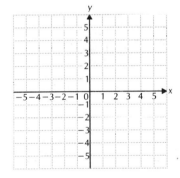

7. $f(x) = x^2 - 6x + 5$

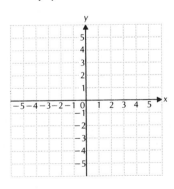

8. $f(x) = 2(x + 1)^2$

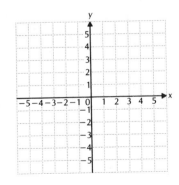

9. $f(x) = -2x^2 - 16x - 37$

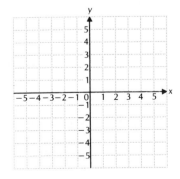

10. $f(x) = (x + 4)^2$

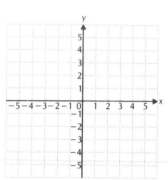

11. $f(x) = -\frac{1}{3}x^2$

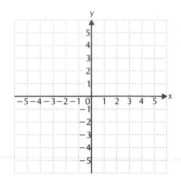

12. $f(x) = (x - 2)^2 - 1$

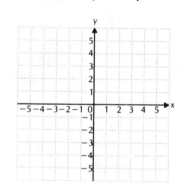

13. $f(x) = 2x^2 - 12x + 19$

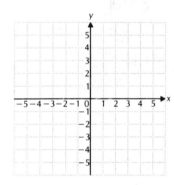

14. $f(x) = 3(x - 2)^2$

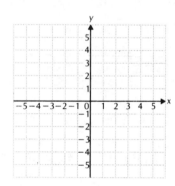

15. $f(x) = (x + 1)^2$

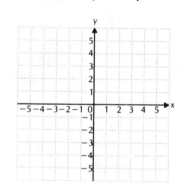

16. $f(x) = 0.5x^2$

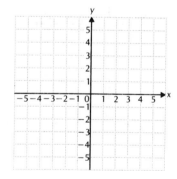

17. $f(x) = -3(x + 2)^2 + 4$

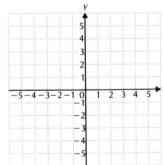

18. $f(x) = x^2 - 2x + 2$

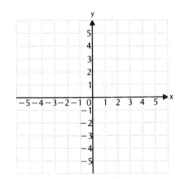

278

19. $f(x) = (x + 2)^2$

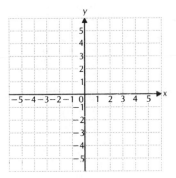

20. $f(x) = (x + 3)^2 - 2$

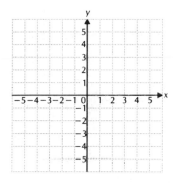

21. $f(x) = -4x^2 + 16x - 10$

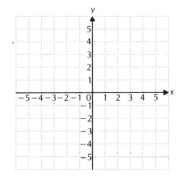

22. $f(x) = -\frac{1}{2}(x - 2)^2 + 4$

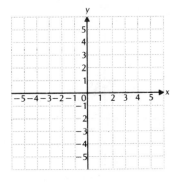

23. $f(x) = -2(x - 3)^2$

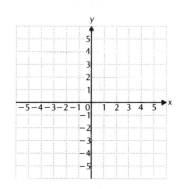

24. $f(x) = -5x^2$

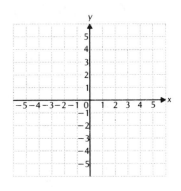

25. $f(x) = x^2 + 4x + 2$

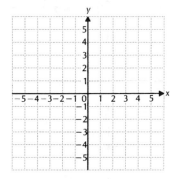

26. $f(x) = -(x + 2)^2$

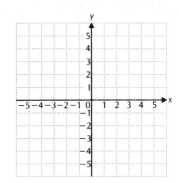

27. $f(x) = 3x^2 - 3x + 1$

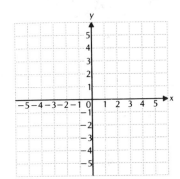

28. $f(x) = \frac{1}{2}(x + 2)^2$

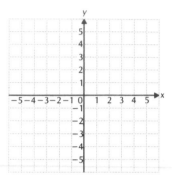

29. $f(x) = -x^2 - 2x - 4$

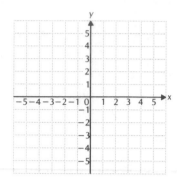

30. $f(x) = 2x^2 - 4x - 1$

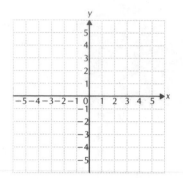

31. $f(x) = (x + 1)^2 - 5$

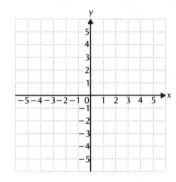

32. $f(x) = -2(x - 2)^2 - 2$

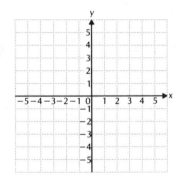

33. $f(x) = \frac{1}{3}(x - 3)^2$

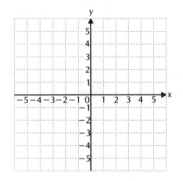

34. $f(x) = -\frac{1}{2}(x + 1)^2$

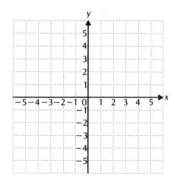

35. $f(x) = x^2 + x - 1$

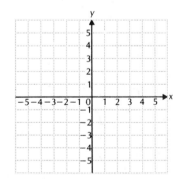

36. $f(x) = -3x^2 - 6x + 1$

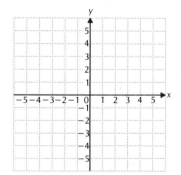

280

Solving Systems Of Equations When One Or Both Equations Are Second Degree
Use after Sections 9.4 and 9.5   Name _____

Example. Solve: $5y^2 = 22 - 2x^2$

$$3x^2 = y^2 - 1$$

$2x^2 + 5y^2 = 22 \longrightarrow \quad 2x^2 + 5y^2 = 22$

$3x^2 - y^2 = -1 \longrightarrow \quad \underline{15x^2 - 5y^2 = -5}$ (Multiplying by 5)
$\qquad\qquad\qquad\qquad\qquad 17x^2 \quad = 17$ (Adding)

$$x^2 = 1$$

$$x = \pm 1$$

If x = 1, x^2 = 1, and if x = -1, x^2 = 1, so substituting 1 or -1 in $3x^2 = y^2 - 1$ we have

$3 \cdot 1 = y^2 - 1$

$\quad 4 = y^2$

$\pm 2 = y$

The solutions are (1, 2), (-1, 2), (1, -2), and (-1, -2).

Solve.

1. $x^2 + y^2 = 13$
   $xy = 6$

   _____

2. $x^2 + y^2 = 81$
   $x^2 - y^2 = 81$

   _____

3. $x^2 - 13 = -y^2$
   $y - x = 1$

   _____

4. $x^2 + y^2 = 37$
   $xy = -6$

   _____

5. $x^2 + 4y^2 = 4$
   $2y = 2 - x$

   _____

6. $x^2 + y^2 = 85$
   $2x - 9y = 0$

   _____

7. $100x^2 + 9y^2 = 900$
   $10x + 3y = 30$

   _____

8. $x^2 = 25 - y^2$
   $x^2 = 25 + y^2$

   _____

9. $y^2 - 8x^2 = 16$
   $8x^2 + y^2 = 16$

   _____

10. $x^2 + y^2 = 41$
    $y - x = 1$

    _____

11. $x^2 - y = 0$
    $y^2 - x = 0$

    _____

12. $x^2 + y^2 = 49$
    $y^2 = x + 7$

    _____

13. A rectangle has perimeter 280 cm, and the length of a diagonal is 100 cm. What are its dimensions? _____

14. The area of a rectangle is $4\sqrt{2}$ m². The length of a diagonal is $2\sqrt{3}$ m. Find the dimensions. _____

15. The product of two numbers is -35. The sum of their squares is 74. Find the numbers. _____

16. The sum of the squares of two positive numbers is 13. Their difference is 1. What are the numbers? _____

17. The sum of the squares of two positive integers is 41. Their difference is 1. What are the integers? _____

18. The perimeter of a rectangle is 46 m and the area is 120 m². What are the dimensions of the rectangle? _____

19. The product of two numbers is $\frac{1}{8}$. The sum of their squares is $\frac{5}{16}$. Find the numbers. _____

20. The area of a rectangle is 0.12 cm². The length of a diagonal is 0.5 cm. Find the dimensions of the rectangle. _____

Examples. Solve.

a) $8^{x-2} = 512$

$8^{x-2} = 8^3$

$x - 2 = 3$

$x = 5$

b) $5^x = 11$

$\log 5^x = \log 11$

$x \log 5 = \log 11$

$x = \dfrac{\log 11}{\log 5}$

$x \approx \dfrac{1.0414}{0.6990}$

$x \approx 1.4898$

c) $e^{-3t} = 0.02$

$\ln e^{-3t} = \ln 0.02$

$-3t \ln e = \ln 0.02$

$-3t = \ln 0.02$

$t = \dfrac{\ln 0.02}{-3}$

$t \approx \dfrac{-3.9120}{-3}$

$t \approx 1.304$

Solve.

1. $2^{3x} = 64$ _____

2. $e^{5t} = 200$ _____

3. $3^x = 5$ _____

4. $5^x = 3$ _____

5. $e^{-2t} = 0.4$ _____

6. $5^{2x-1} = 625$ _____

7. $8^{x-1} = 4$ _____

8. $10^x = 8$ _____

9. $9^x = 3000$ _____

10. $e^{0.06t} = 10$ _____

11. $e^{3t} = 3$ _____

12. $3^x = 1.9$ _____

13. $7^{x+4} = 49$ _____

14. $3^{x-1} = 2$ _____

15. $15^{3x-4} = 10$ _____

16. $10^{4-x} = 10,000$ _____

Example. Solve: $\log_2 (x + 2) - \log_2 (x - 2) = 3$

$\log_2 (x + 2) - \log_2 (x - 2) = 3$ Check:

$$\log_2 \frac{x + 2}{x - 2} = 3$$ $\underline{\log_2 (x + 2) - \log_2 (x - 2) = 3}$

$$\frac{x + 2}{x - 2} = 8$$ $\log_2 \left[\frac{18}{7} + 2\right] - \log_2 \left[\frac{18}{7} - 2\right] \Big| 3$

$$x + 2 = 8x - 16$$ $\log_2 \frac{32}{7} - \log_2 \frac{4}{7}$

$$18 = 7x$$ $\log_2 \left[\frac{32}{7} \div \frac{4}{7}\right]$

$$\frac{18}{7} = x$$

The solution is $\frac{18}{7}$. $\log_2 8$

Solve. $3 \Big|$

17. $\log x + \log (x + 21) = 2$ 18. $\log (x + 4) - \log x = 3$

_____   _____

19. $\log_4 (3x - 5) = 3$ 20. $\log_2 (x - 8) = 5$

_____   _____

21. $\log x + \log (x - 15) = 2$ 22. $\log_2 (x - 3) + \log_2 (x + 3) = 4$

_____   _____

23. $\log (8x + 1) = 1$ 24. $\log (x + 198) - \log x = 2$

_____   _____

25. $\log x - \log (x + 3) = -1$ 26. $\log_3 (x + 5) - \log_3 x = 3$

_____   _____

27. $\log_4 (x - 6) + \log_4 (x + 6) = 3$ 28. $\log_6 x + \log_6 (x + 5) = 2$

_____   _____

29. $\log x + \log (x + 0.48) = -2$ 30. $\log (x + 15) + \log x = 2$

_____   _____

31. $\log_5 x + \log_5 (x + 20) = 3$ 32. $\log_2 (4 - x) = 6$

_____   _____

284

ANSWER KEYS FOR EXTRA PRACTICE SHEETS

Extra Practice 1

1. -32 2. -2.7 3. $-\frac{1}{3}$ 4. -55.5 5. $-\frac{11}{12}$ 6. -22 7. $-\frac{1}{24}$

8. -10 9. 6.46 10. -8 11. 0 12. 35 13. -1.5 14. $-\frac{3}{7}$ 15. 0

16. $-\frac{1}{6}$ 17. -71 18. 3.55 19. 14 20. $\frac{1}{6}$ 21. 0 22. -27.7

23. -17 24. $-\frac{16}{15}$ 25. $-\frac{2}{15}$ 26. 8.1 27. $\frac{23}{42}$ 28. 0 29. $-\frac{1}{5}$

30. 83 31. $-\frac{7}{12}$ 32. -22 33. -30.84 34. -3.003 35. -1 36. $\frac{7}{55}$

37. 3 38. 0.51 39. -36 40. $-\frac{1}{12}$ 41. -82 42. 0.094 43. -3

44. 17 45. -17 46. 3 47. 0 48. 26 49. -26 50. 0 51. 23

52. -52 53. 58 54. -38 55. $-\frac{17}{20}$ 56. 4.5 57. 96 58. -12.7

59. 0 60. -60 61. 39 62. -15.3 63. $\frac{19}{28}$ 64. -45 65. $10\frac{1}{2}$, or $\frac{21}{2}$

66. 4.3 67. -28.02 68. -27 69. $-\frac{5}{6}$ 70. $-\frac{2}{15}$ 71. -19.5 72. -8

73. -143 74. $-\frac{1}{15}$ 75. 3.93 76. -5.76 77. 20 78. $-\frac{3}{20}$ 79. 100

80. $-\frac{41}{20}$ 81. -23 82. $\frac{37}{34}$ 83. -1.8 84. $\frac{4}{3}$

Extra Practice 2

1. 5 2. 6 in. 3. $214 4. -2 5. 120° 6. 3 7. 3, 5 8. 2

9. $16,000 10. 21, 22, 23, 24 11. 13 ft by 8 ft 12. 20 13. $2600

14. 28 in., 70 in. 15. 5 16. $950 17. $210 18. 9, 11, 13 19. $8200

20. 45°, 50°, 85°

Extra Practice 3

<u>1.</u>
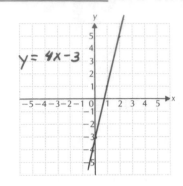
$y = 4x - 3$

<u>2.</u>
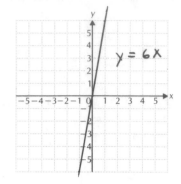
$y = 6x$

<u>3.</u>
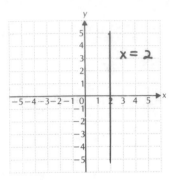
$x = 2$

<u>4.</u>
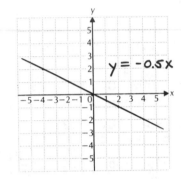
$y = -0.5x$

<u>5.</u>
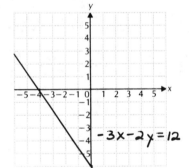
$3x + 6y = 18$

<u>6.</u>
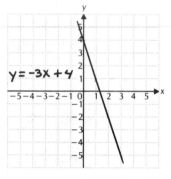
$y = -3x + 4$

<u>7.</u>
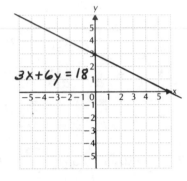
$y = -1$

<u>8.</u>
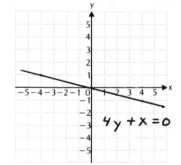
$-3x - 2y = 12$

<u>9.</u>
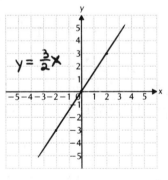
$y = \frac{3}{2}x$

<u>10.</u>
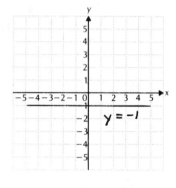
$y = \frac{1}{2}x - 3$

<u>11.</u>
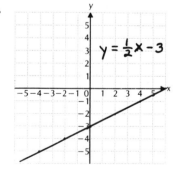
$4y + x = 0$

<u>12.</u>
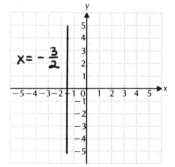
$x = -\frac{3}{2}$

286

13.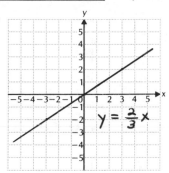

$y = \frac{2}{3}x$

14.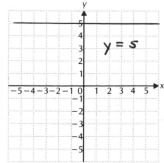

$y = 5$

15.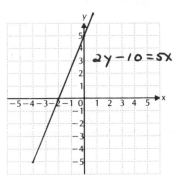

$2y - 10 = 5x$

16.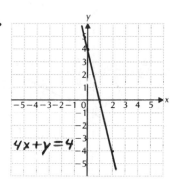

$4x + y = 4$

17.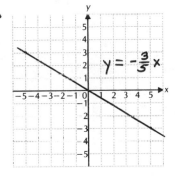

$y = -\frac{3}{5}x$

18.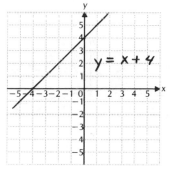

$y = x + 4$

19.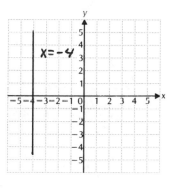

$x = -4$

20.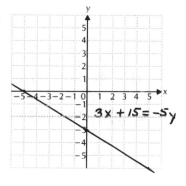

$3x + 15 = -5y$

21.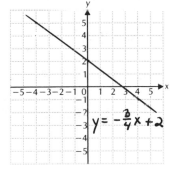

$y = -\frac{3}{4}x + 2$

22.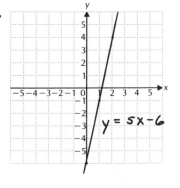

$y = 5x - 6$

23.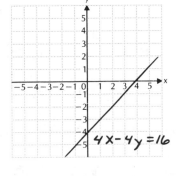

$4x - 4y = 16$

24.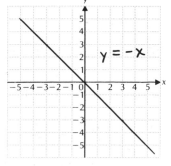

$y = -x$

Extra Practice 3 (continued)

25.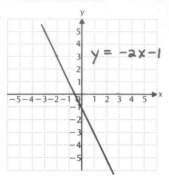

26.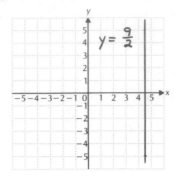

27.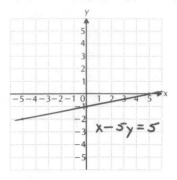

28.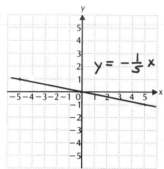

29.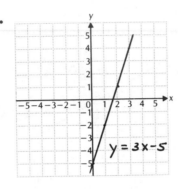

30.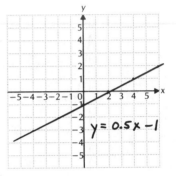

Extra Practice 4

1. (-3, 2)   2. (4, 7)   3. (2, 5)   4. (4, -1)   5. (-1, 2)   6. (1, 1)

7. (-2, -1)   8. (3, -4)   9. (1, 1)   10. (5, -4)   11. (-1, -1)

12. (5, -4)   13. (6, 2)   14. (-3, -3)   15. (1, 2)   16. (-1, 4)

17. $\left(-\frac{8}{7}, -\frac{19}{14}\right)$ 18. (2, 2)   19. $\left(\frac{1}{2}, \frac{1}{3}\right)$ 20. (12, 20)

Extra Practice 5

1. 10, -28   2. 83 pennies, 47 dimes   3. $11,200   4. 8, -4

5. Length is 22 ft; width is 14 ft   6. 18   7. 25, -80   8. 50 polyester,
70 cotton   9. Length is 64 ft; width is 28 ft   10. 40 gallons of 20%,
80 gallons of 65%   11. 54, -32   12. $6500 at 6%, $5500 at 9%

Extra Practice 6

1. $\{x \mid x \leq 6\}$ 2. $\left\{y \mid y \leq -\frac{6}{7}\right\}$ 3. $\left\{y \mid y < -\frac{4}{3}\right\}$ 4. $\{x \mid x < 2.6\}$

5. $\{x \mid x \leq -3\}$ 6. $\{y \mid y > 2\}$ 7. $\left\{x \mid x < \frac{5}{11}\right\}$ 8. $\{y \mid y \geq -1\}$ 9. $\{y \mid y < 52\}$

10. $\{y \mid y < 0\}$ 11. $\{x \mid x \leq 12\}$ 12. $\{y \mid y \leq 7\}$ 13. $\{x \mid x < 7\}$

14. $\{y \mid y \leq -20\}$ 15. $\{y \mid y > -60\}$ 16. $\left\{x \mid x < \frac{1}{4}\right\}$ 17. $\left\{x \mid x \leq -\frac{1}{6}\right\}$

18. $\{y \mid y \geq 4\}$ 19. $\left\{y \mid y > \frac{11}{4}\right\}$ 20. $\left\{x \mid x \geq \frac{7}{8}\right\}$ 21. $\{y \mid y \geq 10\}$

22. $\{x \mid x < -3\}$ 23. $\{x \mid x \geq 2\}$ 24. $\{x \mid x < -1\}$ 25. $\left\{x \mid x > \frac{25}{12}\right\}$

26. $\left\{y \mid y \geq \frac{1}{2}\right\}$ 27. $\{x \mid x \leq 5\}$ 28. $\{y \mid y \geq 4\}$ 29. $\{y \mid y > -20\}$

30. $\{x \mid x \geq 45\}$

Extra Practice 7

1. $\left\{x \mid x < -\frac{25}{9} \text{ or } x > 3\right\}$ 2. $\{y \mid -5 \leq y \leq 11\}$ 3. $\left\{x \mid -\frac{32}{7} < x < 2\right\}$

4. $\left\{\frac{1}{3},\ 5\right\}$ 5. $\{-6,\ 6\}$ 6. $\{y \mid y \leq 0 \text{ or } y \geq 20\}$ 7. $\{y \mid -11 \leq y \leq -3\}$

8. $\{y \mid y < -2 \text{ or } y > 1\}$ 9. $\left\{x \mid x < -\frac{11}{3} \text{ or } x > 5\right\}$ 10. $\{x \mid -25 < x < 25\}$

11. $\{-0.46,\ 0.5\}$ 12. $\left\{x \mid x \leq -\frac{22}{5} \text{ or } x \geq \frac{38}{5}\right\}$ 13. $\{x \mid x < -19 \text{ or } x > 7\}$

14. $\left\{-1,\ \frac{1}{2}\right\}$ 15. $\{y \mid y < -15 \text{ or } y > 25\}$ 16. $\left\{y \mid -\frac{1}{3} \leq y \leq \frac{1}{3}\right\}$

17. $\{y \mid y < -1 \text{ or } y > 1\}$ 18. $\{-2,\ 6\}$ 19. $\left\{x \mid x \leq -\frac{29}{6} \text{ or } x \geq \frac{31}{6}\right\}$

20. $\left\{x \mid -1 < x < \frac{33}{7}\right\}$ 21. $\{-41,\ 45\}$ 22. $\{x \mid x < 0 \text{ or } x > 32\}$

23. $\left\{x \mid -\frac{1}{6} \leq x \leq 1\right\}$ 24. $\{y \mid -4 < y < 7\}$ 25. $\{y \mid y < -5 \text{ or } y > 5\}$

26. $\left\{y \mid \frac{2}{13} \leq y \leq \frac{5}{13}\right\}$ 27. $\left\{y \mid -6 < y < \frac{15}{2}\right\}$ 28. $\{x \mid x \leq -10 \text{ or } x \geq 6\}$

29. $\left\{x \mid x \leq -\frac{1}{7} \text{ or } x \geq \frac{3}{7}\right\}$ 30. $\{y \mid 4 \leq y \leq 18\}$

Extra Practice 8

1. $(5x - 1)(25x^2 + 5x + 1)$ 2. $(w + 7)(w - 7)$ 3. $(y - 5)^2$

4. $(x - 11)(x + 6)$ 5. $a(a - 2)(a - 1)$ 6. Not factorable

7. $(x - 4)(2x + 7)$ 8. $5(x - 2)^2$ 9. $(b - 8)(b - 7)$ 10. $(7 - q)(3 + q)$

11. $2x^2(x^3 - 2)$ 12. $2(4x + 1)(16x^2 - 4x + 1)$ 13. $5y(x^2 + z^2)(x + z)(x - z)$

14. $y^2(3y - 10)(y + 5)$ 15. $(9x - 2)(3x + 5)$ 16. $(w - 2)(w + 18)$

17. $(0.3a + 0.4)^2$ 18. $5x(x + 3)(x + 9)$ 19. $(2y + 5)(4y^2 - 10y + 25)$

20. $\left(\frac{1}{6} + x\right)\left(\frac{1}{6} - x\right)$ 21. Not factorable   22. $(x - 6)(x^2 + 6x + 36)$

23. $2(3y + 1)(7y - 4)$ 24. $a(15d - 10c + b)$

25. $(10c^2 - 3d^2)(100c^4 + 30c^2d^2 + 9d^4)$ 26. $(4 - w)^2$ 27. $x^2(x + 1)^2$

28. $(y - w)(x - z)$ 29. $(y - 2)(y + 20)$ 30. $(x - 15)(x + 1)$

31. $8(a + b)(a - b)$ 32. $(3 - a)(9 + 3a + a^2)$ 33. $(8 + x)^2$

34. $(a - 6)(a + 10)$ 35. $q^2(q - 1)(q - 15)$ 36. $x^2(4x + 3y)(4x - 3y)$

37. $(5 - x)(13 + x)$ 38. Not factorable   39. $5(y + 3)(y^2 - 3y + 9)$

40. $a(a - 10)^2$ 41. $(y - 11)(4y + 3)$ 42. $(b + 3)^2$ 43. $(x + 13)(x - 13)$

44. $(8 - a)(6 + a)$ 45. $y(2y + 5)^2$ 46. $\left(x + \frac{1}{5}\right)\left(x^2 - \frac{1}{5}x + \frac{1}{25}\right)$

47. $(4w - 5)(3w + 2)$ 48. $(2x + 9)(6x - 1)$ 49. $(7x - 5)(2x + 9)$

50. $(x + 1)(x - 1)(x^2 - x + 1)(x^2 + x + 1)$ 51. $(x - 0.1)^2$

52. $(x - 8)(5x + 9)$ 53. Not factorable   54. $x(6x - 1)^2$

55. $(5r + 3)(4r - 1)$ 56. $11(w + 3)(w - 2)$ 57. $(0.1a + 0.5b)(0.1a - 0.5b)$

58. $x^2y(x - 3)(x + 8)$ 59. $3(x^2 - 2y^2)(x^4 + 2x^2y^2 + 4y^4)$ 60. $\left(\frac{1}{2}x - 3\right)^2$

Extra Practice 9

1. $\dfrac{6x + 5}{x^2 - 1}$ 2. $-\dfrac{x}{3y}$ 3. $\dfrac{3x - 2}{x - y}$ 4. $\dfrac{rs - r^2}{2(r + s)}$ 5. $\dfrac{x + 1}{(x - 1)(2x + 1)(3x + 2)}$

6. $2a - 2b$ 7. $\dfrac{ab + b^2 + 4a - 8}{ab - 2b}$ 8. $\dfrac{x^2 + 2x + 2y}{(x + y)x}$ 9. $\dfrac{xy - 2y + x}{xy}$

Extra Practice 9   (continued)

10. $\dfrac{2a}{2a - 3}$ 11. $\dfrac{-7}{(2x - 1)(x - 3)}$ 12. $\dfrac{10x^2 - 3x - 1}{(x + 3)(x - 3)(3x - 1)}$ 13. $\dfrac{x + 5}{x + 2}$

14. $\dfrac{4x^2 + x}{(x + 2)(x + 1)(2x - 3)}$ 15. 0   16. $\dfrac{y^2 + 4}{y^2 - 4}$ 17. $\dfrac{x - 3}{3x}$ 18. $\dfrac{2}{m + 6}$

19. $\dfrac{y^3 - 10y - 2}{y^2 - 9}$ 20. $\dfrac{x}{(x + 1)(x - 1)(x + 2)}$

Extra Practice 10

1. $\dfrac{2}{3}$, -1   2. $\dfrac{78}{7}$ 3. $-\dfrac{1}{7}$ 4. $-\dfrac{3}{2}$, -2   5. $\dfrac{16}{3}$ 6. 5   7. No solution

8. -10   9. 7   10. 10   11. $11\dfrac{1}{9}$ minutes   12. 459 mph   13. $1\dfrac{1}{3}$ hr

14. $3\dfrac{2}{3}$ mph   15. 1½ hr   16. 240 mi   17. 3 hr   18. 270 mph

19. 28 minutes   20. 7560 mi

Extra Practice 11

1. $x - 1$ 2. $a + b$ 3. $\dfrac{w - 2z}{8z - 9w}$ 4. $\dfrac{3ab}{a + b}$ 5. $\dfrac{1 + y}{1 - 2y}$ 6. $\dfrac{r^2s - 2r^2}{s^2 - s^2r}$

7. $\dfrac{1}{ab(a - b)}$ 8. $\dfrac{-5x^2}{2(x^2 + 1)}$ 9. $\dfrac{8}{a - d}$ 10. $\dfrac{x}{1 - x}$ 11. $xy(x + y)$

12. $\dfrac{c - d}{d}$ 13. $\dfrac{x^2 + 8x + 15}{2x^2 + 7x + 5}$ 14. $\dfrac{1 - 2a^2}{1 + 4a^2}$ 15. $\dfrac{4(2x - 1)}{8x - 1}$ 16. $\dfrac{x + 5}{x^2 - x - 2}$

Extra Practice 12

1. $3x^2 + 2x - 4$ 2. $5x - 4$ 3. $x + 2$ 4. $6x^2 - 4x + 3$, R -4

5. $2y^2 - 2y$, R -2   6. $5 + 2x^2 - 3x$ 7. $y^3 - y^2 + y - 1$

8. $a^3 + 4a^2 + 15a + 60$, R 228   9. $r^4 - 2r^3 + 3r^2 - 6r + 14$, R -32

10. $x^2 + 10x + 100$ 11. $2x^2 + 3x^5 - 5x$ 12. $x^6 + x^4 + x^2 + 1$ 13. $2s - 1$

14. $4t - 1$ 15. $2a - 5$ 16. $3x + 5$, R 28   17. $3y^2 - 7$, R -2   18. $3x^2 - 4x$

19. $b^2 - 4b + 13$, R -49   20. $4x^2 + 13x - 6$ 21. $21x^2 - 42x + 98$, R -189

22. $x^6 + x^4 + 6x^2 + 12$ 23. $x^5 + 4x^4 + 16x^3 + 64x^2 + 250x + 1000$, R 4016

24. $x^5 + 4$, R 25

Extra Practice 13

1. $2xz\sqrt{3yz}$ 2. $3y\sqrt[3]{6x^2y^2}$ 3. a^2b^3 4. $\dfrac{6a\sqrt{a}}{b^2}$ 5. $3ab\sqrt{2ac}$ 6. 27

7. $\dfrac{2y\sqrt[3]{3y}}{x^2}$ 8. $2ab^2\sqrt[4]{3a}$ 9. $2ab^2\sqrt{2b}$ 10. $8x^9$ 11. $\dfrac{3x^2\sqrt{x}}{7}$

12. $10z^7\sqrt{3xyz}$ 13. 25 14. $\dfrac{3a\sqrt[3]{a^2}}{4}$ 15. $2xy\sqrt[3]{25y}$ 16. $x^2y^3z^4$

17. $\dfrac{2x\sqrt{5x}}{3}$ 18. 27 19. $27a^3b^6$ 20. $4a^2\sqrt[3]{4}$ 21. $3(x+1)\sqrt[3]{x+1}$

22. $3a\sqrt{ab}$ 23. $4x$ 24. $3x^2\sqrt[3]{y}$ 25. $3x^2y\sqrt{2y}$ 26. $5ab\sqrt[3]{b^2}$ 27. $3x\sqrt[3]{xy}$

28. $2(x+1)^2\sqrt{2}$ 29. $16ab\sqrt[3]{16b}$ 30. $2y\sqrt[3]{y}$ 31. $4xy^2\sqrt[5]{x^3}$

32. $2(y-1)^2\sqrt[3]{(y-1)^2}$ 33. $7a^2b\sqrt{2b}$ 34. $5x$ 35. $9y\sqrt[4]{x^3y}$ 36. $9a^3c^3\sqrt{10a}$

37. $(x+y)^6\sqrt{x+y}$ 38. $21x$ 39. $4y^2$ 40. $4xy\sqrt[3]{3x^2}$

Extra Practice 14

1. $-2, 1$ 2. 4 3. 3 4. 5 5. 1 6. 2 7. 16 8. 5 9. 11

10. 3 11. No solution 12. $-1, 3$ 13. -1 14. 1 15. 2 16. 0

17. No solution 18. 4 19. 5 20. -4

Extra Practice 15

1. $\dfrac{-5 \pm i\sqrt{59}}{7}$ 2. $\dfrac{3 \pm i\sqrt{11}}{2}$ 3. $\dfrac{-1 \pm \sqrt{33}}{4}$ 4. $3 \pm \sqrt{2}$ 5. $1 \pm i\sqrt{7}$

6. $\dfrac{1 \pm \sqrt{13}}{6}$ 7. $\dfrac{4 \pm \sqrt{10}}{3}$ 8. $2 \pm i\sqrt{2}$ 9. $\dfrac{1 \pm i\sqrt{23}}{4}$ 10. $\dfrac{2 \pm i\sqrt{6}}{2}$

11. $\dfrac{3 \pm \sqrt{21}}{2}$ 12. $\dfrac{5 \pm \sqrt{33}}{2}$ 13. $\dfrac{1 \pm i\sqrt{71}}{6}$ 14. $\dfrac{5 \pm i\sqrt{15}}{2}$ 15. $1 \pm \sqrt{5}$

16. $\dfrac{-9 \pm \sqrt{137}}{14}$ 17. $\dfrac{-5 \pm \sqrt{13}}{2}$ 18. $4 \pm \sqrt{2}$ 19. $\dfrac{11 \pm \sqrt{89}}{2}$ 20. $\dfrac{1 \pm \sqrt{17}}{8}$

21. $\dfrac{1 \pm \sqrt{11}}{10}$ 22. $\dfrac{2 \pm 2\sqrt{6}}{5}$ 23. $4 \pm \sqrt{15}$ 24. $\dfrac{-3 \pm \sqrt{35}}{2}$ 25. $\dfrac{1 \pm \sqrt{26}}{5}$

26. $-3 \pm \sqrt{5}$ 27. $5 \pm \sqrt{23}$ 28. $\dfrac{3 \pm \sqrt{33}}{4}$ 29. $\dfrac{1 \pm i\sqrt{95}}{12}$ 30. $\dfrac{1 \pm \sqrt{4001}}{20}$

Extra Practice 16

1. 10 mph   2. Length is 12 in.; width is 7 in.   3. 36 hours   4. 30 m

5. 4 ft   6. Length is 60 in.; width is 15 in.   7. 35 years

8. 8 ft and 15 ft   9. 17 in.   10. 112.31 ft   11. 10 in.   12. 4.3 hr

13. 2.4 in.   14. 6 ft   15. 8.1 mph

Extra Practice 17

1. 100   2. $\pm\sqrt{2}, \pm\sqrt{5}$ 3. $-\frac{1}{2}, \frac{1}{3}$ 4. $-\frac{1}{2}, -5$ 5. 144, 1   6. 25

7. $\pm\sqrt{7}, \pm i\sqrt{2}$ 8. 9, 81   9. -1, 1, 2, 4   10. $\pm\sqrt{3}, \pm i\sqrt{6}$

11. -1, 1, 6, 8   12. 4, 64   13. $\frac{3}{2}$ 14. 225, 256   15. $\pm\sqrt{2}, \pm\sqrt{3}$

16. $-\frac{1}{8}, \frac{2}{5}$

Extra Practice 18

1.
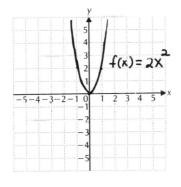

2.
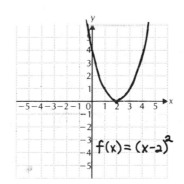

3.
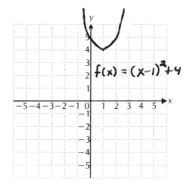

4.
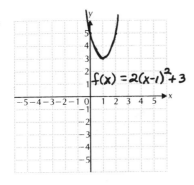

5.
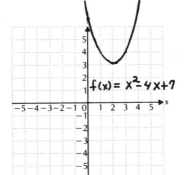

6.
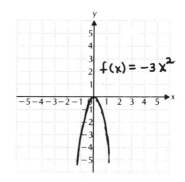

7.

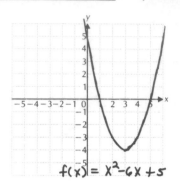

$f(x) = x^2 - 6x + 5$

8.

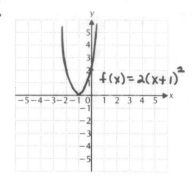

$f(x) = 2(x+1)^2$

9.

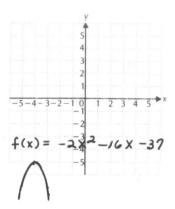

$f(x) = -2x^2 - 16x - 37$

10.

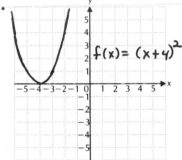

$f(x) = (x+4)^2$

11.

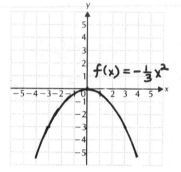

$f(x) = -\frac{1}{3}x^2$

12.

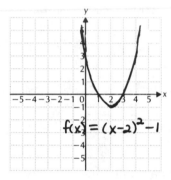

$f(x) = (x-2)^2 - 1$

13.

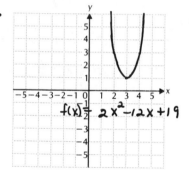

$f(x) = \frac{1}{2}x^2 - 12x + 19$

14.

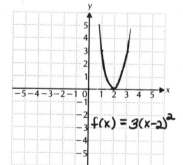

$f(x) = 3(x-2)^2$

15.

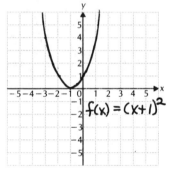

$f(x) = (x+1)^2$

16.

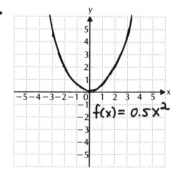

$f(x) = 0.5x^2$

17.

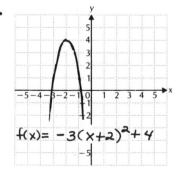

$f(x) = -3(x+2)^2 + 4$

18.

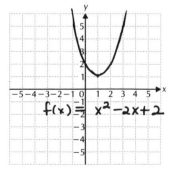

$f(x) = \frac{1}{2}x^2 - 2x + 2$

19.

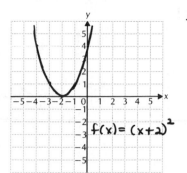

$f(x)= (x+2)^2$

20.

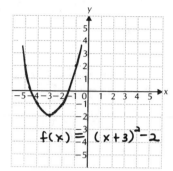

$f(x) = \frac{3}{4}(x+3)^2 - 2$

21.

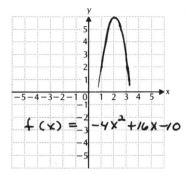

$f(x) = -4x^2 + 16x - 10$

22.

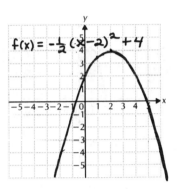

$f(x) = -\frac{1}{2}(x-2)^2 + 4$

23.

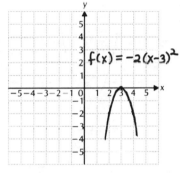

$f(x) = -2(x-3)^2$

24.

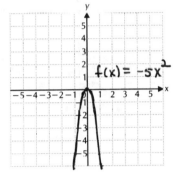

$f(x) = -5x^2$

25.

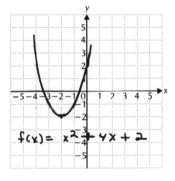

$f(x) = x^2 + 4x + 2$

26.

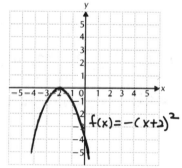

$f(x) = -(x+2)^2$

27.

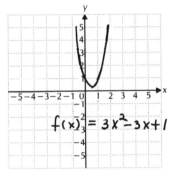

$f(x) = 3x^2 - 3x + 1$

28.

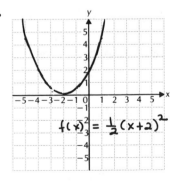

$f(x) = \frac{1}{2}(x+2)^2$

29.

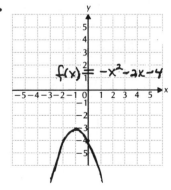

$f(x) = -x^2 - 2x - 4$

30.

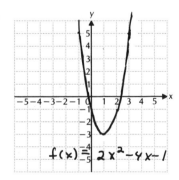

$f(x) = 2x^2 - 4x - 1$

31.
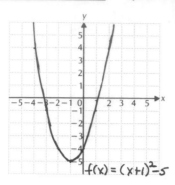

32.
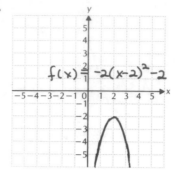

33.
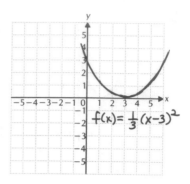

34.
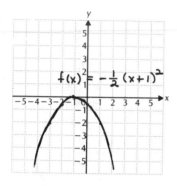

35.
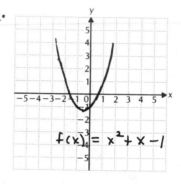

36.
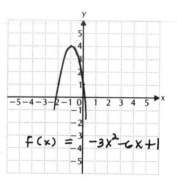

Extra Practice 19

1. (-2, -3), (-3, -2), (2, 3), (3, 2)   2. (9, 0), (-9, 0)

3. (2, 3), (-3, -2)   4. (-1, 6), (1, -6), (-6, 1), (6, -1)   5. (0, 1), (2, 0)

6. (9, 2), (-9, -2)   7. (0, 10), (3, 0)   8. (5, 0), (-5, 0)

9. (0, 4), (0, -4)   10. (4, 5), (-5, -4)   11. (0, 0), (1, 1)

12. (6, $\sqrt{13}$), (6, -$\sqrt{13}$), (-7, 0)   13. 60 cm by 80 cm   14. 2 m by $2\sqrt{2}$ m

15. -5 and 7 or 5 and -7   16. 2 and 3   17. 4 and 5   18. 8 m by 15 m

19. ½ and ¼ or -½ and -¼   20. 0.4 cm by 0.3 cm

<u>Extra Practice 20</u>

<u>1</u>. 2   <u>2</u>. 1.0597   <u>3</u>. 1.4651   <u>4</u>. 0.6825   <u>5</u>. 0.4581   <u>6</u>. 2.5   <u>7</u>. $\frac{5}{3}$

<u>8</u>. 0.9031   <u>9</u>. 3.6440   <u>10</u>. 38.3764   <u>11</u>. 0.3662   <u>12</u>. 0.5844   <u>13</u>. -2

<u>14</u>. 1.6309   <u>15</u>. 1.6168   <u>16</u>. 0   <u>17</u>. 4   <u>18</u>. $\frac{4}{999}$ <u>19</u>. 23   <u>20</u>. 40

<u>21</u>. 20   <u>22</u>. 5   <u>23</u>. $\frac{9}{8}$ <u>24</u>. 2   <u>25</u>. $\frac{1}{3}$ <u>26</u>. $\frac{5}{26}$ <u>27</u>. 10   <u>28</u>. 4

<u>29</u>. 0.02   <u>30</u>. 5   <u>31</u>. 5   <u>32</u>. -60

EVEN ANSWERS FOR THE EXERCISE SETS IN THE TEXT

Exercise Set 1.1, pp. 5 - 6

2. 80 sec, 450 sec, 35 min **4.** 100.1 sq cm **6.** 128 **8.** 12 **10.** 8 **12.** 7

14. $t + 9$, or $9 + t$ **16.** $d - 47$ **18.** $11 + z$, or $z + 11$ **20.** $d + c$, or $c + d$

22. $b - c$ **24.** 67%m **26.** $m + n$ **28.** $4p$ **30.** $9d$ **32.** $p - q$, or $q - p$

34. $m + 1$ **36.** $h - 47$ **38.** $a - 2b$ **40.** 1.11P **42.** 9

Exercise Set 1.2, pp. 13 - 14

2. 0, 2, 14 **4.** -5, 0, 2, -3, 14 **6.** 0.125 **8.** $1.1\overline{6}$ **10.** $\frac{1391}{100}$

12. $\frac{213}{10,000}$ **14.** 28% **16.** 12.5% **18.** 280% **20.** 1.875% **22.** 32.5%

24. 0.25% **26.** 234% **28.** 700% **30.** 0.475, $\frac{475}{1000}$ or $\frac{19}{40}$ **32.** 0.0823, $\frac{823}{10,000}$

34. 1.8, $\frac{9}{5}$ **36.** 0.001, $\frac{1}{1000}$ **38.** $31 < 94$ **40.** $4.7 < 47$ **42.** $-6 > -20$

44. $-16 < -1.6$ **46.** $\frac{7}{8}$ **48.** $\frac{2}{3}$ **50.** 0 **52.** 0.04 **54.** 78%y **56.** $b - 1$

Exercise Set 1.3, pp. 19 - 20

2. -29 **4.** 5 **6.** -12 **8.** -3 **10.** -15 **12.** -34 **14.** 1.9 **16.** -13.26

18. $-\frac{2}{3}$ **20.** $-\frac{5}{4}$ **22.** $-\frac{5}{8}$ **24.** $-\frac{41}{24}$ **26.** 8 **28.** 0 **30.** 8 **32.** $2x$

34. -3 **36.** -21 **38.** 46 **40.** 0 **42.** 5 **44.** 44 **46.** -17.7 **48.** -34.8

50. $-\frac{13}{5}$ **52.** $\frac{3}{4}$ **54.** $-\frac{22}{15}$ **56.** $-\frac{1}{63}$ **58.** Associative law of addition

60. Commutative law of addition **62.** Associative law of addition **64.** 0.89

66. -2 **68.** -19.45

Exercise Set 1.4, pp. 25 - 26

2. -40 **4.** -45 **6.** 21 **8.** -136 **10.** 42.7 **12.** $-\frac{55}{12}$ **14.** 3 **16.** 432

18. 71.04 **20.** $\frac{65}{14}$ **22.** $-\frac{64}{125}$ **24.** -8 **26.** -9 **28.** 8 **30.** 0.7

Exercise Set 1.4, pp. 25 - 26   (continued)

32. Not possible   34. 0   36. Not possible   38. $\frac{10}{9}$ 40. $-\frac{6}{5}$

42. $-\frac{1}{75}$ or $-0.013\overline{3}$ 44. $-\frac{1}{5.5}$ or $0.18\overline{18}$ 46. $-\frac{7}{10}$ 48. 8   50. -3

52. 110   54. -4000   56. 8   58. -42   60. 0.18   62. $\frac{45}{16}$

Exercise Set 1.5, pp. 31 - 32

2. -8   4. -4   6. -14   8. 15   10. $520   12. 8x + 8   14. 9a - 9b

16. -6c - 10d   18. 5xy - 5xz + 5xw   20. P + Prt   22. ¼πr + ¼πrs

24. 5x, -9y, 12   26. 5a, -7b, -9c   28. 7(a + b)   30. 12(x - 1)

32. 6(y - 6)   34. a(b + 1)   36. 3(x + y - z)   38. 4(a + 2b - 1)

40. x(y - z + w)   42. $\frac{1}{2}$h(a + b)   44. 12x   46. -3c   48. 14x   50. 14x

52. -5x   54. -6x   56. 13a - 10b   58. 7a + 9b   60. 9p + 12

62. -11.83a - 36.3b   64. $-\frac{3}{4}x + \frac{3}{4}y - 34$ 66. 1040 ft   68. -900   70. 4050

72. $-\frac{93}{8}$

Exercise Set 1.6, pp. 37 - 38

2. 5x   4. -b - 9   6. -x + 8 or 8 - x   8. -r + s or s - r   10. -x - y - z

12. -9a + 7b - 24   14. 4x - 8y + 5w - 9z   16. $x - 2y + \frac{2}{3}z + 56.3w$

18. 6x + 9   20. a + 3   22. 13x - 16   24. -15y - 45   26. -12y + 33

28. -7t - 26   30. -12t + ½w + 2   32. 47b - 51   34. -1449   36. -8b + 196

38. 23a - 18b + 184   40. -102y - 980z - 301   42. -102   44. 4x + 12y

46. -31a

Exercise Set 1.7, pp. 41 - 42

2. 6^3 4. x^4 6. t^5 8. $(5x)^5$ 10. $2^3r^4t^2$ 12. 7·7·7 or 343

14. (-8)·(-8) or 64   16. y·y·y·y·y·y   18. (-3x)(-3x)(-3x)(-3x)

20. $xyz \cdot xyz \cdot xyz$ **22.** $\sqrt{6}$ **24.** $\frac{9}{7}$ **26.** 1   **28.** 1   **30.** $\frac{1}{8^4}$ **32.** $\frac{1}{16^2}$

34. $\frac{1}{(-4)^3}$ or $-\frac{1}{64}$ **36.** 9^{-2} **38.** 12^{-5} **40.** $(-8)^{-6}$ **42.** 5   **44.** $-\frac{1}{2}$

46. Not equivalent   **48.** $\frac{y^{-2}}{x^{-4}}$ **50.** $y^{-5}x^{-3}$ **52.** $\frac{5}{3}$ **54.** $\frac{328}{3}$

Exercise Set 1.8, pp. 47 - 48

2. 6^8 **4.** 9^{-2} or $\frac{1}{9^2}$ **6.** 9^{-7} or $\frac{1}{9^7}$ **8.** a **10.** 1   **12.** $648y^5$

14. $-18x^7y$ **16.** $-24x^{-12}y$ or $-\frac{24y}{x^{12}}$ **18.** 7^5 **20.** 5^{11} **22.** 12^{-12} or $\frac{1}{12^{12}}$

24. 2^{-2} or $\frac{1}{2^2}$ or $\frac{1}{4}$ or 0.25   **26.** y^9 **28.** $-3ab^2$ **30.** $-\frac{7}{4}a^{-4}b^2$ or $-\frac{7b^2}{4a^4}$

32. $\frac{7}{9}a^{16}b^5$ **34.** 5^{20} **36.** 9^{-12} or $\frac{1}{9^{12}}$ **38.** 7^{40} **40.** $2^5a^{15}b^{20}$ or $32a^{15}b^{20}$

42. $-\frac{1}{27}a^{-6}b^{15}$ or $-\frac{b^{15}}{27a^6}$ **44.** $\frac{1}{8^4}x^{16}y^{-20}z^{-8}$ or $\frac{x^{16}}{8^4y^{20}z^8}$ **46.** $\frac{5^{-6}}{4^9}$ or $\frac{1}{5^6 \cdot 4^9}$

48. $\frac{5^4}{4^4}x^{-20}y^{24}$ or $\frac{5^4y^{24}}{4^4x^{20}}$ **50.** $-23t + 21$ **52.** 8^{120}, or 2^{360}

54. $a^{-14}b^{-27}$ or $\frac{1}{a^{14}b^{27}}$ **56.** 1   **58.** $m^x n^{x^2}$ **60.** $(xy)^{ca+cb}$

Exercise Set 1.9, pp. 51 - 52

2. -16   **4.** -50   **6.** 31   **8.** 64   **10.** -200   **12.** 39   **14.** 290   **16.** 6561

18. 133,128   **20.** 5,354,884   **22.** $A^3 + B^3$ **24.** $(A + B)/(C - D)$

26. $(A^2/B^3)^4$ **28.** $a - \frac{1}{b}$ **30.** $\frac{a + 3}{2a}$ **32.** $a^3 - 2a - 2$ **34.** 80%

36. $8x^{-9}y^{12}z^{-24}$ or $\frac{8y^{12}}{x^9z^{24}}$ **38.** True, $(-a)(-b) = (-1)a(-1)b = (-1)(-1)ab = ab$

Exercise Set 2.1, pp. 65 - 66

2. 12   **4.** -7   **6.** 26   **8.** -52   **10.** 9.17   **12.** $-\frac{11}{12}$ **14.** 7   **16.** -11

18. $\frac{1}{5}$ **20.** 15   **22.** -7   **24.** $\frac{21}{20}$ **26.** 19   **28.** 3   **30.** -23   **32.** 11

34. 3   **36.** 13   **38.** -6   **40.** 5   **42.** -3   **44.** 4   **46.** 0   **48.** -5

50. No solution   **52.** All real numbers   **54.** $-2x^8y^3$ **56.** $2(2x - 5y + 1)$

58. All real numbers   **60.** $\frac{1}{9}$

<u>2</u>. 3   <u>4</u>. 1   <u>6</u>. 7   <u>8</u>. 7   <u>10</u>. -3   <u>12</u>. 6   <u>14</u>. -4, 8   <u>16</u>. 3, 7

<u>18</u>. $\frac{4}{3}, \frac{1}{4}$ <u>20</u>. 0, 5   <u>22</u>. -4, 2   <u>24</u>. -20, 0.02   <u>26</u>. $-\frac{3}{2}$ <u>28</u>. $\frac{7}{6}$

<u>30</u>. No solution <u>32</u>. 8.414

Exercise Set 2.3, pp. 75 - 78

<u>2</u>. 14 ft, 16 ft   <u>4</u>. $1\frac{7}{8}$ m, $3\frac{1}{8}$ m   <u>6</u>. $14.13   <u>8</u>. $3.90   <u>10</u>. 6   <u>12</u>. 8

<u>14</u>. $500   <u>16</u>. $800   <u>18</u>. 25°, 100°, 55°   <u>20</u>. $7 = 110$ m; $w = 45$ m

<u>22</u>. 14, 16   <u>24</u>. $18,500   <u>26</u>. Ground $325; Flight $950   <u>28</u>. $\frac{17}{4}$

<u>30</u>. No solution   <u>32</u>. 25% increase   <u>34</u>. $100

Exercise Set 2.4, pp. 81 - 82

<u>2</u>. $w = \frac{A}{7}$ <u>4</u>. $E = \frac{W}{I}$ <u>6</u>. $a = \frac{F}{m}$ <u>8</u>. $P = \frac{I}{rt}$ <u>10</u>. $c^2 = \frac{E}{m}$ <u>12</u>. $w = \frac{P - 27}{2}$

<u>14</u>. $b^2 = c^2 - a^2$ <u>16</u>. $\pi = \frac{A}{r^2}$ <u>18</u>. $F = \frac{9}{5}C + 32$ <u>20</u>. $\pi = \frac{3V}{4r^3}$

<u>22</u>. $d = \frac{2A - hc}{-h}, \frac{2A}{-h} + c$ <u>24</u>. $v^2 = \frac{Fr}{m}$ <u>26</u>. 250   <u>28</u>. -25

<u>30</u>. $s = \frac{A - \pi r^2}{\pi r}$ <u>32</u>. $T_2 = \frac{P_2 V_2 T_1}{P_1 V_1}$ <u>34</u>. 0.8 yr

Exercise Set 2.5, pp. 89 - 90

<u>2</u>.

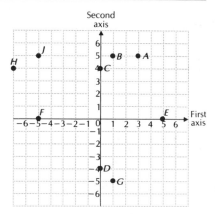

<u>4</u>.

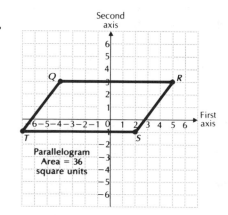

6. No   **8.** Yes   **10.** No   **12.**

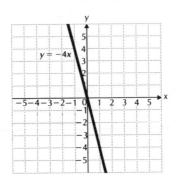

14.

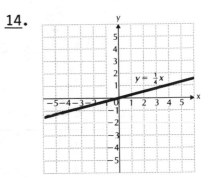

16.

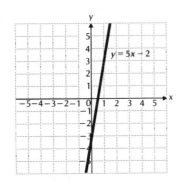

18.

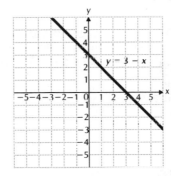

20.

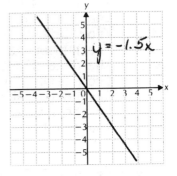

22.

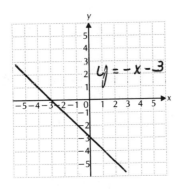

24. $-\dfrac{5}{8}$ **26.** -100

28.

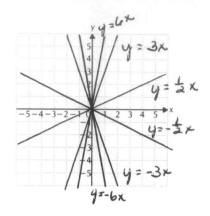

If the number is positive,
the line slants upward
from left to right. If
the number is negative,
the line slants downward
from left to right. The
larger the absolute value
of the number, the steeper
the slant.

Exercise Set 2.6, pp. 97 - 100

<u>2</u>. Slope is 5; y-intercept is (0, 3)   <u>4</u>. Slope is -5; y-intercept is (0, -7)

<u>6</u>. Slope is $\frac{15}{7}$; y-intercept is (0, 2.2)

<u>8</u>. Slope is -0.314; y-intercept is (0, 18.9)

<u>10</u>. Slope is $\frac{2}{5}$;   <u>12</u>. Slope is $-\frac{2}{5}$;   <u>14</u>. Slope is -2;
y-intercept is (0, -4)   y-intercept is (0, 3)   y-intercept is (0, 4)

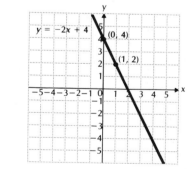

16. Slope is -3;
y-intercept is (0, 6)

18. Slope is 1.5;
y-intercept is (0, -3)

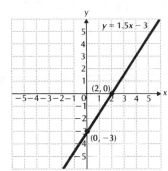

20. Slope is $\frac{4}{5}$;
y-intercept is (0, 0)

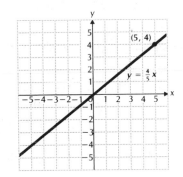

22.

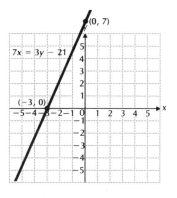

24.

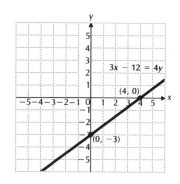

26.

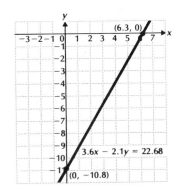

28. Linear, m = $\frac{5}{3}$; y-intercept is (0, -5)   **30.** Linear, m = 0; y-intercept is

(0, -4)   **32.** Not linear   **34.** Not linear   **36.** 6(-2a + 5b)   **38.** -8a + 22b

40. m = -8; y-intercept is $\left(0, -\frac{7}{2}\right)$ **42.** m = $-\frac{3}{7}$; y-intercept is $\left(0, -\frac{6}{77}\right)$

Exercise Set 2.7, pp. 105 - 106

2.

4.

6.

8. $\frac{3}{26}$ 10. $-\frac{3}{4}$ 12. $\frac{98}{269}$ 14. Does not exist   16. Slanted

18. No slope   20. Zero slope   22. Zero slope   24. No slope   26. Slanted

28. No slope   30. Zero slope   32. Slanted   34. $-20a^{-7}b$ or $\frac{-20b}{a^7}$

36. $a = \frac{5}{8}$ 38. $(25, -1)$, $(-25, 1)$, $(50, -2)$, $(-50, 2)$, answers may vary

Exercise Set 2.8, pp. 111 - 112

2. $y - 4 = 5x - 25$ or $y = 5x - 21$ 4. $y - 3 = -3x + 21$ or $y = -3x + 24$

6. $y + 7 = x + 5$ or $y = x - 2$ 8. $y = -3x - 6$ 10. $y - 4 = 0$ or $y = 4$

12. $y = x + 3$ 14. $y = x$ 16. $y = \frac{3}{7}x - 3$ 18. $y = 3x + 5$ 20. $y = -\frac{4}{3}x$

22. $y = 2x + 3$ 24. $y = -2x - 13$ 26. $y = -3x + 13$ 28. $y = -\frac{2}{5}x - \frac{31}{5}$

30. -37.7 32. 7.5 34. $y = \frac{5}{12}x + \frac{41}{12}$ 36. $k = 7$

Exercise Set 2.9, pp. 115 - 116

2. (a) $E = 0.15t + 65$; (b) 71, 72.2   4. (a) $D = 0.2t + 20$;

(b) 27.6 quadrillion joules, 30 quadrillion joules   6. (a) $R = -0.075t + 46.8$;

(b) 42.525 sec, 42.3 sec; (c) 2021   8. (a) $C = 0.15m + 15$; (b) $45

10. 21.1°C

Exercise Set 3.1, pp. 125 - 126

2. No   4. Yes   6. No   8. Yes

10.

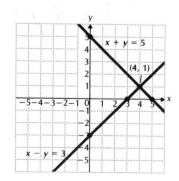

12.

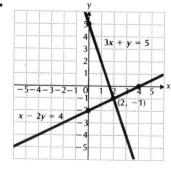

14.

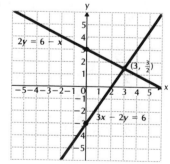

16.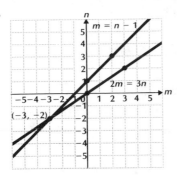

18.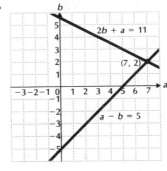

20.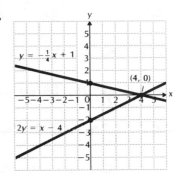

22.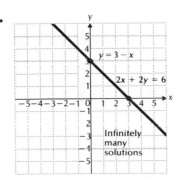

24.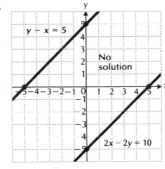

26. -35

28. $\frac{9}{20}$ 30. a = 4Q + b   32. Let b = Burl's age, s = son's age.

Then b = 2s,   b - 10 = 3(s - 10)   34. x + y = 3; answers may vary
                                         x - y = 11

Exercise Set 3.2, pp. 131 - 132

2. (2, -3)   4. $\left[\frac{21}{5}, \frac{12}{5}\right]$ 6. (2, -7)   8. (4, -1)   10. (2, 7)

12. (½, -5)   14. (1, -2)   16. (1, 3)   18. $\left[\frac{10}{21}, \frac{11}{14}\right]$ 20. $\left[\frac{75}{31}, \frac{260}{31}\right]$

22. (2, 3)   24. (-21, 21)   26. (-2, -9)   28. $\left[\frac{1000}{11}, -\frac{1000}{11}\right]$

30. $\left[-\frac{4}{3}, -\frac{19}{3}\right]$ 32. -15y - 39   34. (23.118878, -12.039964)

36. $\left[\frac{a + 2b}{7}, \frac{a - 5b}{7}\right]$

Exercise Set 3.3, pp. 139 - 142

2. -52 and -11   4. 29 and 18   6. $l = 300$ ft, $w = 75$ ft

8. 12 white, 28 printed   10. 4 gallons of 25%, 6 gallons of 50%

12. $6800 at 9%, $8200 at 10%   14. $5200 at 7%, $6400 at 8%

16. 300 nickels, 100 dimes   18. 30 L of 70%, 90 L of 50%

20. Gerry 52, daughter 26   22. Paula 32, Bob 20   24. $l = 138$ ft., $w = 56$ ft.

26. 84 adults, 33 children   28. $12,500 at 6%, $14,500 at 7%

30. 4 boys, 3 girls   32. 82   34. 180   36. $m = -\frac{1}{2}$, $b = \frac{5}{2}$

Exercise Set 3.4, pp. 147 - 148

2. No   4. (4, 0, 2)   6. (2, -2, 2)   8. (3, -2, 1)   10. (7, -3, -4)

12. (2, 1, 3)   14. (2, -5, 6)   16. (17, 9, 79)   18. (3, 4, -1)

20. (2, 5, -3)   22. $d = \frac{2F - tc}{-t}$ or $d = -\frac{2F}{t} + c$ 24. (-2, 0, 0, 1)

Exercise Set 3.5, pp. 151 - 154

2. 12, 27, 18   4. 8, 21, -3   6. 30°, 90°, 60°   8. 32°, 96°, 52°

10. Mon., 20 qt; Tues., 35 qt; Wed., 32 qt   12. Fred, 195; Jane, 180; Mary, 200

14. A, 2200 bd-ft; B, 2500 bd-ft; C, 2700 bd-ft

16. A, 10 ft; B, 12 ft; C, 15 ft   18. 2050 students, 845 adults, 210 children

20. 180°

Exercise Set 3.6, pp. 159 - 160

2. -13   4. 29   6. 1   8. 3   10. -6   12. (-3, 2)   14. $\left(\frac{9}{19}, \frac{51}{38}\right)$

16. $\left(-1, -\frac{6}{7}, \frac{11}{7}\right)$ 18. (-3, 2, 1)   20. (3, 4, -1)   22. -12   24. 12

26. 10

Exercise Set 3.7, pp. 165 - 166

2. (a) P = 45x - 360,000; (b) 8000 units 4. (a) P = 55x - 49,500;

(b) 900 units 6. (a) P = 45x - 22,500; (b) 500 units 8. ($50, 500)

10. ($10, 370) 12. ($40, 7600) 14. (a) C = 20x + 10,000;

(b) R = 100x; (c) P = 80x - 10,000; (d) Profit of $150,000; (e) 125 units

16. -47t + 62 18. 58a - 38 20. -1502t + 82

Exercise Set 3.8, pp. 171 - 172

2. Inconsistent 4. Consistent 6. Consistent 8. Inconsistent

10. Consistent 12. Dependent 14. Independent 16. Dependent

18. Independent 20. Dependent 22. 10 24. Many solutions: 0 par-3,

18 par-4, 0 par-5; 1 par-3, 16 par-4, 1 par-5; 2 par-3, 14 par-4, 2 par-5;

3 par-3, 12 par-4, 3 par-5; and so on.

Exercise Set 4.1, pp. 185 - 186

2. a) Yes b) No c) Yes d) Yes 4. a) Yes b) Yes c) No d) No

6. a) Yes b) Yes c) Yes d) No 8. a) $\{x \mid x < -1\}$ 10. $\{x \mid x \leq 1\}$

12. $\{x \mid 1 \leq x\}$ 14. $\{t \mid 17.6 < t\}$ 16. $\{x \mid x \geq -5\}$ 18. $\{x \mid -2 > x\}$

20. $\{t \mid 9 < t\}$ 22. $\{x \mid x > 6\}$ 24. $\left\{y \mid y \geq \frac{4}{5}\right\}$ 26. $\{x \mid x \leq -3\}$

28. $\{x \mid x < 50\}$ 30. $\{y \mid -0.4 \geq y\}$ 32. $\left\{y \mid y \geq \frac{9}{10}\right\}$ 34. $\{x \mid 4 \leq x\}$

36. $\{y \mid y > 15\}$ 38. -2 40. -4 42. $\{r \mid r > -0.32113\}$ 44. True

Exercise Set 4.2, pp. 189 - 190

2. $\left\{x \mid x < \frac{1}{7}\right\}$ 4. $\{y \mid y \geq 3\}$ 6. $\left\{y \mid y \geq \frac{2}{3}\right\}$ 8. $\left\{x \mid x \geq \frac{7}{6}\right\}$ 10. $\{y \mid y < 5\}$

12. All real numbers 14. $\{S \mid S \geq 84\}$ 16. $\{S \mid S \geq 93\}$ 18. $5000

Exercise Set 4.2, pp. 189 - 190 (continued)

20. {n∣n < 100}   22.

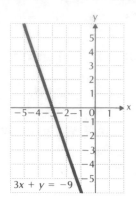

3x + y = −9

24. 0, 9   26. {m∣m ≤ 4.8}

28. $\left\{m\middle|m < \frac{7}{3}\right\}$

Exercise Set 4.3, pp. 195 - 196

2. {11,13,15,17,...}   4. {−4,−7}   6. {x∣x ≤ −15}   8. {x∣x ≥ 0}   10. True

12. False   14. False   16. True   18. False   20. True

22. Ø, {a}, {b}, {c}, {a,b}, {a,c}, {b,c}, {a,b,c}   24. {10}   26. {2,8,9,27}

28. Ø   30. Ø   32. {4,8,11}

34. y ≥ −2

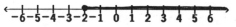

36. −2 > x

38. −4x > 24

40. x + 3 < −2

42. 4y − 9 ≥ 9y + 11

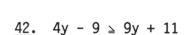

44. $\left(\frac{1}{2}, \frac{15}{2}\right]$ 46. −8   48. Z   50. Ø

Exercise Set 4.4 pp. 201 - 202

2. −1 ≤ y ≤ 3

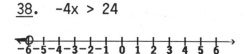

4. 0 > x > −5

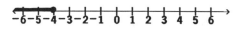

<u>6.</u> $\{x | -2 < x \le 5\}$ <u>8.</u> $\{x | 0 \le x \le 1\}$ <u>10.</u> $\left\{x \left| \frac{11}{2} \ge x \ge -\frac{7}{2}\right.\right\}$

<u>12.</u> $x \le -2$ <u>or</u> $x \ge 2$ <u>14.</u> $x \le -1$ <u>or</u> $x > 3$

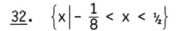

<u>16.</u> $\{x | x < -6$ <u>or</u> $x > 2\}$ <u>18.</u> $\left\{x \left| x \le -3 \text{ <u>or</u> } x \ge -\frac{5}{3}\right.\right\}$ <u>20.</u> $\{x | x < -1$ <u>or</u> $x > 5\}$

<u>22.</u> $\left\{m \left| m < -4 \text{ <u>or</u> } m \ge -\frac{2}{3}\right.\right\}$ <u>24.</u> $-\frac{8}{3}$ <u>26.</u>

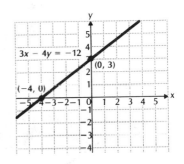

<u>28.</u> $\left\{m \left| m < \frac{6}{5}\right.\right\}$ <u>30.</u> $\left\{x \left| x < \frac{13}{40} \text{ <u>or</u> } x > \frac{17}{40}\right.\right\}$

<u>32.</u> $\left\{x \left| -\frac{1}{8} < x < \frac{1}{2}\right.\right\}$

<u>2.</u> 27   <u>4.</u> 36   <u>6.</u> 55   <u>8.</u> 15   <u>10.</u> $\left\{-\frac{12}{5}, 4\right\}$

<u>12.</u> $\{x | -5 \le x \le 5\}$

<u>14.</u> $\{y | y < -8$ <u>or</u> $y > 8\}$

<u>16.</u> $\{x | -4 < x < 8\}$

<u>18.</u> $\left\{x \left| -1 \le x \le \frac{1}{5}\right.\right\}$

<u>20.</u> $\left\{y \left| y < -\frac{4}{3} \text{ <u>or</u> } y > 4\right.\right\}$

<u>22.</u> $\left\{y \left| y \le -\frac{5}{3} \text{ <u>or</u> } y \ge \frac{19}{9}\right.\right\}$

<u>24.</u> $\left\{x \left| \frac{25}{7} \ge x \ge -5\right.\right\}$ <u>26.</u> $\{y | y < -72$ <u>or</u> $y > 120\}$ <u>28.</u> 132 adults, 118 children

<u>30.</u> No solution   <u>32.</u> All real numbers   <u>34.</u> $\{-\frac{1}{4}, 1\}$ <u>36.</u> $\{x | x \le 1\}$

2. No   4. No

6.
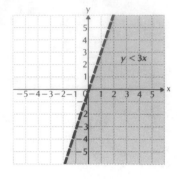

8.
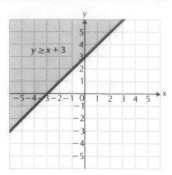

10.
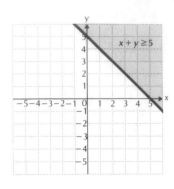

12.
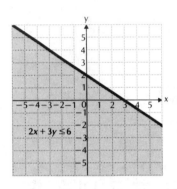

14.
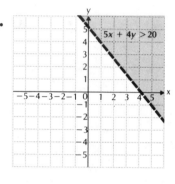

16.
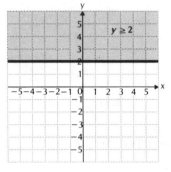

18.
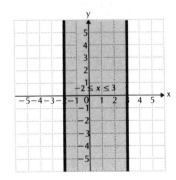

20. $\left(-\dfrac{44}{23}, \dfrac{13}{23}\right)$ 22. $-\dfrac{14}{13}$

24.   26.

28.

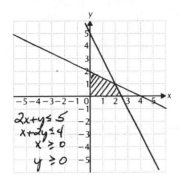

$2x+y \leq 5$
$x+2y \leq 4$
$x \geq 0$
$y \geq 0$

Exercise Set 5.1, pp. 225 - 226

<u>2</u>. 66   <u>4</u>. 187   <u>6</u>. 105   <u>8</u>. 56.52 in²   <u>10</u>. $8y^3$, $-9y^2$, $12y$, 11;

8, -9, 12, 11   <u>12</u>. $-9abc$, $19a^2bc$, $-8ab^2c$, $12abc^2$; -9, 19, -8, 12   <u>14</u>. x

<u>16</u>. None   <u>18</u>. 3, 6, 3, 0; 6; $2y^6$; 2   <u>20</u>. 6, 8, 4, 2, 0; 8; $2x^4y^4$; 2

<u>22</u>. $-4y^2 - 12$ <u>24</u>. $-2a - 6b$ <u>26</u>. $7x + 14$ <u>28</u>. $11a^2 + 3ab - 3b^2$

<u>30</u>. $-4xy^2 + 11xy + x^2y$ <u>32</u>. $-8x^4 - x^3 + x^2 + 9$ <u>34</u>. $7y^5 - 9y^4 + y^2 - y + 18$

<u>36</u>. $-11 + 8y - 2y^2 - 4y^3 + 5y^4$ <u>38</u>. $-42 + 9x - 3x^2 - 6x^3 + 5x^4$

<u>40</u>. $xy^3 - x^2y^2 + x^3y + 6$ <u>42</u>. $-9xy + 5x^2y^2 + 8x^3y^2 - 5x^4$ <u>44</u>. None of these

<u>46</u>. Trinomial   <u>48</u>. $-2x - 92$ <u>50</u>. $\frac{11}{4}$

Exercise Set 5.2, pp. 229 - 230

<u>2</u>. $21y^2 + 3y + 4$ <u>4</u>. $14x + 8y - 6z$ <u>6</u>. $-5x^2 + 4y^2 - 11z^2$

<u>8</u>. $2a^2 + 3b - 4ab + 4$ <u>10</u>. $20ab - 18ac - 3bc$ <u>12</u>. $-3x^2 - x - 3$

<u>14</u>. $-8y^4 + 18y^3 - 4y + 9$ <u>16</u>. $13y + 5$ <u>18</u>. $-13y^2 + 2y + 11$

<u>20</u>. $4x - 10y + 4z$ <u>22</u>. $5y^2 + 6y + 3y^3$ <u>24</u>. $-3y^2 - 6yz - 12z^2$ <u>26</u>. $-33.97a^2$

<u>28</u>. $15y^6$ <u>30</u>. 3, -5   <u>32</u>. $5 + 4x - x^2 + 5x^3$ <u>34</u>. $\frac{1}{2} + \frac{1}{6}y + \frac{1}{12}y^2 + \frac{1}{12}y^3 + \frac{1}{4}y^4$

Exercise Set 5.3, pp. 233 - 234

$\underline{2}$. $-6x^3y$ $\underline{4}$. $-6a^3b^4$ $\underline{6}$. $-56a^3b^4c^6$ $\underline{8}$. $4a^3 - 20a^2$ $\underline{10}$. $4x^2y - 6xy^2$

$\underline{12}$. $-4a^4 + 10a^5$ $\underline{14}$. $8a^2 - 14ab + 3b^2$ $\underline{16}$. $y^2 - 16$ $\underline{18}$. $a^2 + 4ab + 4b^2$

$\underline{20}$. $x^2 - xy - 2y^2$ $\underline{22}$. $6m^4 - 13m^2n^2 + 5n^4$ $\underline{24}$. $y^3 + 27$ $\underline{26}$. $a^3 - b^3$

$\underline{28}$. $x^4 - x^3 + x^2 - 3x + 2$ $\underline{30}$. $2x^4 - 4x^3y - x^2y^2 + 3xy^3 - 2y^4$ $\underline{32}$. $\{y \mid y < -4\}$

$\underline{34}$. $\{x \mid -7 < x < 3\}$ $\underline{36}$. $y^{3n+3}z^{n+3} - 4y^4z^{3n}$ $\underline{38}$. $6x^2 - \frac{1}{2}x^3$

Exercise Set 5.4, pp. 239 - 240

$\underline{2}$. $x^2 + 13x + 40$ $\underline{4}$. $y^2 + 3y - 28$ $\underline{6}$. $x^2 - \frac{3}{4}x + \frac{1}{8}$ $\underline{8}$. $6b^2 - 11b - 10$

$\underline{10}$. $4a^2 - 8ab + 3b^2$ $\underline{12}$. $12a^2 + 399.928ab - 2.4b^2$ $\underline{14}$. $y^2 - 14y + 49$

$\underline{16}$. $9c^2 - 3c + \frac{1}{4}$ $\underline{18}$. $4s^2 + 12st + 9t^2$ $\underline{20}$. $9s^4 + 24s^2t^2 + 16t^4$

$\underline{22}$. $x^4y^2 - 2x^3y^3 + x^2y^4$ $\underline{24}$. $100p^4 + 46p^2q + 5.29q^2$ $\underline{26}$. $x^2 - 9$

$\underline{28}$. $9 - 4x^2$ $\underline{30}$. $9x^2 - 25y^2$ $\underline{32}$. $4a^4 - 25a^2b^2$ $\underline{34}$. $16x^4 - 32x^3 + 16x^2$

$\underline{36}$. $-a^4 - 2a^3b + 25a^2 + 2ab^3 - 25b^2 + b^4$

$\underline{38}$. $y^{12} - 6y^{10} + 15y^8 - 20y^6 + 15y^4 - 6y^2 + 1$ $\underline{40}$. $r^8 - r^2s^4 - r^4s^2 + s^6$

Exercise Set 5.4A, pp. 241 - 242

$\underline{2}$. $16r^2 - \frac{8}{3}r + \frac{1}{9}$ $\underline{4}$. $9x^4 - 4y^2$ $\underline{6}$. $10c^2 - 19cd + 6d^2$ $\underline{8}$. $a^2 - 6ab + 8b^2$

$\underline{10}$. $25y^4 + 70y^2w^3 + 49w^6$ $\underline{12}$. $a^6 - 9b^4$ $\underline{14}$. $6y^2 + 11y - 10$

$\underline{16}$. $9a^4 + 12a^2 + 4$ $\underline{18}$. $x^4 - 81$ $\underline{20}$. $0.04x^2 - 0.16y^2$ $\underline{22}$. $y^4 - 16$

$\underline{24}$. $16x^4 - 8x^2y^2 + y^4$ $\underline{26}$. $m^2 + 2mn + n^2 - 4$ $\underline{28}$. $9a^2 - 12ab + 4b^2 - c^2$

$\underline{30}$. $a^2 + 2ac - b^2 - 2bd + c^2 - d^2$ $\underline{32}$. $\frac{4}{9}x^2 - \frac{1}{9}y^2 - \frac{2}{3}y - 1$

$\underline{34}$. $10y^2 - 38xy + 24x^2 - 212y + 306x + 930$ $\underline{36}$. $_Mx^2 + 2xy + y^2$

$\underline{38}$. 30

Exercise Set 5.5, pp. 245 - 246

2. $3y(2y + 1)$ 4. $5(x^2 - x + 3)$ 6. $4y^2(2 + y^2)$ 8. $2x(4y + 5z - 7w)$

10. $4(3t^5 - 5t^4 + 2t^2 - 4)$ 12. $(a - 2)(x^2 - 3)$ 14. $2m(m - 4)$

16. $6x^2(x - 6)$ 18. $(x + w)(y + z)$ 20. $(y^2 + 3)(y - 1)$

22. $(t^4 - 2)(t + 6)$ 24. $(y + 3)(y - 3)$ 26. $8(x + y)(x - y)$

28. $25a(b^2 + z^2)(b + z)(b - z)$ 30. $x^2(4x^2 + 11y^2)(4x^2 - 11y^2)$

32. $\left[\frac{1}{4} + y\right]\left[\frac{1}{4} - y\right]$ 34. $(0.1x + 0.2y)(0.1x - 0.2y)$ 36. $\left\{x \middle| x \geq 2 \text{ or } \leq -\frac{4}{7}\right\}$

38. $\left\{x \middle| x < \frac{14}{19}\right\}$ 40. $-x(x + 2h)$ 42. 14

Exercise Set 5.6, pp. 255 - 256

2. $(x - 4)^2$ 4. $(x + 8)^2$ 6. $a(a + 12)^2$ 8. $5(2y + 5)^2$ 10. $2(4x + 3)^2$

12. $(0.2x - 0.7)^2$ 14. $(x + 5)(x + 3)$ 16. $2(a - 5)^2$ 18. $(t - 5)(t + 3)$

20. $x(8 - x)(7 + x)$ 22. $(y + 9)(y + 3)$ 24. $(y^2 + 12)(y^2 - 7)$

26. $(3x + 5)(2x - 5)$ 28. $y(5y + 4)(2y - 3)$ 30. $(4a - 1)(3a - 1)$

32. $(3a + 2)(3a + 4)$ 34. $2(5x + 3)(3x - 1)$ 36. $6(3x - 4)(x + 1)$

38. $x(5x + 2)(3x - 5)$ 40. $2x^2(5x - 2)(7x - 4)$ 42. Not factorable

44. $(4m + 3n)(2m - 3n)$ 46. $(6y^2 - 5x)(5y^2 - 12x)$ 48. $(y + 0.5)(y - 0.1)$

50. $c(c^w + 1)^2$ 52. $(2x^a - 3)(2x^a + 1)$

Exercise Set 5.7, pp. 259 - 260

2. $(x - y + 5)(x - y - 5)$ 4. $(c + 2d + 3p)(c + 2d - 3p)$

6. $3(2x + 1 + y)(2x + 1 - y)$ 8. $[4 + (x - y)][4 - (x - y)]$, or

$(4 + x - y)(4 - x + y)$ 10. $y^2 - 24y + 144$ 12. $y^2 + 3.6y + 3.24$

14. $y^2 - \frac{3}{4}ay + \frac{9}{64}a^2$ 16. $(x + 22)(x + 8)$ 18. $(x - 8)(x - 24)$

20. $3(x + 11)(x + 7)$ 22. $3(x - 16b)(x - 4b)$ 24. $(x - 0.6)(x - 2.6)$

26. $\left(x - \dfrac{5}{4}\right)\left(x - \dfrac{9}{4}\right)$ 28. $\left\{\dfrac{6}{7}, \dfrac{10}{7}, -\dfrac{2}{7}\right\}$ 30. $(x - 3a)(x + a)$

32. $5.72(x + 18.6)(x - 12.4)$

Exercise Set 5.8, pp. 263 - 264

2. $(c + 3)(c^2 - 3c + 9)$ 4. $3(z - 1)(z^2 + z + 1)$ 6. $2(3x + 1)(9x^2 - 3x + 1)$

8. $(4 - 5x)(16 + 20x + 25x^2)$ 10. $(3y + 4)(9y^2 - 12y + 16)$

12. $\left(b + \dfrac{1}{3}\right)\left(b^2 - \dfrac{1}{3}b + \dfrac{1}{9}\right)$ 14. $a(b + 5)(b^2 - 5b + 25)$

16. $2(y - 3z)(y^2 + 3yz + 9z^2)$ 18. $(y + 0.5)(y^2 - 0.5y + 0.25)$

20. $(5c^2 - 2d^2)(25c^4 + 10c^2d^2 + 4d^4)$ 22. $(t^2 + 1)(t^4 - t^2 + 1)$

24. $(a - b)(a + b)(a^2 - ab + b^2)(a^2 + ab + b^2)$ 26. $\left\{x \mid -\dfrac{33}{5} \leq x \leq 9\right\}$

28. $7(x - \frac{1}{2})(x^2 + \frac{1}{2}x + \frac{1}{4})$ 30. $y(3x^2 + 3xy + y^2)$

32. $(x - 1)^3(x - 2)(x^2 - x + 1)$ 34. $3(x^a + 2y^b)(x^{2a} - 2x^ay^b + 4y^{2b})$

36. $(ax - by)(a^2x^2 + axby + b^2y^2)$

Exercise Set 5.9, pp. 267 - 268

2. $(y + 9)(y - 9)$ 4. $(4a - 1)(2a + 5)$ 6. $2x(y + 5)(y - 5)$ 8. $(p + 8)^2$

10. $3(y - 12)(y + 7)$ 12. $(4a + 9b)(4a - 9b)$ 14. $(10b + a)(7b - a)$

16. $(3m^2 + 8)(m + 3)$ 18. $(3a - 7b)(9a^2 + 21ab + 49b^2)$

20. $(x + 6)(x - 6)(x + 1)(x - 1)$ 22. $(w + z)(x - y)$

24. $(2t + 1)(4t^2 - 2t + 1)(2t - 1)(4t^2 + 2t + 1)$ 26. $(t + 5 + p)(t + 5 - p)$

28. $-2b(7a + 1)(2a - 1)$ 30. $2(x^2 + 4)(x + 2)(x - 2)$ 32. $xy(x + 5y)(x - 5y)$

34. $3(x + 3)(x - 3)(x + 2)$ 36. $2(5a + 3b)(25a^2 - 15ab + 9b^2)$

38. $(11 + y^2)(2 + y)(2 - y)$ 40. $(x + 1)(x^2 + 1)(x - 1)^3$

Exercise Set 5.9, pp. 267 - 268   (continued)

42. $5(c^{50} + 4d^{50})(c^{25} + 2d^{25})(c^{25} - 2d^{25})$ **44.** $(c^2d^2 + a^8)(cd - a^4)(cd + a^4)$

46. $y(y^4 + 1)(y^2 + 1)(y + 1)(y - 1)$ **48.** $3(a + b - c - d)(a + b + c + d)$

50. $3x(x + 5)$

Exercise Set 5.10, pp. 271 - 274

2. 9, -5 **4.** 1 **6.** -5, -3 **8.** 0, -9 **10.** -9, 9 **12.** -8, -4 **14.** 9, 5

16. 8, 1 **18.** 8, -3 **20.** 11, -12 **22.** l = 100 ft; w = 75 ft

24. 13 and 15 **26.** $-\frac{5}{2}, \frac{9}{2}$ **28.** l = 12 m; w = 9 m **30.** 6

32. h = 9 cm; b = 4 cm **34.** 16, 18, and 20 **36.** (2, -2, -4)

38. $x = \dfrac{b^2 - 3b - c}{2b - 3}$ **40.** Length is 28 cm, width is 14 cm

42. length = 40 in., width = 30 in., depth = 20 in. **44.** 54 cm^2

Exercise Set 5.11, pp. 281 - 284

2. Yes **4.** No **6.** -3 **8.** -6.4 **10.** 3 **12.** 12 **14.** -6 **16.** 0

18. 4 **20.** 7 **22.** Below 57.5° stopping distance is negative; above 32° there

is no ice **24.** About 284.3 in.^{3} **26.** a) 1 b) 6 c) 22 d) $3t^2 - 2t + 1$

e) $3a^2 + 6ah + 3h^2 - 2a - 2h + 1$ **28.** a) -6 b) -7 c) 0 d) Not possible

e) -3

30.
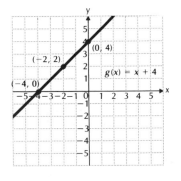

32.
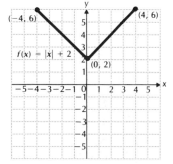

34.
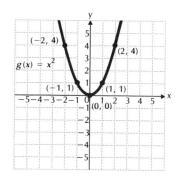

Exercise Set 5.11, pp. 281 - 284   (continued)

36. No   38. Yes   40. $x^2 + x - 1$; $x^2 - x - 3$; $x^3 + x^2 - 2x - 2$; $\dfrac{x^2 - 2}{x + 1}$;

$x^4 - 4x^2 + 4$ 42. $x^2 + 2x$; $-x^2 - 2$; $x^3 - 1$; $\dfrac{x - 1}{x^2 + x + 1}$; $x^2 - 2x + 1$

44. $28x^5 + 7x^2$, $28x^5 - 7x^2$, $196x^7$, $4x^3$, $784x^{10}$ 46. 41, 9, 400, 1.5625, 625

48. $\{x \mid x < -8 \text{ or } x > 32\}$ 50. 3   52. 0

Exercise Set 6.1, pp. 295 - 298

2. All real numbers except 6 and 9   4. All real numbers except 13

4. a) $\dfrac{(t - 3)(t + 3)}{(t + 2)(t + 3)}$ b) $\dfrac{(p - 4)(p + 5)}{(p - 5)(p + 5)}$ 6. $\dfrac{x}{3}$ 8. $a - 2$ 10. $\dfrac{x + 2}{x - 2}$

12. $\dfrac{p - 5}{p + 5}$ 14. $\dfrac{y + 5}{y - 3}$ 16. $\dfrac{m + n}{4}$ 18. $\dfrac{1}{y + 1}$ 20. $\dfrac{x^2 - 6x + 9}{x + 3}$

22. $\dfrac{1}{2x + 3y}$ 24. $6x^2$ 26. $\dfrac{x^2 + 6x + 8}{x}$ 28. $\dfrac{5x + 2}{x - 3}$ 30. $\dfrac{y^2 + 9y + 18}{3y - 12}$

32. $\dfrac{a^3 + 4a}{a^2 + 7a + 12}$ 34. $\dfrac{4y^2 - 6y + 9}{8y^2 - 14y + 3}$ 36. $\dfrac{d^2 - 6d + 5}{5d^2 + 25d}$ 38. $-\dfrac{14}{15}$ 40. $-\dfrac{16}{15}$

42. $\dfrac{246{,}636}{x^2 - 8811.5769}$ 44. $\dfrac{-4}{x - 2}$ 46. $\dfrac{a^2 + 2}{a^2 - 3}$ 48. $\dfrac{(u^2 - uv + v^2)^2}{u - v}$

Exercise Set 6.2, pp. 301 - 302

2. 60   4. 270   6. 150   8. 945   10. $\dfrac{25}{72}$ 12. $\dfrac{93}{150}$ or $\dfrac{31}{50}$ 14. $\dfrac{89}{60}$

16. $36r^2s^3$ 18. $b(a - b)(a + b)$ 20. $90x^3y^3$ 22. $(x + 5)(x + 5)(x - 3)$

24. $(y + 3)(y - 3)$ or $(y + 3)(3 - y)$ 26. $(2x + 1)(x - 1)(x - 3)(x - 3)$

28. $3y^2(4y - 1)(y - 1)$ 30. $(x - 7)^2$

32. $x^4(x - 1)(x + 1)(x^2 + x + 1)(x^2 - x + 1)(x^2 + 1)$

Exercise Set 6.3, pp. 307 - 310

2. 2   4. $\dfrac{2t + 6}{t - 4}$ 6. $r + s$ 8. $\dfrac{7}{a}$ 10. $\dfrac{-2}{y^2 - 16}$ 12. $\dfrac{2x^2 - x + 14}{x^2 - x - 12}$

14. $\dfrac{a^2 + 7ab + b^2}{a^2 - b^2}$ 16. $\dfrac{3y^2 + 7y + 14}{(2y - 5)(y + 2)(y - 1)}$ 18. $\dfrac{4y + 17}{y^2 - 4}$ 20. $\dfrac{y - 34}{20(y + 2)}$

22. $\dfrac{-x^2 + 4xy - y^2}{x^2 - y^2}$ 24. $\dfrac{2x^2 + 21x}{(x - 4)(x - 2)(x + 3)}$ 26. $\dfrac{11y - 3}{(y - 3)(y + 3)(y + 3)}$

Exercise Set 6.3, pp. 307 – 310 (continued)

28. $\dfrac{5y^2 - 11y - 6}{(y - 5)(y - 2)(y - 3)}$ 30. $\dfrac{2p^2 + 7p + 10}{(p + 6)(p - 4)(p + 4)}$ 32. $\dfrac{-y}{y^2 + 2y - 3}$

34. $\dfrac{4y - 11}{y^2 - 16}$ 36. $\dfrac{-14y^2 - 3y + 3}{4y^2 - 1}$ 38. $a^5 + 3a^4 - 3a^3 - 9a^2 + 2a + 6$

40. $\dfrac{8a^2}{a^4 - b^4}$

Exercise Set 6.4, pp. 315 – 318

2. $\dfrac{51}{5}$ 4. $\dfrac{40}{9}$ 6. $-\dfrac{225}{2}$ 8. $-4, -1$ 10. $-\dfrac{1}{2}$ 12. 14 14. -11

16. No solution 18. 3 20. $\dfrac{3}{4}$ 22. -1 24. -23 26. 11 28. 4

30. 3 32. No solution 34. 2 36. No solution

38. $4(t + 5)(t^2 - 5t + 125)$ 40. $(y - 30)(y + 20)$ 42. $-\dfrac{7}{2}$

44. All real numbers except -4 and -3.

Exercise Set 6.5, pp. 325 – 328

2. $-3, -2$ 4. $\dfrac{35}{12}$ 6. $1\dfrac{5}{7}$ hours 8. $9\dfrac{9}{10}$ hours 10. $2\dfrac{19}{40}$ hours

12. A, $1\dfrac{1}{3}$ hours; B, 4 hours 14. 12 mph 16. 450 km

18. Passenger, 80 mph; Freight, 66 mph 20. $1\dfrac{1}{5}$ km/h 22. 12 mi

24. $21\dfrac{9}{11}$ min. until 11:00 26. 1400 mi round trip 28. 30 mi 30. 51.4 mph

Exercise Set 6.6, pp. 331 – 332

2. $W_2 = \dfrac{d_2 W_1}{d_1}$ 4. $v_1 = \dfrac{2s - v_2 t}{t}$ 6. $R = \dfrac{r_1 r_2}{r_1 + r_2}$ 8. $r = \dfrac{2V - IR}{2I}$

10. $f = \dfrac{pq}{q + p}$ 12. $n = \dfrac{IR}{E - Ir}$ 14. $t_1 = \dfrac{H + Smt_2}{Sm}$ 16. $r = \dfrac{eR}{E - e}$

18. $R = \dfrac{3V + \pi h^3}{3\pi h^2}$ 20. $(3x + 5)(2x - 7)$ 22. $-\dfrac{5}{3}, \dfrac{7}{2}$ 24. $t = \dfrac{ab}{a + b}$

26. $b = \dfrac{at}{a - t}$

Exercise Set 6.7, pp. 337 – 338

2. $\dfrac{5}{12}$; $y = \dfrac{5}{12}x$ 4. $\dfrac{2}{5}$; $y = \dfrac{2}{5}x$ 6. $\dfrac{3}{2}$; $y = \dfrac{3}{2}x$ 8. $66\dfrac{2}{3}$ cm 10. 204,000,000

12. 40 kg 14. 64; $y = \dfrac{64}{x}$ 16. 45; $y = \dfrac{45}{x}$ 18. 0.45; $y = \dfrac{0.45}{x}$

<u>20</u>. 27 minutes   <u>22</u>. 450 m   <u>24</u>. h(2x + h)   <u>26</u>.

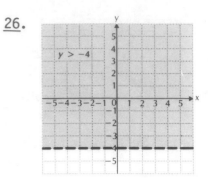

<u>28</u>. a) Inversely b) Neither c) Directly

d) Directly e) Directly

Exercise Set 6.8, pp. 341 - 342

<u>2</u>. $\dfrac{1 + 7y}{1 - 5y}$ <u>4</u>. $\dfrac{y^2 + 1}{y^2 - 1}$ <u>6</u>. $\dfrac{2z + 5y}{z - 4y}$ <u>8</u>. $\dfrac{a + b}{a}$ <u>10</u>. $\dfrac{3}{3x + 2}$ <u>12</u>. $\dfrac{1}{x - y}$

<u>14</u>. $\dfrac{1}{a(a - h)}$ <u>16</u>. $\dfrac{(x - 4)(x - 7)}{(x - 5)(x + 6)}$ <u>18</u>. $\dfrac{-4a - 4}{8a - 5}$ <u>20</u>. $\dfrac{x^4}{81}$ <u>22</u>. $\dfrac{x}{x^3 - 1}$

<u>24</u>. $\dfrac{1}{a^2 - ab + b^2}$

Exercise Set 6.9, pp. 347 - 348

<u>2</u>. $4y^4 + 3y^3 - 6$ <u>4</u>. $12a^2 + 14a - 10$ <u>6</u>. y - 4

<u>8</u>. y - 5, R -50; or $y - 5 + \dfrac{-50}{y - 5}$ <u>10</u>. t - 4, R -21; or $t - 4 + \dfrac{-21}{t - 3}$

<u>12</u>. $2x^2 - 3x + 4$, R -26; or $2x^2 - 3x + 4 + \dfrac{-26}{3x + 4}$

<u>14</u>. $3x^2 - x + 4$, R 10; or $3x^2 - x + 4 + \dfrac{10}{2x - 3}$

<u>16</u>. $3x^2 + 2x - 5$, R(2x - 5); or $3x^2 + 2x - 5 + \dfrac{2x - 5}{x^2 - 2}$

<u>18</u>. $\dfrac{8}{5}$, $-\dfrac{8}{5}$ <u>20</u>. $-\dfrac{7}{4}$ <u>22</u>. $2y^3 + 6y^2 + 17y + 45$, R 116y - 48   <u>24</u>. $a^2 + ab$

<u>26</u>. $a^6 - a^5b + a^4b^2 - a^3b^3 + a^2b^4 - ab^5 + b^6$

Exercise Set 6.10, pp. 351 - 352

<u>2</u>. $x^2 - 3x + 5$, R -10   <u>4</u>. a + 15, R 41   <u>6</u>. $x^2 - 9x + 5$, R -7

<u>8</u>. $3x^2 + 16x + 44$, R 135   <u>10</u>. $x^2 - 4x + 8$, R -8   <u>12</u>. $6y^3 - 3y^2 + 9y + 1$, R 3

<u>14</u>. $y^2 - 3y + 9$ <u>16</u>. $x^4 + 2x^3 + 4x^2 + 8x + 16$

18.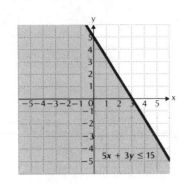

20.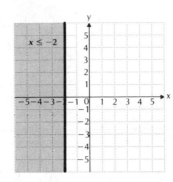

22. $5.032x^4 - 85.89624x^3 + 1477.6628x^2 - 25,223.704x + 430,568.62$, R $-7,349,589$

Exercise Set 7.1, pp. 365 - 366

2. 1   4. $y^3 + z$ 6. $-16s^4t^{-2}$ or $\dfrac{-16s^4}{t^2}$ 8. $9x^{-6}y^{10}$ or $\dfrac{9y^{10}}{x^6}$ 10. $8z^{-2}$ or $\dfrac{8}{z^2}$

12. $-35c^2d^{-1}$ or $\dfrac{-35c^2}{d}$ 14. $-25x^{-2}y^2$ or $-\dfrac{25y^2}{x^2}$ 16. $\dfrac{x^{-1}y^{-1}}{3}$ or $\dfrac{1}{3xy}$

18. $-\dfrac{a^{12}b^{15}}{64}$ 20. $\dfrac{8}{27}x^{-18}y^{-27}$, or $\dfrac{8}{27x^{18}y^{27}}$ 22. 2.6×10^{12} 24. 1.095×10^6

26. 2.63×10^{-7} 28. 9×10^{-11} 30. $92,400,000$

32. $0.00000000000000000000000000000911$ 34. $234,000,000$ 36. 0.07034

38. 3.38×10^{-4} 40. 2.6732×10^4 42. 1.5×10^3 44. 3×10^{-5}

46. 2.0951×10^8; 8.953×10^{-1} 48. 8.10^{-90}, 7.1×10^{-90} 50. 8

52. $c = \dfrac{7 - 2a}{4 - a}$ 54. $\dfrac{2}{27}$

Exercise Set 7.2, pp. 371 - 372

2. 15, -15   4. 3, -3   6. 9, -9   8. $-\dfrac{19}{3}$ 10. 21   12. $-\dfrac{9}{12}$ or $-\dfrac{3}{4}$

14. 0.6   16. 0.12   18. $y^2 - 8$ 20. $\dfrac{a}{a^2 - b}$ 22. $|5t|$ or $5|t|$

24. $|6b|$ or $6|b|$ 26. $|5 - b|$ 28. $|y + 8|$ 30. $|3x - 5|$ 32. -4

34. $-5y$ 36. 10   38. $0.02(y - 2)$ 40. -4   42. 2   44. $-\dfrac{1}{2}$ 46. $|y|$

48. $|7b|$ or $7|b|$ 50. 10 52. $|2a + b|$ 54. -6 56. 2xy 58. $4x^2 - 9$

60. $2(x - 4)(x - 9)$

Exercise Set 7.3, pp. 379 - 380

2. $\sqrt{35}$ 4. $\sqrt[3]{14}$ 6. $\sqrt[4]{18}$ 8. $\sqrt{26xy}$ 10. $\sqrt[5]{80y^4}$ 12. $\sqrt{y^2 - b^2}$

14. $3\sqrt{2}$ 16. $2\sqrt{5}$ 18. $3\sqrt{10}$ 20. $5y^3\sqrt{7}$ 22. $2y\sqrt[3]{5}$ 24. 8

26. $2\sqrt[3]{5}$ 28. $30\sqrt{2}$ 30. $2x^2y\sqrt{6}$ 32. $25t^3\sqrt[3]{t}$ 34. $(x + y)^2\sqrt[3]{(x + y)^2}$

36. $6xy^3\sqrt{3xy}$ 38. Rational 40. Irrational 42. Irrational

44. Irrational 46. Rational 48. Rational 50. Rational 52. Irrational

54. 11.136 56. -3.071 58. $x^2 - \frac{2}{3}x + \frac{1}{9}$ 60. (a) 20 mph; (b) 37.4 mph;

(c) 42.4 mph 62. $572\sqrt{3}$

Exercise Set 7.4, pp. 383 - 384

2. $\frac{10}{9}$ 4. $\frac{7}{8}$ 6. $\frac{11}{x}$ 8. $\frac{6a^2\sqrt{a}}{b^3}$ 10. $\frac{4x^2\sqrt[3]{x}}{6y^2}$ 12. $\sqrt{7}$ 14. 2

16. $2b\sqrt{2b}$ 18. $3xy\sqrt[3]{y^2}$ 20. $\frac{5\sqrt{ab}}{3}$ 22. $\sqrt{r^2 - rs + s^2}$ 24. $7y\sqrt{7y}$

26. $5r\sqrt[3]{5r}$ 28. $24x^3y\sqrt{3y}$ 30. $3x\sqrt[3]{3xy^2}$ 32. $\frac{15}{2}$

34. (a) 1.62 sec; (b) 1.99 sec; (c) 2.20 sec 36. $9\sqrt[3]{9n^2}$

Exercise Set 7.5, pp. 387 - 388

2. $17\sqrt{5}$ 4. $8\sqrt[5]{2}$ 6. $3\sqrt[4]{t}$ 8. $7\sqrt{6}$ 10. $6\sqrt{7} + \sqrt[4]{11}$ 12. $41\sqrt{2}$

14. $66\sqrt{3}$ 16. $4\sqrt{5}$ 18. -7 20. $55\sqrt{2}$ 22. $(4x - 2)\sqrt{3x}$

24. $(3 - x)\sqrt[3]{2x}$ 26. $3\sqrt{3t + 3}$ 28. $(2 - x)\sqrt{x - 1}$ 30. 15 ft by 12 ft

32. $(25x - 30y - 9xy)\sqrt{2xy}$ 34. $(7x^2 - 2y^2)\sqrt{x + y}$

2. $4\sqrt{3} + 3$ 4. $5 - \sqrt{10}$ 6. $6\sqrt{5} - 4$ 8. $3 - 4\sqrt[3]{63}$ 10. $-2x\sqrt[3]{3}$ 12. -1

14. -45 16. $x - y$ 18. $2 + 2\sqrt{6}$ 20. $2 - 3\sqrt{3}$ 22. $24 - 7\sqrt{15}$

24. $2 - 3\sqrt{x} + x$ 26. $6\sqrt[4]{63} - 9\sqrt[4]{42} + 2\sqrt[4]{54} - 3\sqrt[4]{36}$ 28. $6 + 2\sqrt{5}$ 30. $\dfrac{x - 2}{x + 3}$

32. $2x - 2\sqrt{x^2 - 4}$ 34. $\sqrt[3]{y} - y$ 36. $12 + 6\sqrt{3}$

38. $16(a + 3) + 38a\sqrt{3(a + 3)} - 15a^2$ 40. $2\sqrt{34}$

2. $\dfrac{\sqrt{66}}{6}$ 4. $\dfrac{\sqrt{154}}{7}$ 6. $\dfrac{\sqrt{6}}{5}$ 8. $\dfrac{\sqrt[3]{9}}{3}$ 10. $\dfrac{\sqrt[3]{63xy^2}}{3y}$ 12. $\dfrac{a\sqrt[3]{147ab}}{7b}$

14. $\dfrac{\sqrt[4]{a^3b^3}}{ab}$ 16. $\dfrac{6}{\sqrt{30x}}$ 18. $\dfrac{2}{\sqrt{5}}$ 20. $\dfrac{35}{2\sqrt{14}}$ 22. $\dfrac{5}{\sqrt[3]{100}}$ 24. $\dfrac{3a}{\sqrt{3ab}}$

26. $\dfrac{3a^2}{\sqrt[3]{63ab^2}}$ 28. $\dfrac{xy}{5\sqrt{xy}}$ 30. $\dfrac{7(9 - \sqrt{10})}{71}$ 32. $\dfrac{3\sqrt{2}(\sqrt{3} + \sqrt{5})}{2}$

34. $-\dfrac{3\sqrt{2} + 2\sqrt{42} - 3\sqrt{15} - 6\sqrt{35}}{25}$ 36. $\dfrac{a + 2\sqrt{ab} + b}{a - b}$ 38. $\dfrac{4\sqrt{6} + 9}{3}$

40. $\dfrac{7}{5(3 + \sqrt{2}}$ 42. $\dfrac{-3}{3\sqrt{2} + 3\sqrt{3} + 7\sqrt{6} + 21}$ 44. $\dfrac{x - y}{x - 2\sqrt{xy} + y}$

46. $\dfrac{53}{75\sqrt{6} - 187}$ 48. 1 50. $\dfrac{15y + 20y\sqrt{z} + 6\sqrt{yz} + 8z\sqrt{y}}{25y - 4z}$ 52. $\dfrac{36 + 12\sqrt{3} - y}{6 + y}$

54. $\dfrac{1}{\sqrt{y + 18} + \sqrt{y}}$ 56. $\dfrac{-3\sqrt{a^2 - 3}}{a^2 - 3}$ 58. $1 - \sqrt{w}$

2. $\sqrt[5]{y}$ 4. 4 6. $\sqrt[4]{x^3y^3}$ 8. 128 10. $19\frac{1}{3}$ 12. $(x^3y^2z^2)^{1/7}$

14. $(7xy)^{4/3}$ 16. $(2a^5b)^{7/6}$ 18. $\dfrac{1}{y^{1/4}}$ 20. $x^{5/6}$ 22. $11^{7/6}$ 24. $9^{2/11}$

26. $3.9^{7/20}$ 28. $5^{5/21}$ 30. $\sqrt[3]{y}$ 32. x^2y^3 34. $\sqrt{3}$ 36. $2x\sqrt{y}$

38. $2x^3y^4$ 40. $\dfrac{x^3y^4}{2}$ 42. $\sqrt{2ts}$ 44. $3x^2y^2$ 46. $\sqrt[12]{7^45^3}$ 48. $\sqrt[15]{27y^8}$

50. $\sqrt[4]{3xy^2 + 24xy + 48x}$ 52. $\sqrt[12]{(x + y)^{-1}}$ 54. $\sqrt[12]{x^4y^3z^2}$ 56. $\sqrt[5]{xy^8}$

Exercise Set 7.8, pp. 405 - 406   (continued)

58. $x^3 \cdot \sqrt[6]{x}$ **60.** $\sqrt[4]{2xy^2}$ **62.** $\sqrt[6]{p + q}$ **64.** x^3

Exercise Set 7.9, pp. 411 - 412

2. 123   **4.** 84   **6.** -64   **8.** No solution   **10.** $-\dfrac{5}{3}$ **12.** 2

14. No solution   **16.** 7, 3   **18.** $\dfrac{15}{4}$ **20.** 1   **22.** h = 7 in., b = 9 in.

24. -8, 8   **26.** -4, 3   **28.** 1, 8   **30.** $\dfrac{1}{36}$, 36   **32.** 25   **34.** 3

Exercise Set 7.10, pp. 415 - 416

2. $\sqrt{164}$; 12.806   **4.** $\sqrt{200}$; 14.142   **6.** $\sqrt{119}$; 10.909   **8.** 4

10. $\sqrt{19}$; 4.359   **12.** $\sqrt{4 - n}$ **14.** $\sqrt{8450}$; 91.924 ft

16. $\sqrt{10{,}561}$; 102.77 ft   **18.** $s + s\sqrt{2}$ **20.** 8.9 ft   **22.** 3, 4, 5

24. $x^2 + \dfrac{b}{a}x + \dfrac{b^2}{4a^2}$ **26.** 50 ft²

Exercise Set 7.11, pp. 421 - 422

2. $i\sqrt{17}$ or $\sqrt{17}i$ **4.** 5i   **6.** $-2i\sqrt{5}$ or $-2\sqrt{5}i$ **8.** 5 + 11i   **10.** -1 - 8i

12. 8 + i   **14.** -9 + 5i   **16.** -3 + 2i   **18.** 4 - 7i   **20.** -7 + 26i

22. 16 + 7i   **24.** 40 + 13i   **26.** 8 + 31i   **28.** 1   **30.** -243i   **32.** 21 - 20i

34. 12 + 16i   **36.** 21 + 20i   **38.** $\dfrac{15}{26} + \dfrac{29}{26}i$ **40.** $\dfrac{6}{25} - \dfrac{17}{25}i$ **42.** $\dfrac{8}{5} - \dfrac{3}{5}i$

44. Yes   **46.** No   **48.** $\dfrac{70}{29}$ **50.** -4 - 8i   **52.** -3 - 4i   **54.** -88i   **56.** 8

58. $\dfrac{3}{5} + \dfrac{9}{5}i$ **60.** 1

Exercise Set 8.1, pp. 433 - 436

2. $\pm\sqrt{7}$ **4.** $\pm\dfrac{4}{3}i$ **6.** $\pm\dfrac{\sqrt{21}}{3}$ **8.** 0, $-\dfrac{8}{19}$ **10.** 0, -4   **12.** 6, 1

14. $-\dfrac{3}{2}$, -5   **16.** -7, -2   **18.** $-\dfrac{3}{4}$, -2   **20.** 15, 1   **22.** 3 cm

24. Length is 8 m; width is 3 m   **26.** Length is 26 cm; width is 13 cm

28. 24 m, 7 m   **30.** 5 m, 12 m   **32.** 400 ft   **34.** 8.3 sec   **36.** $2\sqrt{22}$

38. $\dfrac{\sqrt{10}}{5}$ **40.** $-\dfrac{5}{3}, 4, \dfrac{5}{2}$ **42.** $\dfrac{1}{18}, \dfrac{1}{3}$ **44.** 5, 6, 7

Exercise Set 8.2, pp. 441 - 442

2. $3 \pm \sqrt{13}$ **4.** $3 \pm \sqrt{7}$ **6.** $\dfrac{-1 \pm i\sqrt{7}}{2}$ **8.** $3 \pm 2i$ **10.** $3 \pm \sqrt{5}$

12. $1 \pm 2i$ **14.** 0, -1   **16.** 2, -3   **18.** $-1 \pm 2i$ **20.** $-1, \dfrac{1 \pm i\sqrt{3}}{2}$

22. -0.8, -5.2   **24.** 1.5, -0.5   **26.** 0.5700731, -0.7973459   **28.** $\dfrac{22 \pm 4i\sqrt{31}}{7}$

30. $-\sqrt{3} \pm \sqrt{2}$ **32.** $\sqrt{3}, \dfrac{3 - \sqrt{3}}{2}$

Exercise Set 8.3, pp. 447 - 450

2. -7, 4   **4.** -8, 2   **6.** 2, -1   **8.** 6, -3   **10.** $\pm 5\sqrt{2}$

12. First part 60 mph; Second part 50 mph   **14.** 40 mph   **16.** A, 200 mph

B, 250 mph; or A, 150 mph B, 200 mph   **18.** 12 hours   **20.** 9.34 mph   **22.** $\dfrac{1}{x - 2}$

24. A, 24.0 hours; B, 51.0 hours   **26.** $\dfrac{-3 \pm \sqrt{57}}{2}$ **28.** $\dfrac{-i \pm \sqrt{23}}{4}$

Exercise Set 8.4, pp. 453 - 454

2. One real   **4.** Two nonreal   **6.** Two real   **8.** Two real   **10.** Two nonreal

12. Two real   **14.** Two real   **16.** Two real   **18.** $x^2 - 16 = 0$

20. $x^2 + 10x + 25 = 0$ **22.** $8x^2 + 6x + 1 = 0$ **24.** $12x^2 - (4k + 3m)x + km = 0$

26. $x^2 - \sqrt{3}x - 6 = 0$ **28.** The sum of the solutions is $\dfrac{-b + \sqrt{b^2 - 4ac}}{2a} +$

$\dfrac{-b - \sqrt{b^2 - 4ac}}{2a} = \dfrac{-2b}{2a} = -\dfrac{b}{a}.$ **30.** (a) k = 2; (b) $\dfrac{11}{2}$ **32.** -1

Exercise Set 8.5, pp. 457 - 458

2. $r = \dfrac{1}{2}\sqrt{\dfrac{A}{\pi}}$ **4.** $s = \sqrt{\dfrac{kQ_1Q_2}{N}}$ **6.** $r = \sqrt{\dfrac{A}{\pi}}$ **8.** $c = \sqrt{d^2 - a^2 - b^2}$

10. $t = \dfrac{-v_0 + \sqrt{v_0^2 + 2gs}}{g}$ **12.** $r = \dfrac{-\pi s + \sqrt{\pi^2 s^2 + 4\pi A}}{2\pi}$ **14.** $L = \dfrac{1}{W^2 C}$

16. $R = \sqrt{\dfrac{6.2A^2}{Np + p^2}}$ 18. $C = \dfrac{vm}{\sqrt{m^2 - m_0^2}}$ 20. $\dfrac{x - 9}{(x + 7)(x + 9)}$

Exercise Set 8.6, pp. 461 - 462

2. $\dfrac{1}{4}$, 16   4. $\pm\sqrt{2}$, ± 1 6. 1   8. $-\dfrac{3}{2}$, 1, $\dfrac{1}{2}$, -1   10. $\pm\sqrt{\dfrac{5 + \sqrt{5}}{2}}$,

$\pm\sqrt{\dfrac{5 - \sqrt{5}}{2}}$ 12. $\dfrac{4}{5}$, -1   14. $-\dfrac{1}{10}$, 1   16. 4L of A, 8L of B   18. 28.5

20. $3 \pm \sqrt{10}$, $-1 \pm \sqrt{2}$ 22. 259

Exercise Set 8.7, pp. 467 - 468

2. $y = \dfrac{2}{3}x^2$ 4. $y = \dfrac{54}{x^2}$ 6. $y = \dfrac{5x}{z}$ 8. $y = \dfrac{xz}{w}$ 10. $y = \dfrac{5xz}{4w^2}$

12. 624.24 in²   14. $22.5\dfrac{W}{m^2}$ 16. 220 cm³   18. $7.20

Exercise Set 8.8, pp. 475 - 476

2.
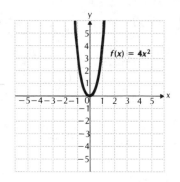

4.
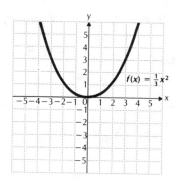

6.
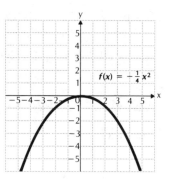

8.
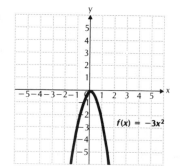

10.
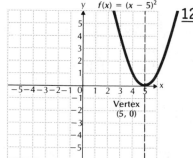

12.
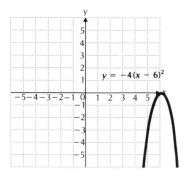

14.

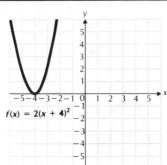

$f(x) = 2(x + 4)^2$

16.

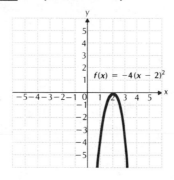

$f(x) = -4(x - 2)^2$

18.

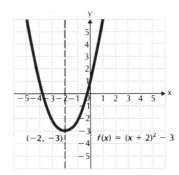

$(-2, -3)$ $f(x) = (x + 2)^2 - 3$

20.

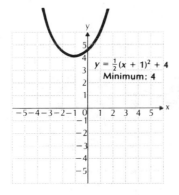

$y = \frac{1}{2}(x + 1)^2 + 4$
Minimum: 4

22.

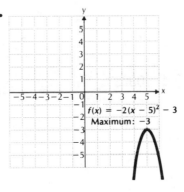

$f(x) = -2(x - 5)^2 - 3$
Maximum: −3

24.

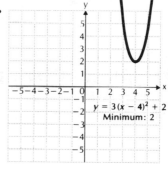

$y = 3(x - 4)^2 + 2$
Minimum: 2

26.

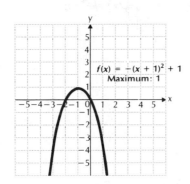

$f(x) = -(x + 1)^2 + 1$
Maximum: 1

Exercise Set 8.9, pp. 481 - 482

2. $f(x) = (x + 1)^2 - 6$

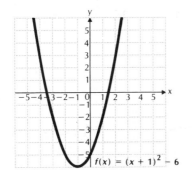

$f(x) = (x + 1)^2 - 6$

4. $f(x) = -(x + 2)^2 + 7$

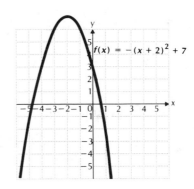

$f(x) = -(x + 2)^2 + 7$

6. $f(x) = 4(x + 1)^2 - 7$

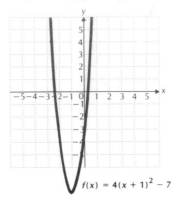

8. $f(x) = -2\left[x + \frac{1}{2}\right]^2 + \frac{7}{2}$

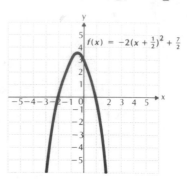

10. $(2 - \sqrt{3}, 0)$, $(2 + \sqrt{3}, 0)$ 12. $(-1, 0)$, $(3, 0)$ 14. None   16. $\left[-\frac{3}{2}, 0\right]$

18. 5   20. $(3.136756, 0)$, $(-1.008083, 0)$ 22.

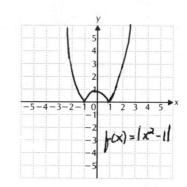

24. $x = \dfrac{p + q}{2}$

Exercise Set 8.10, pp. 485 - 488

2. 17 ft by 17 ft; 289 ft²   4. 506.25; 22.5 and 22.5   6. -9; 3 and -3

8. $-\dfrac{49}{4}$; $\dfrac{7}{2}$ and $-\dfrac{7}{2}$ 10. $f(x) = 3x^2 - x + 2$ 12. $f(x) = x^2 - 5x$

14. (a) $f(x) = 2500x^2 - 6500x + 5000$; (b) $19,000

16. (a) $f(x) = \dfrac{3}{16}x^2 - \dfrac{135}{4}x + 1750$; (b) 531.25   18. $P(x) = -x^2 + 980x - 3000$;

Max = $237,100 at x = 490   20. $5xy^2 \sqrt[4]{x}$ 22. b = 19 cm, h = 19 cm, A = $180\frac{1}{2}$ cm²

24. 4050 ft²

Exercise Set 9.1, pp. 497 - 498

2. 10   4. 10   6. $\sqrt{464} \approx 21.541$ 8. $\sqrt{98.93} \approx 9.946$ 10. $\sqrt{13} \approx 3.606$

12. $\left[\frac{13}{2}, -1\right]$ **14.** $\left[0, -\frac{1}{2}\right]$ **16.** $\left[\frac{5}{2}, 1\right]$ **18.** (4.65, 0)   **20.** $\left[-\frac{27}{80}, \frac{1}{24}\right]$

22. $\left[\frac{5}{2}, \frac{7}{2}\sqrt{3}\right]$ **24.** $\pm 2, \pm 4$

26. 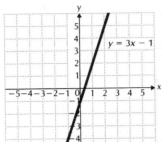   **28.** $2\sqrt{a^2 + b^2}$ **30.** $2\sqrt{3}c$ **32.** Yes   **34.** (0, 4)

Exercise Set 9.2, pp. 503 - 504

2. $(x - 2)^2 + (y + 3)^2 = 1$
Center: (2, -3)
Radius: 1

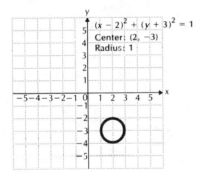

4. $x^2 + (y - 1)^2 = 3$
Center: (0, 1)
Radius: $\sqrt{3}$

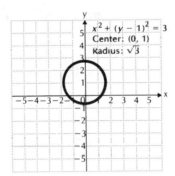

6. $x^2 + y^2 = 9$
Center: (0, 0)
Radius: 3

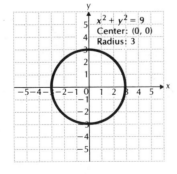

8. $x^2 + y^2 = 16$ **10.** $(x - 5)^2 + (y - 6)^2 = 12$

12. $(-3, 2), r = 2\sqrt{7}$ **14.** $(-3, -2), r = 1$

16. $(0, -5), r = 10$ **18.**

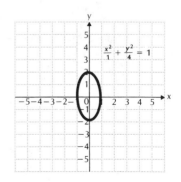

20.

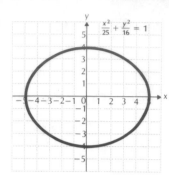

22. $(x + 4)^2 + (y - 1)^2 = 72$

24. $(x - 3)^2 + y^2 = 25$

26. $\dfrac{(x - 1)^2}{25} + \dfrac{(y + 1)^2}{4} = 1$, c: (1, -1),

v: (6, -1), (-4, -1), (1, 1), (1, -3)

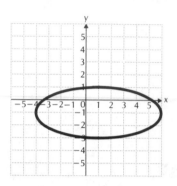

Exercise Set 9.3, pp. 511 - 512

2.

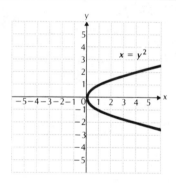

4.

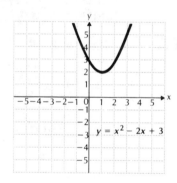

6.

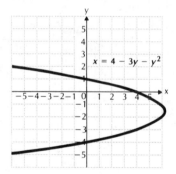

8.

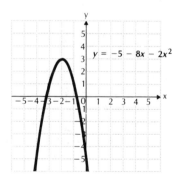

10.

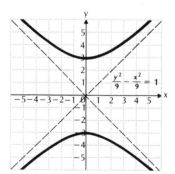

12.

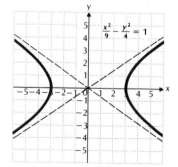

Exercise Set 9.3, pp. 511 - 512 (continued)

14. 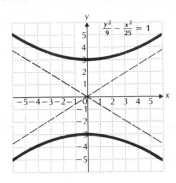 16. 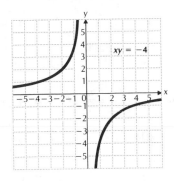 18.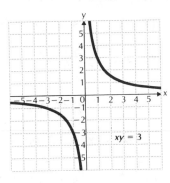

20. $\pm i\sqrt{5}$ 22. 400 mph, 720 mph 24. Parabola 26. Hyperbola 28. Circle

Exercise Set 9.4, pp. 517 - 518

2. $(-8, -6)$, $(6, 8)$ 4. $(2, 0)$, $(0, 3)$ 6. $(2, 4)(1, 1)$

8. $\left(\frac{11}{4}, -\frac{9}{8}\right)$, $(1, -2)$ 10. $\left(-\frac{9}{5}, \frac{8}{5}\right)$, $(3, 0)$

12. $\left(\frac{7 + \sqrt{33}}{2}, \frac{7 - \sqrt{33}}{2}\right)$, $\left(\frac{7 - \sqrt{33}}{2}, \frac{7 + \sqrt{33}}{2}\right)$ 14. 8 and 7

16. Length is 2 in.; width is 1 in. 18. Length is 12 ft, width is 5 ft

20. $\frac{5 \pm \sqrt{97}}{6}$ 22. $2a^6d^2 \sqrt[4]{2d}$ 24. -2

Exercise Set 9.5, pp. 521 - 522

2. $(0, 0)$ $(1, 1)$ 4. $(0, 2)$, $(0, -2)$ 6. $(2, 4)$, $(-2, -4)$, $(4, 2)$, $(-4, -2)$

8. $(2, 1)$, $(-2, -1)$ 10. $(2, 1)$, $(-2, -1)$, $(1, 2)$, $(-1, -2)$

12. $(3, \sqrt{5})$, $(-3, -\sqrt{5})$, $(\sqrt{5}, 3)$, $(-\sqrt{5}, -3)$ 14. 6 and 10, -6 and -10

16. Length is $\sqrt{2}$ m, width is 1 m 18. $125, 6% 20. $\frac{x - 2\sqrt{xh} + h}{x - h}$

22. ½, ¼; ½, -¼; -½, ¼; -½,-¼ 24. 10 in. by 7 in. by 5 in.

Exercise Set 9.6, pp. 527 - 528

2. $\{x \mid x < -1 \text{ or } x > 4\}$ 4. $\{x \mid -3 \leqslant x \leqslant 5\}$ 6. $\{x \mid -2 < x < 1\}$

8. $\{x \mid -2 \leqslant x \leqslant 2\}$ 10. No solution 12. $\{x \mid x < -2 \text{ or } x > 6\}$

14. $\{x|-1 < x < 0 \text{ or } x > 1\}$ 16. $\{x|x < -2 \text{ or } 1 < x < 4\}$

18. $\{x|x < -1 \text{ or } 2 < x < 3\}$ 20. $\{x|x > -5\}$ 22. $\{x|-5 < x < 2\}$

24. $\left\{x\left|x < -\frac{3}{4} \text{ or } x \geqslant \frac{5}{2}\right.\right\}$ 26. $\left\{x\left|x < \frac{3}{2} \text{ or } x \geqslant 4\right.\right\}$

28. $\{x|-4 < x < -3 \text{ or } x > 1\}$ 30. $\{x|-3 \leqslant x < 0\}$ 32. $\{x|1 < x < 2\}$

34. $\{x|-7 < x < -2 \text{ or } x > 2\}$ 36. $\left\{x\left|x < 0 \text{ or } x \geqslant \frac{1}{3}\right.\right\}$

38. $\{x|x < -1 - \sqrt{5} \text{ or } x > -1 + \sqrt{5}$

Exercise Set 10.1, pp. 539 - 540

2.

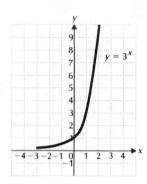

$y = 3^x$

4.

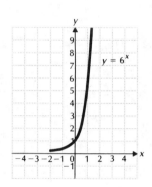

$y = 6^x$

6.

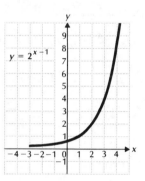

$y = 2^{x-1}$

8.

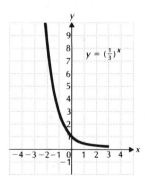

$y = \left(\frac{1}{3}\right)^x$

10.

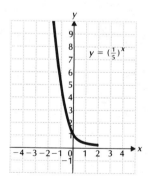

$y = \left(\frac{1}{5}\right)^x$

12.

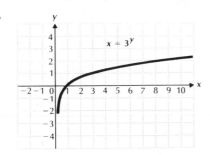

14. x^{-2} or $\frac{1}{x^2}$ 16. x^{-7} or $\frac{1}{x^7}$

18.

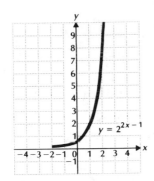

20.

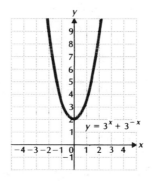

22.

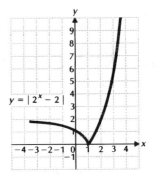

Exercise Set 10.2, pp. 545 - 546

2.

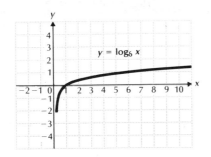

4. $2 = \log_{10} 100$ 6. $-5 = \log_4 \frac{1}{1024}$

8. $\frac{1}{4} = \log_{16} 2$ 10. $0.4771 = \log_{10} 3$

12. $7^h = 10$ 14. $6^1 = 6$ 16. $10^{-2} = 0.01$

18. $10^{0.4771} = 3$ 20. 64   22. 4   24. $\frac{1}{9}$

26. 2   28. 5   30. -3   32. 1   34. 6

36. -4   38. 0   40. 8.45×10^{-2} 42. $\sqrt[5]{x^4}$

44.

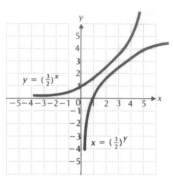

46.

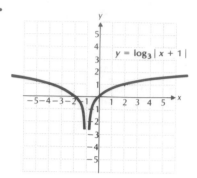

48. 25   50. -25, 4   52. $\frac{2}{3}$ 54. x^2 56. 0

Exercise Set 10.3, pp. 551 - 552

2. $\log_3 27 + \log_3 81$ 4. $\log_5 25 + \log_5 125$ 6. $\log_t 5 + \log_t y$

8. $\log_b (65.2)$ 10. $\log_t (H \cdot M)$ 12. $\frac{1}{4} \log_b t$ 14. $\log_t T - \log_t 7$

16. $\log_b \frac{42}{7}$ or $\log_b 6$ 18. $\log_a 5 + \log_a x + 4 \log_a y + 3 \log_a z$

20. $\frac{1}{3}\left[4 \log_c x - 3 \log_c y - 2 \log_c z\right]$

22. $2 \log_b p + 5 \log_b q - 4 \log_b m - 7 \log_b n$ 24. $\log_a \frac{\sqrt{x}\ y^3}{x^2}$ or $\log_a \frac{y^3}{x\sqrt{x}}$

26. $\log_a x$ 28. $\log_a \frac{\sqrt{a}}{x}$ 30. 5   32. $23 - 18i$ 34. $\log_a (x^3 + y^3)$

36. $\frac{1}{2} \log_a (c - d) - \frac{1}{2} \log_a (c + d)$

Exercise Set 10.4, pp. 559 - 562

2. $\log 3 \times 5 = \log 3 + \log 5 \approx 0.4771 + 0.6990 = \log 1.1761$; antilog $1.1761 \approx 15$

4. $\log \frac{16}{8} = \log 16 - \log 8 \approx 1.2041 - 0.9031 = 0.3010$; antilog $0.3010 \approx 2$

6. 0.8837   8. 0.9330   10. 0.6628   12. 3.9405   14. 1.3139   16. 4.7952

18. 0.3345 + (-3)   20. 0.5403 + (-3)   22. 83,600   24. 426   26. 0.0973

28. 0.00599   30. 346   32. 0.0346   34. 0.00000426   36. 4.7543

38. 4.0914   40. 1.2487   42. -1.6421   44. -3.6990   46. -0.2981

Exercise Set 10.4, pp. 559 - 562   (continued)

48. 36,897.76 **50.** 1,000,000,000 **52.** 0.0045 **54.** 0.01 **56.** 0.00001

58. 0.0631 **60.** 2.1878 **62.** 1000 **64.** 11.5129 **66.** -7.0470 **68.** 2.9339

70. -0.9188 **72.** 5.6419 **74.** 22,026.47 **76.** 25.662 **78.** 0.0316

80. 0.0389 **82.** 0, $\frac{b}{a}$ **84.** $\frac{1}{4}$, 9 **86.** True **88.** False

Exercise Set 10.5, pp. 567 - 568

2. 4.9069 **4.** 5.0444 **6.** -1 **8.** -3, $\frac{1}{2}$ **10.** 1.1073 **12.** 6.9078

14. 4.6052 **16.** 9.9021 **18.** $-\frac{25}{6}$ **20.** 1 **22.** 1 **24.** $\frac{83}{15}$ **26.** 4

28. (3, 3), $\left[\frac{9}{2}, 2\right]$ **30.** (3, -5), (3, 5), (-3, 5), (-3, -5) **32.** $\frac{12}{5}$

34. $\pm\sqrt{34}$ **36.** $\frac{16}{5}$, $-\frac{2}{5}$ **38.** $\frac{1}{100,000}$, 100,000

Exercise Set 10.6, pp. 573 - 574

2. 0.9 ft/sec **4.** 1.9 ft/sec **6.** 6.31 billion **8.** \$724.27 **10.** 76¢, \$1.99

12. 878 yr **14.** 8.69 yr **16.** 6.7 **18.** 4.95 yr

Exercise Set, Appendix A, pp. 593 - 594

2. $f^{-1}(x) = x - 7$ **4.** $f^{-1}(x) = 9 - x$ **6.** $g^{-1}(x) = x + 8$ **8.** $f^{-1}(x) = \frac{1}{4}x$

10. $g^{-1}(x) = \frac{x - 7}{4}$ **12.** $h^{-1}(x) = \frac{x + 3}{-5}$ **14.** $f^{-1}(x) = \frac{x - 9}{-4}$

16. $f^{-1}(x) = \frac{5x - 2}{3}$ **18.** $g^{-1}(x) = -\frac{3}{2}x + \frac{21}{2}$ **20.** $f^{-1}(x) = \sqrt{\frac{x + 2}{3}}$

22. $f^{-1}(x) = \log_{10} x$ **24.**   **26.**

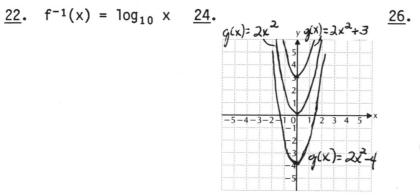

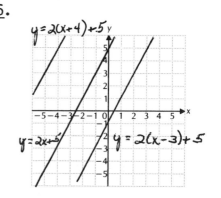

Exercise Set, Appendix A, pp. 593 - 594   (continued)

<u>28</u>.

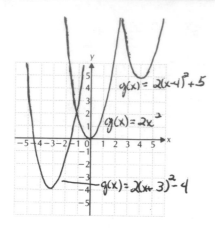

$g(x) = 2(x-4)^2 + 5$

$g(x) = 2x^2$

$g(x) = 2(x+3)^2 - 4$

<u>30</u>. Yes. $f^{-1}(x) = \sqrt[3]{x}$

<u>32</u>. $\dfrac{-2x - h}{x^2(x + h)^2}$

<u>Exercise Set, Appendix B, pp. 601 - 602</u>

<u>2</u>. 8.222   <u>4</u>. 0.1569   <u>6</u>. 26.04   <u>8</u>. 7.142   <u>10</u>. 0.3173   <u>12</u>. 2.6740

<u>14</u>. 1.3377   <u>16</u>. 1.5725   <u>18</u>. 8.9564 - 10   <u>20</u>. 3.6549   <u>22</u>. 8.9220 - 10

<u>24</u>. 2.9032   <u>26</u>. 224.5   <u>28</u>. 14.53   <u>30</u>. 70,030   <u>32</u>. 0.09245   <u>34</u>. 0.5343

<u>36</u>. 0.007295   <u>38</u>. 2.347

COMPUTER CORNER   Chapter 1

Enter the following program into your computer.

```
1   REM Chapter 1 Intermediate Algebra Texts by Keedy, Bittinger
10  PRINT
20  PRINT "Program: TO FIND THE AREA OF A TRAPEZOID"
30  INPUT "Enter the length of the first base :";B1
40  INPUT "Enter the length of the second base :";B2
50  INPUT "Enter the height :";H
60  PRINT "The AREA is .5(";B1;"+";B2;")(";H;") =";.5*(B1+B2)*H
70  PRINT:PRINT
80  PRINT "Do you wish to enter another set of data -- y/n";
90  INPUT A$
100 IF A$ = "Y" OR A$ = "y" THEN 20
110 END
```

EXERCISES

Use the program to find the areas of the trapezoids with the
following dimensions.

1. $h = 10$, $b_1 = 45$, $b_2 = 67$ 2. $h = 12345$, $b_1 = 5689$, $b_2 = 6788$

3. $h = 12.7896$, $b_1 = 78.2343$, $b_2 = 0.004376$

4. $h = 234567$, $b_1 = 66667778$, $b_2 = 787000000$

Enter the following program into your computer.

```
1   REM Chapter 2 Intermediate Algebra Texts by Keedy, Bittinger
10  PRINT "Program: GIVEN TWO POINTS, THIS PROGRAM WILL COMPUTE"
20  PRINT "THE SLOPE OF THE LINE AND GIVE THE SLOPE-INTERCEPT"
30  PRINT "EQUATION OF THE LINE"
40  PRINT
50  INPUT "Enter X1 :";X1
60  INPUT "Enter Y1 :";Y1
70  INPUT "Enter X2 :";X2
80  INPUT "Enter Y2 :";Y2
90  PRINT
100 IF X2 = X1 THEN PRINT "No slope":GOTO 150
110 IF Y2 = Y1 THEN PRINT "Zero slope. The equation of the line
              is y =";Y1:GOTO 150
120 M = (Y2 - Y1)/(X2 - X1)
130 PRINT "Slope = (";Y2;"-";Y1;") / (";X2;"-";X1;") = ";M
140 PRINT "An equation of the line is y = ";M;"x +";Y1 - M*X1
150 PRINT:PRINT
160 PRINT "Do you wish to enter another set of data -- y/n";
170 INPUT A$
180 IF A$ = "Y" OR A$ = "y" THEN 20
190 END
```

EXERCISES

Use the program to find the slope of the lione containing each pair
or points and the slope-intercept equation of the line.

1. (3,8) and (9,-4)   2. (17,-12) and (-9,-15)
3. (-8,-7) and (-9,-12)   4. (14,3) and (2,12)
5. (15,-3) and (15,-9)   6. (-23,-17) and (-89,-17)
7. (3.256,-12.6789) and (-5.5758,8.7665)
8. (0.0089,0.12305) and (-0.0078,-00995)

Enter the following program into your computer.


```
1 REM Chapter 3 Intermediate Algebra Texts by Keedy, Bittinger
10 PRINT "Program: SOLVING 2X2, 3X3, AND 4X4 SYSTEMS"
15 PRINT "USING DETERMINANTS."
20 DIM A(4,6)
30 PRINT
40 P = 0
50 INPUT "Do you want a 2 x 2, 3 x 3, or 4 x 4 system (2,3,4) ";QQ
60 IF QQ < 2 THEN 30
70 IF QQ > 4 THEN 30
80 PP = QQ + 1
90 GOSUB 230
100 GOSUB 330
110 IF P = PP THEN PRINT "INFINITELY MANY SOLUTIONS"
120 IF P = PP THEN 200
130 IF DX = 0 THEN PRINT "NO SOLUTION"
140 IF DX = 0 GOTO 200
150 PRINT "ANSWERS FOLLOW  "
160 FOR J = 1 TO QQ
170 PRINT "X";J;"= ";D(J)/DX
172 PRINT "            ";D(J);"          ";DX
180 NEXT J
190 PRINT:PRINT
200 INPUT "Do you wish to enter another set of data -- y/n";A$
210 IF A$ = "y" OR A$ = "Y" THEN 30
220 END
230 REM input & echo data
240 FOR I = 1 TO QQ
250 FOR J = 1 TO PP
260 IF J = PP THEN PRINT "COLUMN ";PP;" IS TO THE RIGHT OF THE = SIGN"
270 PRINT "Enter ROW ";I;", COLUMN ";J
280 INPUT A(I,J)
290 IF J = PP THEN PRINT
300 NEXT J
310 NEXT I
320 RETURN
330 REM compute answer
340 IF QQ = 2 THEN GOSUB 600
350 IF QQ = 2 THEN 390
360 IF QQ = 3 THEN GOSUB 640
370 IF QQ = 3 THEN 390
380 GOSUB 510
390 DX = D
400 FOR K = 1 TO QQ
410 GOSUB 680
420 IF QQ = 2 THEN GOSUB 600
430 IF QQ = 2 THEN GOTO 470
440 IF QQ = 3 THEN GOSUB 640
450 IF QQ = 3 THEN GOTO 470
```

```
460 GOSUB 510
470 D(K) = D
480 GOSUB 740
490 NEXT K
500 RETURN
510 REM compute d = determ of matrix a
520 D = (A(3,1)*A(4,2)-A(4,1)*A(3,2))*(A(1,3)*A(2,4)-A(1,4)*A(2,3))
530 D = D+(A(3,1)*A(4,3)-A(4,1)*A(3,3))*(A(1,4)*A(2,2)-A(1,2)*A(2,4))
540 D = D+(A(3,1)*A(4,4)-A(4,1)*A(3,4))*(A(1,2)*A(2,3)-A(1,3)*A(2,2))
550 D = D+(A(3,2)*A(4,3)-A(4,2)*A(3,3))*(A(1,1)*A(2,4)-A(1,4)*A(2,1))
560 D = D+(A(3,2)*A(4,4)-A(4,2)*A(3,4))*(A(1,3)*A(2,1)-A(1,1)*A(2,3))
570 D = D+(A(3,3)*A(4,4)-A(4,3)*A(3,4))*(A(1,1)*A(2,2)-A(1,2)*A(2,1))
580 IF D = 0 THEN P = P + 1
590 RETURN
600 REM compute d = determ of matrix a
610 D = A(1,1)*A(2,2)-A(2,1)*A(1,2)
620 IF D = 0 THEN P = P + 1
630 RETURN

640 REM compute d = determ of matrix a
650 D = A(1,1)*(A(2,2)*A(3,3)-A(3,2)*A(2,3))-A(1,2)*(A(2,1)*
    A(3,3)-A(3,1)*A(2,3))+A(1,3)*(A(2,1)*A(3,2)-A(3,1)*A(2,2))
660 IF D = 0 THEN P = P + 1
670 RETURN
680 REM replace col k by constants column
690 FOR KK = 1 TO QQ
700 A(KK,6) = A(KK,K)
710 A(KK,K) = A(KK,PP)
720 NEXT KK
730 RETURN
740 REM swap back columns
750 FOR KK = 1 TO QQ
760 A(KK,K) = A(KK,6)
770 NEXT KK
780 RETURN
```

EXERCISES

1. Use the program to solve the systems in Exercise Set 3.2. Check your answers against those you found in your homework.

2. Use the program to solve the systems in Exercise Set 3.4. Check your answers against those you found in your homework. Be certain to do Exercises 23 and 24.

Enter the following program into your computer.

```
1 REM Chapter 4 Intermediate Algebra Texts by Keedy, Bittinger
10 PRINT "Program: DOES A POINT SOLVE A 2X2 SYSTEM OF INEQUALITIES"
20 PRINT
30 PRINT "Enter A,B,C,D,E,F for the equations Ax + By >=C,
                                               Dx + Ey <=F"
31 PRINT "Enter your six inputs separated by commas."
32  PRINT "For example, 3,-4,16,5,6,14"
40 INPUT A(1),A(2),A(3),A(4),A(5),A(6)
140 PRINT "Inequalities to consider:";A(1);"x +";A(2);"y >=";A(3)
145 PRINT "                          :";A(4);"x +";A(5);"y <=";A(6)
150 PRINT "Enter (x,y) coordinates, example 2,7: ":INPUT X,Y
152 IF A(1)*X+A(2)*Y>=A(3) AND A(4)*X+A(5)*Y<=A(6) THEN
    PRINT "This is a solution" ELSE PRINT "This is not a solution"
170 PRINT
180 PRINT "Do you wish another set of data -- y/n";
190 INPUT A$
200 IF A$="y" OR A$="yes" THEN GOTO 150
210 END
```

EXERCISES

Determine whether the give pairs are solutions of the given inequalities.

1. $3x - 5y \geqslant 4$; $(-10,10)$, $(8,9)$, $(13,-12)$, $(-23.4,-37.8)$
      $-7x + 8y \leqslant 11$

2. $45x + 67y \geqslant 234$; $(-10,10)$, $(8,9)$, $(13,-12)$, $(-23.4,-37.8)$
      $89x - 78y \leqslant -88$

Enter the following programn into your program.


```
1 REM Chapter 5 Intermediate Algebra Texts by Keedy, Bittinger
10 PRINT "Program: FACTORING TRINOMIALS OF THE TYPE ax^2 + bx + c"
20 PRINT "Enter a,b,c where a is a positive integer, and c is nonzero."
30 INPUT "a = ";A
40 IF A < 1 THEN 20
50 INPUT "b = ";B:INPUT "c = ";C
60 IF A <>1 THEN QQ$=MID$(STR$(A),2) ELSE QQ$=""
70 QQ$=QQ$+"x^2 "
80 IF B = -1 THEN QQ$ = QQ$+"- x ":GOTO 110
90 IF B = 1 THEN QQ$ = QQ$+"+ x ":GOTO 110
100 XX = B:GOSUB 620:QQ$ = QQ$+ XX$+"x "
110 XX = C:GOSUB 620:QQ$ = QQ$+XX$
120 REM
130 PRINT
140 FOR X = 1 TO A
150 X1 = A/X
160 IF X1<>INT(X1) THEN 350
170 REM
180 PRINT
190 FOR D = 1 TO ABS(C)
200 D1 = C/D
210 IF D1<>INT(D1) THEN 340
220 REM
230 K = 0
240 D2 = D
250 GOSUB 370
260 D2 = -D2
270 D1 = -D1
280 GOSUB 370
290 IF K = 0 THEN 340 ELSE K = 1
300 T = D1
310 D1 = D2
320 D2 = T
330 GOTO 250
340 NEXT D
350 NEXT X
360 GOTO 490
370 M = X*D1 + X1*D2
380 PRINT "(";
390 IF X <> 1 THEN PRINT MID$(STR$(X),2);
400 XX = D1:GOSUB 620
410 PRINT "x ";XX$;")(";
420 IF X1 <> 1 THEN PRINT MID$(STR$(X1),2);
430 XX = D2:GOSUB 620
440 PRINT "x ";XX$;") = ";
450 XX = M:GOSUB 660:PRINT XX$
460 IF M = B THEN 510
470 REM
480 RETURN
```

342

```
490 NEXT K
500 RETURN
510 REM compute d = determ of matrix a
520 D = (A(3,1)*A(4,2)-A(4,1)*A(3,2))*(A(1,3)*A(2,4)-A(1,4)*A(2,3))
530 D = D+(A(3,1)*A(4,3)-A(4,1)*A(3,3))*(A(1,4)*A(2,2)-A(1,2)*A(2,4))
540 D = D+(A(3,1)*A(4,4)-A(4,1)*A(3,4))*(A(1,2)*A(2,3)-A(1,3)*A(2,2))
550 D = D+(A(3,2)*A(4,3)-A(4,2)*A(3,3))*(A(1,1)*A(2,4)-A(1,4)*A(2,1))
560 D = D+(A(3,2)*A(4,4)-A(4,2)*A(3,4))*(A(1,3)*A(2,1)-A(1,1)*A(2,3))
570 D = D+(A(3,3)*A(4,4)-A(4,3)*A(3,4))*(A(1,1)*A(2,2)-A(1,2)*A(2,1))
580 IF D = 0 THEN P = P + 1
590 RETURN
600 REM compute d = determ of matrix a
610 D = A(1,1)*A(2,2)-A(2,1)*A(1,2)
620 IF D = 0 THEN P = P + 1
630 RETURN
640 REM compute d = determ of matrix a
650 D = A(1,1)*(A(2,2)*A(3,3)-A(3,2)*A(2,3))-A(1,2)*(A(2,1)*
    A(3,3)-A(3,1)*A(2,3))+A(1,3)*(A(2,1)*A(3,2)-A(3,1)*A(2,2))
660 IF D = 0 THEN P = P + 1
670 RETURN
680 REM replace col k by constants column
690 FOR KK = 1 TO QQ
700 A(KK,6) = A(KK,K)
710 A(KK,K) = A(KK,PP)
720 NEXT KK
730 RETURN
740 REM swap back columns
750 FOR KK = 1 TO QQ
760 A(KK,K) = A(KK,6)
770 NEXT KK
780 RETURN
```

EXERCISES

Use the program to factor the following trinomials.

1. $x^2 + 2x + 1$ 2. $49x^2 - 64$ 3. $x^2 - 4x - 21$

4. $45x^2 + 23x + 78$ 5. $45x^2 - 119x + 78$

6. $256x^2 - 1000x + 6400$

Enter the following program into your computer. This program will
carry out the division of a cubic polynomial by a divisor of the type
x - a. It uses synthetic division.

```
1 REM Chapter 6 Intermediate Algebra Texts by Keedy, Bittinger
10 PRINT "Program: SYNTHETIC DIVISION"
20 PRINT "EX.  (-7X^3 + 3X^2 - 4X + 3) / (X+2)"
30 INPUT "YOUR FIRST INPUT WILL BE THE NUMBER A
            IN THE DIVISOR X - A ";A
40 PRINT
50 PRINT "ENTER THE COEFFICIENTS OF THE POLYNOMIAL IN DESCENDING ORDER"
60 PRINT "PRESS 'RETURN' AFTER EACH COEFFICIENT"
70 I = 0:Z = 0:X = 0
80 FOR I = 4 TO 1 STEP -1
90 INPUT P(I)
100 NEXT I
110 IF A > 0 THEN AA$="-" ELSE AA$="+"
120 PRINT "DIVIDED BY X ";AA$" ";MID$(STR$(A),2);" YIELDS"
130 PRINT
140 Q(4) = P(4)
150 PRINT STR$(Q(4));"X^2 ";
160 FOR X = 3 TO 1 STEP -1
170 Q(X) = P(X) + Q(X+1)*A
180 Z = Z + 1
190 IF Z <> 1 THEN 230
200 IF Q(X) > 0 THEN QQ$ = "+ " ELSE QQ$ = "- "
210 PRINT QQ$;MID$(STR$(Q(X)),2);"X ";
220 GOTO 270
230 IF Z = 3 THEN PRINT "   REMAINDER OF "Q(X) ELSE GOTO 250
240 GOTO 270
250 IF Q(X) > 0 THEN QQ$ = "+ " ELSE QQ$ = "- "
260 PRINT QQ$;MID$(STR$(Q(X)),2);
270 NEXT X
280 PRINT
290 INPUT "DO YOU WISH TO ENTER ANOTHER SET OF DATA -- Y/N ";A$
300 IF A$ = "Y" OR A$ = "y" THEN 10
310 END
```

EXERCISES

Use the program to do Exercises 5-10 of Exercise Set 6.9. See if you
can devise a way to use the program for Exercises 11-14.

Enter the following program into your computer. This program will
either tell you whether a set of three numbers are the lengths of the
sides of a right triangle, or it will generate sets of Pythagorean
Triples.

```
1 REM Chapter 7 Intermediate Algebra Texts by Keedy, Bittinger
10 PRINT "Program: PYTHAGOREAN TRIPLES"
20 PRINT
30 PRINT "Do you wish to test for a right triangle or create
                a pythagorean triple"
40 INPUT "Enter 1 (right triangle) or 2 (pythagorean) ";A1
50 IF A1 = 2 THEN 200
60 PRINT
70 INPUT "Enter a ";A
80 INPUT "Enter b ";B
90 INPUT "Enter c ";C
100 X = A^2
110 Y = B^2
120 Z = C^2
130 PRINT "A^2,B^2,C^2 are ";A^2;B^2,C^2
140 PRINT
150 IF X+Y=Z THEN PRINT "These are the sides of a right triangle."
     ELSE PRINT "These are not the sides of a right triangle."
160 PRINT "Do you wish to test another set of data -- y/n ";
170 INPUT A$
180 IF A$ = "Y" OR A$ = "y" THEN 20
190 GOTO 310
200 PRINT
210 PRINT"If u and v are numbers, then the sides of a right"
220 PRINT "triangle can be represented by a = v^2 - u^2, b = 2uv,"
225 PRINT "c = u^2 + v^2."
230 PRINT:PRINT
240 INPUT "Enter u ";U
250 INPUT "Enter v ";V
260 Z = V^2
270 X = U^2
280 Y = Z - X
290 PRINT "A, B, C are ";Y; 2*U*V; X + Z
300 GOTO 160
310 END
```

EXERCISES

Use the program to determine whether each set of three numbers are
the lengths of the sides of a right triangle.

1. 3, 4, 5   2. 3, 5, 7   3. 5, 12, 13

4. 1200, 3500, 3700   5. 45667, 32568, 54322

Use the program to generate several sets of Pythagorean Triples.

Enter the following program into your computer.

```
1 REM Chapter 8 Intermediate Algebra Texts by Keedy, Bittinger
10 PRINT "Program: QUADRATIC FORMULA WITH COMPLEX SOLUTIONS"
20 PRINT "ENTER COEFFICIENTS A,B, AND C WHERE A IS NONZERO"
30 PRINT
40 PRINT"THIS PROGRAM SOLVES QUADRATIC EQUATIONS WHERE THE"
50 PRINT "DISCRIMINANT B^2 - 4*A*C IS EITHER NEGATIVE OR POSITIVE."
60 PRINT "IF THE DISCRIMINANT IS NEGATIVE THEN THE SOLUTION(S)
                ARE COMPLEX NUMBERS."
70 PRINT "Enter a,b, and c "
80 INPUT "a = ";A
90 IF A = 0 THEN 10
100 INPUT "b = ";B:INPUT "c = ";C
110 IF A = 0 THEN GOTO 10
120 D = B^2 - 4*A*C
130 PRINT "THE DISCRIMINANT IS ";D
140 IF D < 0 THEN I$ = "i":D = -D ELSE I$ = " "
150 PRINT
160 IF I$ = "i" THEN 240
170 P1 = (-B/(2*A))
180 P2 = D^.5/(2*A)
190 A1 = P1 + P2
200 A2 = P1 - P2
210 PRINT " a"," b"," c","    x1 = ";A1
220 PRINT A,B,C,"   x2 = ";A2
230 GOTO 290
240 XX$ = STR$(-B/(2*A)):XY$ = STR$((D^.5)/(2*A))
250 X1$ = XX$+" + "+XY$+I$
260 X2$ = XX$+" - "+XY$+I$
270 PRINT " A"," B"," C","    X1 = ";X1$
280 PRINT A,B,C,"    X2 = ";X2$
290 PRINT:INPUT "DO YOU WISH TO ENTER ANOTHER
                SET OF COEFFICIENTS -- Y/N ";A$
300 IF A$ = "Y" OR A$ = "y" THEN 30
310 END
```

EXERCISES

Use the program to solve the following equations.

1. $3x^2 + x - 2 = 0$ 2. $4x^2 + 9 = 0$ 3. $5x^2 - 8x = 3$

Use the program to solve the equations in Exercises 1-24, 26, 27 of Exercise Set 8.2. Check the answers against those you found in your homework.

Enter the following program into your computer.

```
1 REM Chapter 9 Intermediate Algebra Texts by Keedy, Bittinger
10 PRINT "Program: DISTANCE BETWEEN TWO POINTS IN A PLANE"
20 PRINT
30 PRINT "D = [(X2 - X1)^2 + (Y2 - Y1)^2]^.5
40 INPUT "Enter X1 :";X1
50 INPUT "Enter Y1 :";Y1
60 INPUT "Enter X2 :";X2
70 INPUT "Enter Y2 :";Y2
80 PRINT "D = [(";X2;" -";X1;")^2 + (";Y2;" -";Y1;")^2]^.5 =";
           ((X2 - X1)^2+(Y2 - Y1)^2)^.5
90 PRINT:PRINT
100 PRINT "Do you wish to enter another set of data -- y/n";
110 INPUT A$
120 IF A$ = "Y" OR A$ = "y" THEN 20
130 END
```

EXERCISES

Use the program to find the distance between each pair of points in
Exercises 1-10 of Exercise Set 9.1. Compare your answers against
those you found in your homework.

Enter the following program into your computer.

```
1 REM Chapter 10 Intermediate Algebra Texts by Keedy, Bittinger
10 PRINT "Program: LOGARITHMS OF NUMBERS TO ANY BASE"
20 PRINT
30 PRINT "The logarithm, base b, = ln n divided by ln b."
40 INPUT "Enter Base b = ";B
50 INPUT "Enter Number n = ";N
60 PRINT "The log of "N", base "B", = ";LOG(N);" /";LOG(B);" =";
           LOG(N)/LOG(B)
70 PRINT :PRINT
80 PRINT "Do you wish to enter another set of data -- y/n";
90 INPUT A$
100 IF A$ = "Y" OR A$ = "y" THEN 20
110 END
```

EXERCISES

Use the program to find the following.

1. $\log_5 17$ 2. $\log_e 345$ 3. $\log_{10} 0.987$ 4. $\log_{23.7} 567895$

VIDEO CASSETTE REVIEWS
for
BASIC MATHEMATICS, FIFTH EDITION
by
Keedy and Bittinger

Section references for the text follow the listing of each objective.

Counter readings may vary slightly with the equipment used and the condition of the tapes. The tapes are thirty minutes in length.

VIDEO CASSETTE NUMBER	COUNTER READINGS	OBJECTIVES
1	0010	a. Add whole numbers. (1.2)
	0112	b. Solve problems involving addition of whole numbers. (1.8)
	0238	c. Subtract whole numbers. (1.3)
	0291	d. Solve equations like t + 28 = 54 by writing a related subtraction. (1.7)
2	0015	a. Solve problems involving subtraction. (1.8)
	0120	b. Round to the nearest ten, hundred, or thousand. (1.4)
	0120	c. Estimate sums and differences by rounding. (1.4)
	0227	d. Multiply whole numbers. (1.5, 11.7)
	0307	e. Solve problems involving multiplication. (1.8)
3	0016	a. Divide whole numbers. (1.6)
	0102	b. Solve equations like 8·n = 96 by writing a related division. (1.7)
	0160	c. Solve problems involving division. (1.8)
4	0012	a. Simplify fractional notation. (2.3)
	0080	b. Test fractions for equality. (2.3)
	0115	c. Multiply and simplify, using fractional notation. (2.4-2.6)
	0162	d. Solve problems involving multiplication. (2.6)
	0221	e. Find the reciprocal of a number. (2.7)
	0245	f. Divide and simplify, using fractional notation. (2.7)
	0275	g. Solve problems involving division. (2.7)
5	0018	a. Find the LCM of two or more numbers using a list of multiples or factorizations. (3.1)
	0140	b. Add by finding least common denominators. (3.2)
	0218	c. Subtract using fractional notation. (3.3)
	0238	d. Determine which of two numbers is greater. (3.2)
	0276	e. Solve problems involving subtraction. (3.3)

VIDEO CASSETTE NUMBER	COUNTER READINGS	OBJECTIVES
6	0013	a. Convert from mixed numerals to fractions. (3.4)
	0064	b. Convert from fractional notation to mixed numerals. (3.4)
	0101	c. Add using mixed numerals. (3.5)
	0168	d. Subtract using mixed numerals. (3.5)
	0226	e. Solve problems involving addition and subtraction with mixed numerals. (3.5, 3.6)
	0305	f. Multiply using mixed numerals. (3.6)
	0324	g. Divide using mixed numerals. (3.6)
7	0034	a. Given a pair of numbers names by decimal notation, tell which is larger. (4.2)
	0129	b. Round to the nearest thousandth, hundredth, tenth, one, ten, hundred, or thousand. (4.2)
	0255	c. Add using decimal notation. (4.3)
	0415	d. Subtract using decimal notation. (4.3)
	0510	e. Solve problems involving addition and subtraction with decimals. (4.4)
8	0033	a. Multiply using decimal notation. (5.1)
	0175	b. Convert from dollars to cents and cents to dollars. (4.1)
	0283	c. Divide using decimal notation. (5.2)
	0497	d. Solve problems involving multiplication and division with decimals. (5.3)
9	0011	a. Estimate sums, differences, products, and quotients. (5.4)
	0128	b. Convert from fractional notation to decimal notation. (4.1, 5.5)
	0235	c. Solve proportions. (6.1)
10	0012	a. Solve problems involving proportions. (6.3)
	0172	b. Write three kinds of notation for percent. (7.1)
	0219	c. Convert from percent to decimal notation. (7.1, 7.2)
	0237	d. Convert from decimal to percent notation. (7.1, 7.2)
	0262	e. Convert from fractional to percent notation. (7.1, 7.2)
	0308	f. Convert from percent to fractional notation. (7.1, 7.2)
11	0011	a. Translate percent problems to number sentences. (7.3A, 7.3B)
	0095	b. Solve percent problems. (7.3A, 7.3B)
	0187	c. Solve percent problems. (7.3A, 7.3B)
	0296	d. Solve percent problems involving percent increase or decrease. (7.3A, 7.3B)
12	0009	a. Solve percent problems involving percent increase or decrease. (7.4-7.7)
	0070	b. Find the average of a set of numbers and solve problems involving averages. (8.1)
	0212	c. Find the median of a set of numbers and solve problems involving medians. (8.1)
	0275	d. Write exponential notation for products such as $4 \cdot 4 \cdot 4$. (8.2)
	0298	e. Convert from exponential to standard notation. (8.2)

VIDEO CASSETTE NUMBER	COUNTER READINGS	OBJECTIVES
13	0012	a. Write a number with an exponent of 1, and conversely write standard notation for an expression a^1. (8.2)
	0039	b. Write standard notation for an expression with 0 as an exponent. (8.2)
	0076	c. Convert from one metric unit to another. (9.1, 9.2)
	0238	d. Find the area of a rectangle or square. (9.3-9.5)
	0288	e. Solve problems involving area. (9.3-9.5)
14	0011	a. Solve problems involving area. (9.3-9.5)
	0137	b. Find areas of parallelograms, triangles, and trapezoids. (9.3-9.5)
	0264	c. Solve problems involving areas of parallelograms, triangles, and trapezoids. (9.3-9.5)
15	0012	a. Find the length of a radius of a circle given the length of a diameter, and find the length of a diameter given the length of a radius. (9.6)
	0063	b. Find the circumference of a circle given the length of a diameter or a radius. (9.6)
	0154	c. Find the area of a circle given the length of a radius. (9.6)
	0216	d. Solve problems involving circles. (9.6)

Section references for the text follow the listing of each objective.

Counter readings may vary slightly with the equipment used and the condition of the tapes. The tapes are thirty minutes in length.

VIDEO CASSETTE NUMBER	COUNTER READINGS	OBJECTIVES
1	0028	a. Solve simple equations using both the addition and multiplication principles. (1.8, 3.1-3.2)
	0254	b. Solve equations in which like terms are to be collected. (3.3)
	0370	c. Solve simple equations containing parentheses. (2.8, 3.4)
2	0053	a. Solve equations (already factored) using the principle of zero products. (5.7)
	0291	b. Solve problems by translating to equations. (1.9, 3.5, 6.5)
3	0034	a. Solve problems by translating to equations. (1.9, 3.5, 6.5)
	0497	b. Solve formulas for a specified letter. (3.6)
4	0034	a. Multiply a monomial and polynomial mentally. (4.5)
	0087	b. Multiply two binomials mentally. (3.6, 4.5)
	0296	c. Multiply the sum and difference of two expressions mentally. (4.6)
	0405	d. Square a binomial mentally. (4.7)
5	0027	a. Factor monomials. (1.5, 5.1)
	0092	b. Factor polynomials when the terms have a common factor. (1.5, 5.1)
	0301	c. Factor certain expressions with four terms by grouping. (1.5, 5.1)
	0428	d. Factor trinomials of the type $x^2 + px + q$ by examining the last coefficient, q. (5.4, 5.5)
6	0030	a. Factor trinomials of the type $ax^2 + bx + c$, $a \neq 1$. (5.4, 5.5)
	0317	b. Recognize squares of binomials (also called trinomial squares). (5.3)
	0423	c. Factor squares of binomials (or trinomial squares). (5.3)
	0470	d. Factor differences of squares. (5.2)

VIDEO CASSETTE NUMBER	COUNTER READINGS	OBJECTIVES
7	0041	a. Solve certain equations by factoring. (5.7, 5.8)
	0229	b. Solve applied problems involving equations that can be solved by factoring. (5.7, 5.8)
8	0038	a. Determine whether an ordered pair of numbers is a solution of an equation with two variables. (6.1-6.3)
	0131	b. Graph equations of the type $y = mx$ and $y = mx + b$. (6.1-6.3)
	0314	c. Solve a system of two equations by the substitution method when one of them has a variable alone on one side. (7.3)
	0410	d. Solve a system of two equations by the substitution method when neither equation has a variable alone on one side. (7.3)
9	0047	a. Solve a system of two equations by the substitution method when neither equation has a variable alone on one side. (7.3)
	0207	b. Solve a system of two equations using the addition method when no multiplication is necessary. (7.4)
	0375	c. Solve a system of two equations using the addition method when the multiplication principle must be used. (7.4)
10	0041	a. Solve problems by translating them to systems of equations. (7.5)
11	0031	a. Solve motion problems using the formula $d = rt$. (7.5, 7.6)
	0367	b. Solve coin and mixture problems. (7.5, 7.6)
12	0037	a. Multiply two binomials mentally. (5.9)
	0151	b. Square a binomial mentally. (5.9)
	0250	c. Multiply the sum and difference of two expressions mentally. (5.9)
	0320	d. Factor polynomials when the terms have a common factor. (5.9)
	0365	e. Factor by grouping. (5.9)
	0431	f. Factor trinomials that are squares of binomials. (5.9)
	0501	g. Factor trinomials that are not squares. (5.9)
13	0033	a. Factor differences of squares. (5.9)
	0184	b. Factor polynomials completely. (5.9)
	0402	c. Solve a formula for a letter. (5.9)
14	0034	a. Find the LCM of several numbers by factoring. (9.4)
	0106	b. Add fractions, first finding the LCM of the denominators. (9.4)
	0186	c. Find the LCM of algebraic expressions by factoring. (9.4)
	0408	d. Add fractional expressions with different denominators and simplify the result. (9.5, 9.6)

VIDEO CASSETTE NUMBER	COUNTER READINGS	OBJECTIVES
15	0037	a. Subtract fractional expressions with different denominators. (9.5, 9.6)
	0213	b. Simplify combined additions and subtractions of fractional expressions. (9.5, 9.6)
	0386	c. Solve fractional equations. (9.7)
16	0033	a. Solve fractional equations. (9.7)
	0300	b. Solve applied problems using fractional equations. (9.8, 9.9)
17	0041	a. Find the ratio of one quantity to another. (6.4, 9.8, 9.12)
	0084	b. Solve proportional problems. (6.4, 9.8, 9.12)
	0308	c. Solve problems involving direct variation. (6.4, 9.8, 9.12)
18	0041	a. Multiply with radical notation. (10.3)
	0104	b. Factor radical expressions and where possible simplify. (10.3)
	0215	c. Simplify radical expressions by factoring, assuming all expressions under radicals represent non-negative numbers. (10.4)
	0333	d. Multiply and simplify radical expressions. (10.4)
	0439	e. Simplify radical expressions with fractional radicands, when numerator and denominator are perfect squares (or can be so simplified). (10.5)
	0503	f. Simplify radical expressions with fractional radicands when numerator and denominator are not perfect squares so that there will only be a whole number radicand. (10.5)
19	0040	a. Add or subtract with radical notation, using the distributive law to simplify. (10.7)
	0360	b. Divide with radical notation. (10.6)
	0419	c. Rationalize denominators. (10.5, 10.6)
20	0040	a. Solve quadratic equations of the type $ax^2 + bx = 0$, $a \neq 0$, $b \neq 0$, by factoring. (11.1, 11.2)
	0104	b. Solve quadratic equations of the type $ax^2 + bx + c = 0$, $a \neq 0$, $b \neq 0$, $c \neq 0$, by factoring. (11.1, 11.2)
	0254	c. Solve quadratic equations using the quadratic formula. (11.5)
21	0035	a. Solve certain fractional equations by first deriving a quadratic equation. (11.8)
	0207	b. Solve certain radical equations by first using the principle of squaring to derive a quadratic equation. (10.9)
	0387	c. Use quadratic equations to solve applied problems. (11.2, 11.3, 11.8)

VIDEO CASSETTE NUMBER	COUNTER READINGS	OBJECTIVES
22	0033	a. Use quadratic equations to solve applied problems. (11.2, 11.3, 11.8)
	0231	b. Without graphing, tell whether the graph of an equation of the type $y = ax^2 + bx + c$ opens upward or downward. Then graph the equation. (11.9)

VIDEO CASSETTE NUMBER	APPROX. COUNTER READING	DESCRIPTION
23	0000	Introduction to the 5 steps of Problem-Solving: FAMILIARIZE, TRANSLATE, CARRY OUT, CHECK, and STATE THE ANSWER.
	0350	PROBLEM 1: The sum of two consecutive integers is 47. What are the integers?
	1000	PROBLEM 2: A 5000 liter fuel tank is to be filled with two different fuel mixtures. One mixture is 40% kerosene, while the other is 65% kerosene. Both are mixtures of kerosene and oil. When the tank is full it is required to contain a mixture which is 55% kerosene. How much of each mixture should be used to fill the tank?
24	0000	Quick review of Problem-Solving techniques.
	0020	PROBLEM 1: A motorboat took 3 hours to make a downstream trip with a 5 km/h current. The return trip against the same current took 7 hours. Find the speed of the boat in still water.
	0705	PROBLEM 2: The head of a paint crew knows that it will take Troy 5 hours to paint a new room on her house while Hutch can paint the same room in 4 hours. How long would it take Troy and Hutch, working together, to paint this room?

VIDEO CASSETTE REVIEWS
for
INTERMEDIATE ALGEBRA, FIFTH EDITION
by
Keedy and Bittinger

Section references for the text follow the listing of each objective.

Counter readings may vary slightly with the equipment used and the condition of the tapes. The tapes are thirty minutes in length.

VIDEO CASSETTE NUMBER	COUNTER READINGS	OBJECTIVES
1	0013	a. Rewrite expressions with or without whole number exponents. (1.7, 7.2)
	0106	b. Rewrite expressions with or without negative integers as exponents. (1.7)
	0160	c. Use exponential notation in multiplication and division. (1.8)
	0258	d. Use exponential notation in raising a power to a power. (1.8)
2	0015	a. Solve equations using the addition principle. (2.1)
	0064	b. Solve equations using the multiplication principle. (2.1)
	0097	c. Solve equations using the principles together. (2.1)
	0176	d. Solve certain equations containing parentheses. (2.2)
	0251	e. Solve equations using the principle of zero products. (2.2)
3	0015	a. Solve problems by translating to equations. (1.1, 2.3)
	0268	b. Solve formulas for a specified letter. (2.4)
4	0014	a. Given an equation $y = mx + b$, determine the slope and y-intercept and graph the equation. (2.8)
	0092	b. Graph linear equations with a missing variable. (2.5)
	0135	c. Determine which equations are linear. (2.6)
	0180	d. Graph linear equations using intercepts. (2.7)
	0226	e. Given two points of a line, find its slope. (2.7)
	0323	f. Identify lines with zero slope and lines that do not have a slope. (2.7)
5	0014	a. Determine whether an ordered pair is a solution of system of two equations. (3.1)
	0052	b. Solve systems of two linear equations graphically. (3.1)
	0215	c. Solve systems of equations in two variables using the substitution method. (3.2)
	0307	d. Solve systems of equations in two variables by the addition method. (3.2)

VIDEO CASSETTE NUMBER	COUNTER READINGS	OBJECTIVES
6	0014	a. Solve systems of equations in two variables by the addition method. (3.2)
	0074	b. Solve problems by translating them to systems of two equations and solving the system. (3.3)
7	0013	a. Solve systems of three equations in three variables. (3.4)
	0206	b. Solve problems by translating them to systems of three equations and solving the system. (3.5)
8	0011	a. Multiply two binomials mentally. (5.3)
	0078	b. Square a binomial mentally. (5.4)
	0149	c. Multiply, mentally, the product of the sum and the difference of the same two expressions. (5.4)
	0216	d. Factor polynomials whose terms have a common factor. (1.5, 5.5)
	0253	e. Factor certain polynomials with four terms by grouping. (1.5, 5.5)
	0311	f. Factor differences of two squares. (5.5)
9	0015	a. Factor trinomial squares. (5.4)
	0086	b. Factor trinomials of the type $x^2 + bx + c$. (5.6)
	0146	c. Factor trinomials of the type $ax^2 + bx + c$, $a \neq 1$. (5.6)
	0208	d. Factor sums and differences of two cubes. (5.3)
	0291	e. Factor polynomials using any of the methods that you have learned. (5.9)
10	0017	a. Multiply fractional expressions. (6.1)
	0048	b. Multiply a fractional expression by 1, using an expression like A/A. (6.1)
	0121	c. Simplify fractional expressions. (6.1)
	0186	d. Multiply fractional expressions and simplify. (6.1)
	0283	e. Divide fractional expressions and simplify. (6.1)
11	0016	a. Find the LCM of several algebraic expressions by factoring. (6.2)
	0114	b. Add and subtract fractional expressions having the same denominator. (6.3)
	0144	c. Add and subtract fractional expressions whose denominators are additive inverses of each other. (6.3)
	0203	d. Add and subtract fractional expressions having different denominators. (6.3)
	0316	e. Simplify complex fractional expressions. (6.8)
12	0017	a. Simplify complex fractional expressions. (6.8)
	0135	b. Solve fractional equations. (6.4)
13	0022	a. Solve work problems. (6.5)
	0173	b. Solve motion problems. (6.6)

VIDEO CASSETTE NUMBER	COUNTER READINGS	OBJECTIVES
14	0016	a. Simplify radical expressions with perfect-square radicands. (7.2)
	0055	b. Find cube roots, simplify certain expressions. (7.2)
	0092	c. Simplify expressions involving odd and even roots. (7.2)
	0154	d. Multiply with radical notation. (7.3, 7.6)
	0196	e. Simplify radical expressions by factoring, assuming that all expressions represent non-negative numbers. (7.3, 7.6)
	0263	f. Multiply and simplify radical expressions. (7.3, 7.6)
15	0019	a. Simplify radical expressions having a quotient for a radicand. (7.4, 7.7)
	0066	b. Divide and simplify radical expressions. (7.4, 7.7)
	0101	c. Calculate combinations of roots and powers. (7.10)
	0164	d. Add or subtract with radical notation and simplify. (7.5)
	0209	e. Rationalize the denominator of a radical expression. (7.7)
	0268	f. Rationalize the numerator of a rational expression. (7.7)
	0299	g. Rationalize denominators or numerators having two terms. (7.7)
16	0016	a. Rationalize denominators or numerators havings two terms. (7.7)
	0124	b. Write expressions with or without fractional exponents. (7.8)
	0177	c. Write expressions without negative exponents. (7.8)
	0200	d. Use the laws of exponents with fractional exponents. (7.8)
	0247	e. Use fractional exponents to simplify radical expressions. (7.8)
17	0015	a. Solve radical equations with one radical term. (7.9)
	0113	b. Solve radical equations with two radical terms. (7.9)
	0259	c. Solve equations of the type $ax^2 = k$. (8.1)
	0281	d. Solve equations of the type $ax^2 + bx = 0$. (8.1)
	0302	e. Solve equations of the type $ax^2 + bx + c = 0$. (8.1)
18	0015	a. Translate problems to quadratic equations and solve. (8.1, 8.3)
	0191	b. Solve quadratic equations using the quadratic formula. (8.2)
19	0017	a. Solve fractional equations that are quadratic after clearing of fractions. (8.3)
	0118	b. Solve problems that translate to this kind of equation (fractional equation that is quadratic after clearing of fractions). (8.3)
20	0016	a. Determine the nature of the solutions of a quadratic equation with real-number coefficients, without solving it. (8.4)
	0153	b. Write a quadratic equation having two numbers specified as solutions. (8.4)
	0205	c. Solve a formula for a given letter. (8.5)
	0270	d. Solve equations that are reducible to quadratic. (8.6)

VIDEO CASSETTE NUMBER	COUNTER READINGS	OBJECTIVES
21	0015	a. Solve equations that are reducible to quadratic. (8.6)
	0077	b. Graph functions of the form $y = ax^2$ or $f(x) = ax^2$. (8.8, 8.9)
	0158	c. Graph functions like $f(x) = a(x - h)^2$. (8.8, 8.9)
	0215	d. Graph functions like $f(x) = a(x - h)^2 + k$. (8.8, 8.9)
	0245	e. Solve systems of one first-degree and one second-degree equation. (9.4, 9.5)
22	0014	a. Solve systems of one first-degree and one second-degree equation. (9.4, 9.5)
	0091	b. Solve problems involving such systems of equations (one first-degree and one second-degree equations). (9.4, 9.5)
	0250	c. Solve systems of two second-degree equations. (9.4, 9.5)
23	0013	a. Solve problems involving such systems (two second-degree equations). (9.4, 9.5)
	0211	b. Graph exponential functions. (10.1)
24	0014	a. Graph inverses of exponential functions. (10.1)
	0119	b. Graph logarithm functions. (10.2)
	0202	c. Convert from exponential to logarithmic equations. (10.3)
	0237	d. Convert from logarithmic to exponential equations. (10.3)
	0263	e. Solve certain logarithmic equations. (10.3)
25	0017	a. Express the logarithm of a product as a sum of logarithms, and conversely. (10.3)
	0057	b. Express a logarithm of a power as a product. (10.3)
	0084	c. Express the logarithm of a quotient as a difference of logarithms, and conversely. (10.3)
	0130	d. Convert from logarithms of products, quotients, and powers to expressions in terms of individual logarithms, and conversely. (10.3)
	0276	e. Use interpolation and a common logarithm table to find logarithms when four digits occur. (10.4, Appendix B)
26	0014	a. Use interpolation and a common logarithm table to find logarithms when four digits occur. (10.4, Appendix B)
	0084	b. Use the interpolation and a common logarithm table to find anti-logarithms when four digits occur. (10.4, Appendix B)
	0165	c. Solve exponential equations. (10.5)
	0220	d. Solve logarithmic equations. (10.5)
	0261	e. Solve certain applied problems involving exponential and logarithmic equations. (10.6)
27	0016	a. Solve equations and inequalities with absolute value. (4.5)
	0157	b. Determine whether an ordered pair is a solution of an inequality in two variables. (4.6)
	0196	c. Graph, on a plane, linear inequalities in two variables. (4.3, 4.4)

VIDEO CASSETTE NUMBER	APPROX. COUNTER READING	DESCRIPTION
28	0000	Review of 5 steps of Problem-Solving: FAMILIARIZE, TRANSLATE, CARRY OUT, CHECK, and STATE THE ANSWER.
	0120	PROBLEM 1: Three numbers are such that the second is 38 less than twice the first and the third is 20 more than 1/17 the first. The sum of the three numbers is 34. Find the smallest of these three numbers.
	0580	PROBLEM 2: John has 2 paint solutions. One of these is 30% linseed oil while the other is 60% linseed oil. He wants to paint his cabin with a 36 liter mixture of these two paint solutions which will be exactly 50% linseed oil. How many liters of each solution should be mixed to get his desired solution?
29	0000	Brief review of the 5 steps of Problem-Solving.
	0020	PROBLEM 1: A refinery receives a crude oil order through two different pipelines. When the oil is flowing through both of these lines at the same time, the order can be filled in 30 hours. One of these lines will deliver oil three times as fast as the other. Determine how long it would take each pipeline to deliver the order alone.
	0508	PROBLEM 2: Two airplanes leave the same airport at the same time flying in opposite directions. One flies due east with a tail wind while the other flies due west against a head wind of the same speed as the first airplane's tail wind. The airplane with the tail wind flies 850 km in the same length of time as the other plane flies 500 km. The speed in still air of the eastbound airplane is 200 km/h while the westbound airplane has a still airspeed of 220 km/h. Find the speed of the wind.

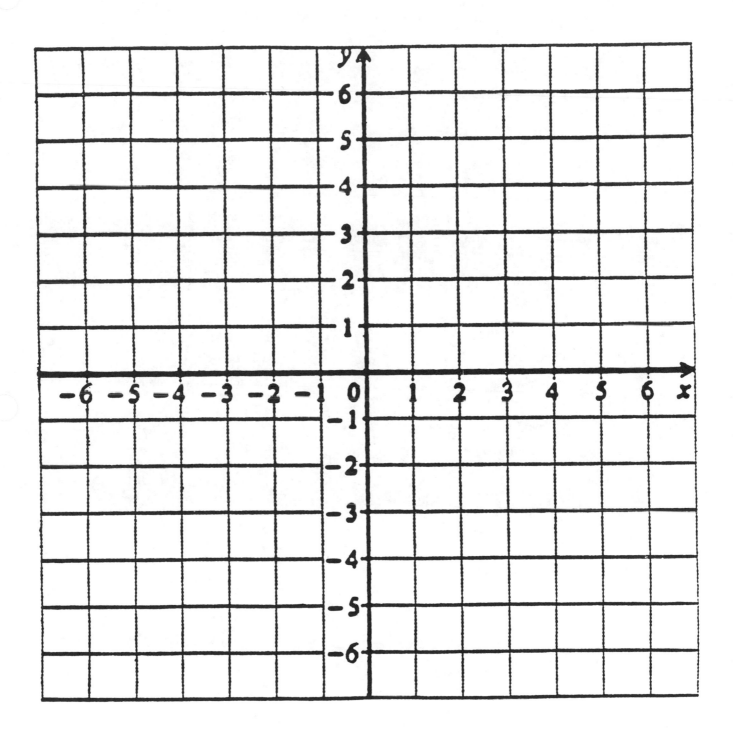

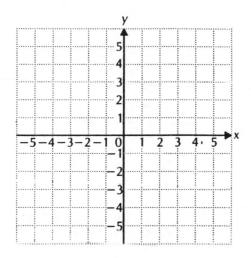

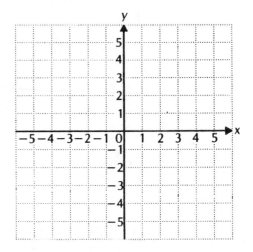

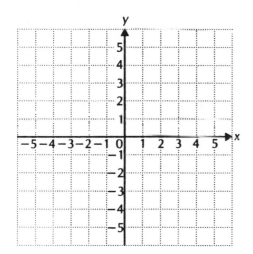

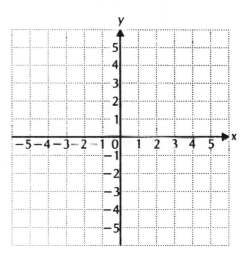

TRANSPARENCY MASTER: NUMBER LINES

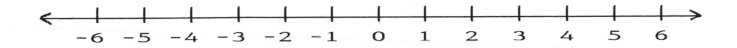

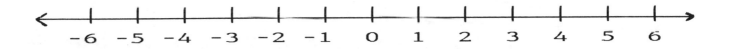

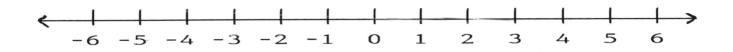

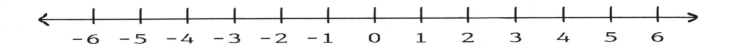

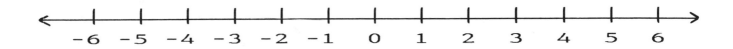

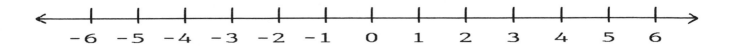

TEST AID: RECTANGULAR COORDINATE GRIDS

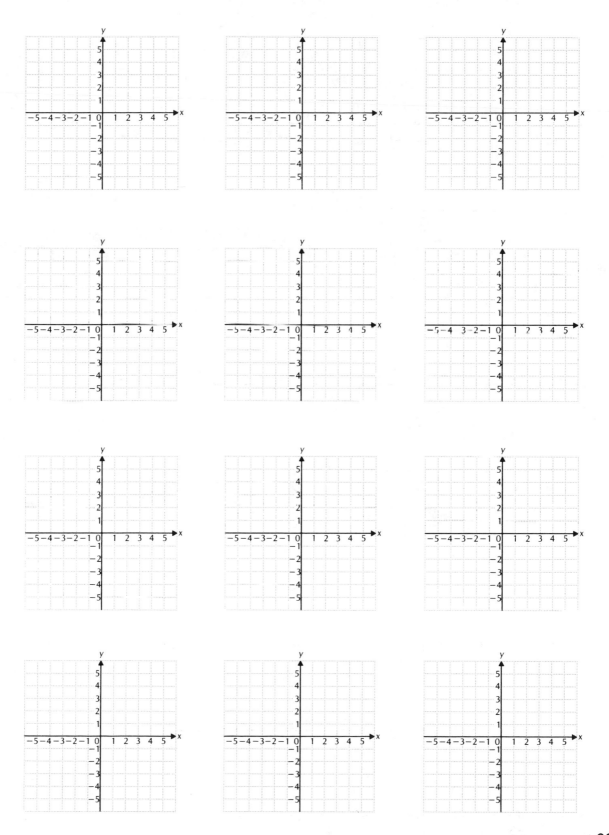

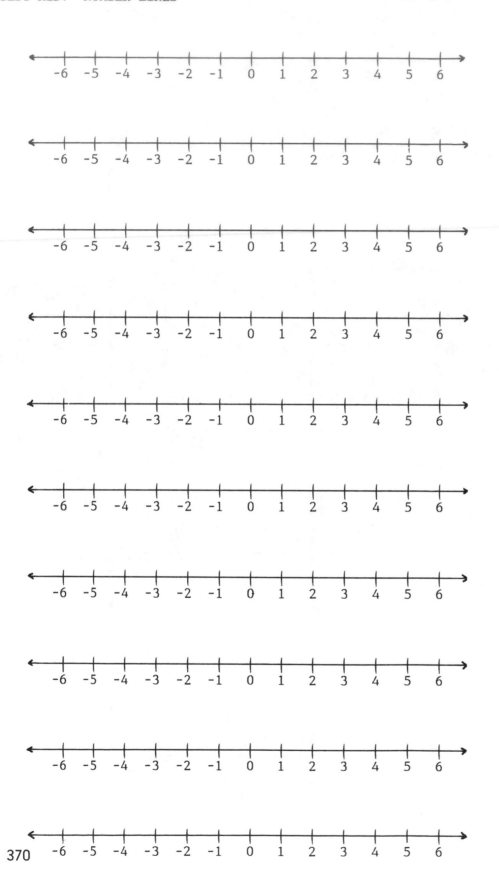

370